To Jay, with our fond hope that your search f... trut... B...

M000290363

With One Heart
is a very special tale:

"An amazing book from an amazing family! This is one of the most honest, thoughtful and moving true stories I have ever read. It is an inspiring account of lives centered in God, in the way that only the most truthful and realistic accounts are."

Dr. Richard J. Wood
Dean, Yale Divinity School 1996-2001; now President, United Board for Christian Higher Education in Asia

"What a love story! Only a person with an incredibly faith-filled heart could write such a compelling book. I am deeply moved by Timber's amazing experiences with his beautiful wife, Annette, and their magnificent family. I am in awe of their dedication and personally inspired to renew my own commitment to my family and faith."

Kathie Lee Gifford
Actress, musician and television host

"I expected to skim this book, but instead found myself entranced. Extremely well written, this is simply a wonderful sketch of the beauty of family love – even when that love is tested to the utmost. You may not share their religion, but you will be awed to encounter people of such rich faith. The power of the struggle to discover and embrace the gift of the twins was greatly moving to me as a Catholic convinced that new life is always – no matter the appearances – a confirmation of God's love. It's an eloquent testimony. I'll be recommending it to many friends."

Father Michael J. Sheeran
Society of Jesus; President, Regis University

"This book is a delightful and profoundly poignant reminder to us all to reflect upon the priorities in our lives and cherish that which is of immeasurable value – the love and constancy of family."

Lt. Colonel Frederick A. "Bud" Bromley III
United States Air Force

"There exists a silent underground of women who whisper 'I know...' when a pregnant mother loses her unborn child.

"Each year, thousands upon thousands of women endure this pain, yet it is rarely written of at a heartfelt, personal level. Timber Dick and his remarkable wife, Annette, have brought such a story into the light, so all of us who have lived through this sorrow can shout, 'I know!'

Like an excellent mystery, *With One Heart* kept me reading through the night. This amazing book, however, is about the greatest mystery of all: the Mystery of Life. Like a good detective, Timber Dick delves into the darkest corners of the soul to find his answers to some of life's most perplexing questions.

"The portrait of the family, particularly the wondrous wife/mother, Annette, is at once charming and extraordinary. As a writer, I would be afraid to make up such astonishing characters. The fact that they actually live and breathe leaves me smiling with delight."

Anna Sandor
Award-winning film and television screenwriter

"An emotional tour de force! This is a rare and illuminating insight into one of today's great families."

Lord Greville Janner of Braunstone,
Queen's Council, London
Author and Statesman

"As a mother, but also as a writer and college professor, I was astonished by the emotional resonance and profound spirituality of this book – and how the saga of this extraordinary family continually took my breath away. The narrative about the twins is a deeply moving tale of discovery and loss simultaneously matched by the equally compelling story of family devotion and unity. In these times, as we re-evaluate our national values, it is a great comfort to read a book so simply wonderful and filled with heartfelt, timeless wisdom.

"I found that I just *had* to read it in one sitting (and then reread it!) and was not at all surprised to feel a sense of peace at the end, having both wept at the pain and struggles and rejoiced at the faith and trust conveyed by the author."

Dr. Susan P. Casteras
Professor, University of Washington;
Former Curator, Yale Center for British Art

"What an emotionally compelling story of a family steeped in the turmoil of a hauntingly troubled pregnancy! I held my breath, laughed, cried, and was thoroughly captivated throughout. You'll want to set aside a whole day to enjoy this gripping, heart-moving story of a family's trials and adventures as they press on to discover their way in life, their God, and make perhaps the biggest decision of their lives!"

Gary A. Wayne
Investment Executive;
former Major League Baseball pitcher

"Heart-wrenching at points, and then heart warming with the same ferocity. This is a truly compelling story of real beauty – there's poetry in the language. It's an exciting page-turner with stunning imagery."

Saul Nadata
Author and playwright

* * * * *

With One Heart

Timber Dick

Tendix Press
a division of
TENDIX, LLC
Denver, Colorado

With One Heart

Copyright 2001 by Timber Dick
All rights reserved, including
the right of reproduction
in whole or in part
in any form

First Tendix Press edition 2002

Manufactured in the United States of America

The Tendix Press website can be accessed at:
www.tendixpress.com

ISBN: 0-9716682-0-5

Cover design by Karey Christ-Janer
Boulder, CO   [karey@boulder.net]

Tendix Press
a division of
TENDIX, LLC
P.O. Box 12376
Denver, Colorado 80212

This work is dedicated to those who have sacrificed to build a more peaceful, merciful and respectful world.

My deepest gratitude to Dr. John Clark Pratt and Mr. Saul Nadata for their insightful and incisive editorial work. Their encouragement nourished me while their considerate direction, correction and rejection kept this story true and focused. My thanks also to Marjory Dick, who offered her 100 years of wisdom in support of this effort.

And most precious and appreciated, I thank my beloved wife for her faith, forgiveness, fortitude and sustaining love through the challenging times of this tale and many others untold.

Timber Dick
Denver 2001

Prologue

Every effort has been made to accurately and faithfully portray the following events, including intents, actions and dialogues. Where feasible, we verified the story with concurrent journals and tapes. The identities of a few individuals have been intentionally obscured, but most people described herein are represented by their own names.

In this account, I sought to convey both the simple and the subtle meanings we derived from our experience. We hope that the reader will join us in honor, enjoyment and awe as we try to appreciate what happened, and why.

Before I formed thee in the belly, I knew thee;
and before thou camest forth out of the womb I sanctified
thee...
Then said I, Ah, Lord God! Behold, I cannot speak:
for I am a child.
— Jeremiah 1:5-6

With One Heart

*   *   *   *   *

Chapter 1

Faces on the Shrouded Screen

Tuesday Afternoon 16 May 1995
Denver, Colorado

Gray-blue rays flickered weakly from the hulking console's monitor, creating an aura of light without warmth and defining shapes without color. The boundaries of the sterile examination room were shown not by its darkened walls, but by the reach of the fragile shards of light and shadow stabbing out from the cold, convex pane on the face of the machine. Its rays probed and quivered across the perforated ceiling tiles and caressed the pale, undulating furrows of the blackout curtains clinging to the far wall. I squinted to make sense of the images on the glass as they flashed and faded. Sometimes they were almost intelligible – then the glimmering phosphors and ghostly silhouettes would collapse into confused splotches that barely reflected the creased brow and pursed lips of the operator hunched over the screen. He fingered the controls and fought the darkness to scribble notes on the pad at his side, his every move mocked by the nebulous apparitions lurking on the walls and ceiling.

He wore a lab coat. His face was ashen except for a series of thin silver crescents at the periphery of his form, indistinct highlights from the machine's fluorescing facade. His right hand deftly manipulated a compact signal transducer along my wife's acquiescent body. Seeking. Stroking. Pausing. Pressing. A swaying coil of black wire tied the device in his grasp to the equipment he attended, feeding it tiny electrical impulses, pulsing energy echoing from the life within her.

The phantoms of the console danced to his every move.

1

My neck ached. I shifted position and the smooth contours of Annette's bare midriff partially eclipsed my view of the inscrutable shapes on the screen. My gaze flowed along the soft curves of her torso. She was looking away from me, her attention focused on the fleeting forms of the tube glowing before her. Her face was resolute, her jaw set. I felt, more than heard, the low, electronic hum emanating from the apparatus filling a large area of the room. Somewhere deep in the bowels of the refrigerator-sized box beside her a muffled fan whispered. Otherwise the room was still. She squeezed my hand more tightly as the technician again ran the transponder across her rounded stomach.

"There!" she exclaimed."What was that? Wasn't that a foot?"

She needn't have asked. After twelve pregnancies and too many hours with her heels in the stirrups of an obstetrical bench, she had learned to recognize her babies' fingers and toes on the equipment beside her.

The radiology specialist grunted affirmatively in reply. To him, she seemed a distraction, largely irrelevant as he sought to interpret his transient electronic hieroglyphs. Every few moments he winced and would let out a sigh, as if breathing were somehow difficult for him. Otherwise he was uncommunicative. Annette was only mildly successful in disguising her growing irritation with the situation. She was sympathetic with the intense concentration he required to decipher the ambiguous shapes and textures shown on the ultrasonic test apparatus. Nonetheless, she was the one who had to lay frozen on the table as he squirted frigid electrolyte gel on her and smeared the clammy probe all over her abdomen. The least he could do was tell her what was going on.

Finally, the tech took another deep breath and exhaled slowly. He depressed the switch of the small lamp on the console and drafted some additional notation by its subservient but meager glow. I searched his face for clues as to the meaning of the traces on the screen. He exuded pride – perhaps arrogance? – in his skill at the controls of the ultrasonic imaging system. I had been told this was one of the most sophisticated units in the region, and the operators had to train for years before they were fully qualified to serve in this branch of the clinic. The job came with unique responsibilities and a peculiar kind of power. The tech could see babies while they were invisible to anyone else. In this high-risk obstetrical practice, he was usually the first to know if there were twins or triplets, or to fully grasp the scope of the challenges of any particular pregnancy. Sometimes the babies he saw on the screen would come back to visit the staff, a year or two later, with parents beaming with gratitude for the care they had received. Some of the babies, however, never got a chance to take a breath. This was, after all, high risk.

He looked over at me for an instant, and then seemed to stare in the space above my left shoulder.

"Would you ask Dr. Porter to come in?" he said curtly and nodded his head toward the closed door.

Even as I moved to comply, I was startled to realize I had completely forgotten there was a fourth person in the room. A woman also garbed in a plain white lab suit had been standing motionless behind me. My incredulity at being ordered around by the machine's operator dissolved into chagrin. Annette and I instinctively turned to watch the woman as she exited, but we were unprepared for the light that blazed from the hallway into the cramped room. The brilliance of the hall's cold fluorescent ceiling fixtures was blinding as the nurse opened the door and silently slipped out.

With a click of the latch, the dim room again took shape around me. I focused on Annette. She didn't seem to share my sense of foreboding. Although her brow was knit with frustration at the lack of comment from the tech and the discomfort of the spare, sanitary surroundings, my wife's eyes looked somehow peaceful. She had been here previously, in this same room, and had watched with fear and fascination the figures glowing on the computerized screen. Three years before, the doctors thought our unborn daughter Mercina had problems. I brought Annette in during her fifth month for an ultrasound and amniocentesis. The results of those tests were fine, and Mercina was born in good health only a few days past her due date in January of 1992. If her sense of ease could be correlated with her experience, Annette had reason to feel calm as she lay on the table. So far, she had delivered ten healthy babies, and experienced only one miscarriage.

Three-month old Lincoln died in 1989, but that had nothing to do with the pregnancy.

Dr. Porter was not our regular obstetrician. We had been referred to his practice. Two months earlier, in March, Annette had listened carefully through the earphones of a Doppler stethoscope, with the sensor head positioned firmly just below her belly button.

"Can you hear it?" Linda had asked Annette. Dr. Linda Irwin had attended Annette's last three pregnancies, and they'd developed a close bond over the years. Annette was in for a regular prenatal visit groaning under the load of this pregnancy. It seemed to her that this time she was gaining weight and inches at a breathtaking clip. Annette was relieved to hear a heartbeat that was vibrant and strong – easily distinguishable from the whooshings and gurglings of the other goings-on inside her. This baby was obviously big, and it certainly sounded healthy.

Dr. Irwin's phone call a few weeks later didn't bother either of us much. Linda explained that a routine blood test indicated some protein levels were abnormally high. The test was not by itself conclusive.

"I'm going to refer you to Dr. Porter's clinic downtown to have things checked out. They won't do an amnio," Linda had said. "We'll just run an ultrasound to make sure everything's OK."

Dr. Irwin was well aware that Annette was profoundly committed to motherhood in every sense of the word. She and Annette had on several occasions discussed the increasing risks of childbearing as a woman passed forty. If an amnio indicated Down syndrome or some other problem, she knew Annette and I had long ago decided to offer the baby everything we afforded our other children. We were well acquainted with the challenges of teaching and raising a child with Down syndrome, and statistically that was the most probable birth defect we might be facing.

"If there's a problem, we'll want to know so we can do all we can to take care of the baby," Dr. Irwin had counseled Annette on the phone.

Annette was sometimes a little embarrassed to admit it, but she really wanted another child. Most of her friends – even those several years her junior – had stopped having children after two or three or four. While other moms gasped in astonishment, my wife got pregnant again and again, and said she loved every minute. She was sick and had aches like everyone else, but she obviously thrived in her role as mother. When our oldest, Tomicah, reached school age, his sister Kimber and brother Levi were still toddlers. Our littlest at the time, Charity, was a plump armful only a few months old. Since the school year was out of synch with Tomicah's December birthdate, Annette and I decided to begin teaching him at home. Annette had earned a teaching certificate along with her bachelor's degree from Yale, plus a master's from Stanford and another from Yale's Divinity School, so there was no real question about her teaching qualifications. Still, she came from a very

4

traditional, education-oriented family and our approach elicited a chorus of skeptical critiques. There's no question that it was a formidable task to educate first Tomicah, then each of the other children in turn as they grew to school age. While the kids soon formed a literate and articulate group, Annette's anxieties about their education persisted. It was only after Tomicah was admitted to college at age 14 that she felt a sense of security in her accomplishments as a teacher of our children.

The kids have formed a family that to look at is pretty remarkable. Each baby came according to some inspired program: They kept alternating by sex, by hair color, even by intellectual interest. The first six were born a boy, a girl, a boy, and so on. Lincoln, our baby number seven, came right according to plan. His siblings promptly anointed him the most enchanting of the crew, and we were devastated when he died of Sudden Infant Death Syndrome at three months. When the next pregnancy resulted in another son – Shiloh – some nine months later, the symmetry of the family was retained. He was in turn followed by brown-haired, green-eyed Mercina. Mia, as she chose to call herself, was slight but wiry, small but strong in her will and capabilities. Not until 1993 when baby number ten was born – a girl – was the pattern broken. Glorianna was a blue-eyed bombshell, like her mother, and was similarly charming. Mia and Glori were a complementary pair, straight-haired brunette and ringleted blonde, almost like different versions of the same doll. They were adored by all of us, and everyone was comfortable with the prospect that Glori might remain the youngest Tillemann-Dick.

Everyone, that is, except Annette. In her most private moments, even as she thanked God for the abundance of love, health, and happiness that graced our her home, Annette confided to me that she nurtured a secret wish. Maybe "wish" was too strong a word, but it was more than a fantasy. Annette had always hoped she would be blessed with twins. Now that Mercina and Glori had arrived as two baby girls in a row, it had seemed only fitting to her that the wished-for twins would be little boys.

Perhaps that was the explanation for the lack of worry in her eyes. As Annette lay chilled and uncomfortable on the table, she knew of one reason why the protein enzyme test results could be off. When a close friend had similar test results, she gave birth four months later to a lovely baby boy – and a lovely little girl. As much as Annette was committed to a life devoid of envy and covetousness, she could scarcely imagine anything more wonderful. If it were somehow possible (and she dared not even pray for it), she would love to hear the doctor say, "Well, are you ready for two little armfuls?"

As I gazed into her face amidst the shadows cast by the ultrasound machine, she looked paradoxically excited and yet at peace. Anxious, yet calm? It made me reflect upon her recent craving for hot dogs. She was generally inclined to a vegetarian diet, but for the past two months from morning through the night she craved the big, juicy quarter-pound franks from the 7-11 down the street. "I can't believe I'm eating this," she had explained to me as she smeared mustard along the length of the steaming meat. "Just the thought makes me a little nauseous." Then she glanced back with a playful grin, "But every time we drive past here, my mouth starts to water – and you can't believe how good they taste!"

Light blazed into the room once again as the nurse returned with a slightly portly man in his late fifties wearing a white lab coat and grey-framed bifocals. One of the most highly regarded perinatal geneticists in the Rocky Mountain states, Dr. Albert Porter was the doctor who had given our unborn Mercina a clean bill of health when Annette had last been in this room. Perhaps as a result of his experience, he accorded Annette special status. When I looked at my wife, I saw her as someone little changed from the time we met. Between pregnancies she retained the figure she had cultivated as a co-ed, and except for a few tiny crows-feet, she looked remarkably like the woman I found so appealing in college. Dr. Porter, however, saw my wife as an *ancient ultra multi-gravida.* I choked on his terminology, but he simply meant in medical terms that she was over forty and was mother to <u>lots</u> of kids – a rarity in our times. Thus, independent of any appreciation the doctor may have had for her physically and intellectually, her history made Annette a pretty exciting patient.

Dr. Porter followed the tech around the table and the two of them stared intently into the machine as the probe was once again swiped over Annette's bare midriff. For several long moments, Dr. Porter said nothing. The tech made several unintelligible comments as he pointed to specific areas of the screen. The doctor bent over to look more closely, his face gray and lined in the cold light thrown off by the CRT.

"Did you make a tape?" he asked, referring to the videotape used to record the images on the screen before them.

6

"Yeah. I got all three axes, multiple sections, discrete frequencies," the tech replied.

Dr. Porter stood erect, thin-lipped and grim. He spoke without removing his gaze from image on the terminal.

"Annette," he said uncomfortably, measuring his words as he raised his arm to rub his temples with his thumb and fingertips, "With this equipment we can see a lot, but not everything. Steve is probably the most experienced ultrasound technician in the region. He's the best – " Then his voice trailed off and his attention was again drawn to the screen of the console. The figures squirmed and swirled as the tech swept the sensory probe across the smooth, pale globe of my wife's torso.

I. *The Letter*

1963-1975
Aspen, Colorado

My family's first home in Aspen wasn't very large. It was located just half a block from the creaking Little Nell ski lift that climbed up Ajax Mountain from the heart of the resurrected mining town. We moved to Aspen when I was a chubby, freckled seven year old. My father had been killed a couple of years earlier in a wreck with a drunk driver. My mother was looking to escape the pain of her loss and start her life anew. My parents loved Colorado, and they had often driven together in their1952 MG-TD on sports car rallies through the Roaring Fork River's emerald valley. When my mother realized she could afford to move to the brown, two-bedroom bungalow at the base of Ajax, she quickly decided to pack up her cat, her dog and her kids.

The valley's beauty served as a balm to her grief and she felt confident that my brother, sister and I couldn't get in too much trouble growing up in such a lovely small town. Her expectations were generally met by my siblings. Margot was a year and a half older than I was.

Slender, with long brown hair, she was smart, studious and sociable. In no time, she had a broad circle of friends and was elected to the Aspen Elementary School Student Council. My brother Justin was eighteen months younger than I was. Colorado's Rockies proved to be his natural habitat. His good looks were complimented by his remarkable athletic ability. For Justin, skiing was a completely natural act. He would flit down the slopes like a swift through the trees or a trout in one of the nearby streams. In a town of skiers, my brother was soon eliciting spontaneous applause from tourists and locals alike with his spectacular aerial stunts and mercuric mogul maneuvers.

To my mom's continuing frustration, however, I was a bit of a mess. Things got off to a bad start when I shattered my left wrist while doing bedroom acrobatics shortly after we arrived in town. It was the first of seven broken limbs over the next decade. The town's leading orthopedic surgeon became one of my good friends.

"Your bones are just fine," he said quizzically as he examined my X-rays for the umpteenth time. He repositioned his glasses from their perch atop his forehead to their conventional resting place and stared at me gravely. "What the heck are you doing to yourself out there?"

Most of the breaks were nasty. No compound fractures, but I usually managed to break a couple of bones simultaneously. I'd be knocked out of commission for three to six months, and then I'd scramble all the harder to keep up with my friends and classmates. Before too long I'd crash again. Skiing was my riskiest activity, but I also managed to break bones playing football and just horsing around.

Aspen in wintertime was a lonely place for a kid in a cast up to his hip. I spent a lot of time reading and doing my own special research and development projects. I'd send away for the latest information on our national space race to the moon. I studied every word of my monthly issue of Popular Science. Scale model rockets, planes and missiles whizzed over our house. My little brother grew sick of testing my special recipes for the astronauts, so I put on a few more pounds in my attempts to devise ways to keep them well nourished.

"Timber – Come in here, please." Mom's voice was serious, a little weary, and conveyed something indefinable. Even as an eight-year-old, I could tell that she was concerned with a matter more weighty than mud on the floor or the gloves I'd left on the kitchen table. The interplanetary cruiser I had been building with Legos would have to wait. I grabbed my crutches and hopped into the living room.

8

A stranger wearing a suit was standing near my mom inside the front door. They looked at me gravely as I approached. I caught a meaningful glance between the two of them as my mom motioned me forward and introduced him.

"This is Mr. Bowles, Timber. He works in Senator Dominick's office in Glenwood, and he has something he wants to talk to you about."

Mr. Bowles was older than my mom, tall, and very impressive. Kind of intimidating, in fact. His voice was not particularly friendly.

"Timber, do you recognize this? Your mother thinks you might have written it." He handed me four sheets of paper, all Xerox copies. I examined them carefully, but it took me only a moment to see that the originals were indeed my own work.

The first was a copy of the front of an envelope. In my tortured scrawl, it was addressed to The President of the United States, The White House, 1600 Pennsylvania Avenue, Washington, DC. My hands quivered perceptibly as I flipped to the second page. It showed the back of the same envelope. Although it originally had my mom's name and return address artfully engraved on the flap, the copy showed it just as I had sent it – all you could see was a large black smear. I hadn't wanted it to be easy for the President to figure out who had written the message inside. As I turned to the third page, I was stunned to see that my efforts to communicate with the President incognito were of little effect: The copy showed the same image of the back of the envelope, but the smear of black ink I had so laboriously applied had somehow been magically removed.

"We originally thought your mother might have sent this, and the Secret Service in Washington was somewhat concerned about her intent," Mr. Bowles intoned soberly.

My Mom???? What did she know about space flight? How in the world could they have thought that SHE would have written the President?

I was getting nervous. I remembered quite clearly what I had put in the envelope – and what I was now certain I would see on the fourth copy in my shaking hands. I paused to shove my sturdy, black plastic-framed glasses into place before turning the page.

9

Dear Mr. President –
Our country has a big problem. We must get to the moon before the Russians! Regular rockets will take too long and use too much fuel.
I have plans for an atomic powered rocket engine. It is the most powerful engine ever made by man!
I will contact you again soon.
Signed,
Mister X

There it was. I took a deep breath before looking at either Mr. Bowles or my mom. Clearly, I had to play my cards carefully. It seemed like the folks in Washington were indeed interested – after all, they had wasted no time in figuring out where the letter originated – but I had a bit of a problem. I had to find a way to tell the President that I had overstated my position just a little. I didn't really have detailed plans for the rocket. I just had some drawings. Actually, I had two drawings. They were hidden under my bed. Still, he would understand: It was an utterly brilliant idea.

"So, who do you think this mysterious Mister X is?" I asked the man in the suit. I had to see just what they knew.

"Timber! YOU wrote this letter!" My mom sounded like she was mad at me. She obviously didn't understand the importance of these negotiations. She was going to blow the whole deal if she wasn't more careful.

"Mom!" I had to get her to focus on the issue at hand. "Did you check this guy's ID? What if he's a spy?"

She grabbed me firmly by the shoulder as she knelt down to look me squarely in the eye.

"Timber, tell Mr. Bowles everything you know about this letter – Now!" Her voice was icy. She glared at me as her lips merged into a thin bloodless seam. By this time I was getting scared. As a matter of fact, I suddenly felt an urgent need to go to the bathroom. Mr. Bowles was also very grim. He didn't look like he'd let me leave to use the toilet. Maybe he knew there was a window in there. It occurred to me that he was the kind of guy who might be carrying a gun in a shoulder holster under that gray suitcoat.

It was an excruciating moment in my young life.

If Mr. Bowles had been a spy, the fate of the free world would have been in jeopardy. I caved in under the pressure – I spilled my guts. But I didn't surrender my drawings. It soon became clear that Mr. Bowles had precious little interest in my rocket design, anyway. He said he was asked by the FBI to find out whether an adult had written the letter. He said if it was an adult, the FBI would have had some sort of a "security concern." Once he was convinced that I – and not my mom – was the one with the rocket plans, he seemed to completely lose interest in my atomic engine.

My opinion of our President suffered considerably as a result. And that night before she'd let me eat dinner, my mom had me promise that I'd never use her stationery again without asking, and that I'd talk with her before writing any government officials.

Nonetheless, the mail continued to fascinate me with its power. It was about year later that I fell deeply in love with Debbie Nimrod. At age eleven, she was older than me, beautiful and popular – but she had a boyfriend. I figured I needed to impress her. There was a box in the attic that contained some old jewelry, so I took the nicest ring and mailed it – along with my proposal of marriage – to Debbie. The U.S. Mail empowered me. I never would have had the guts to ask her to marry me face-to-face, but I sure wrote her a great letter. I was more than a little embarrassed when her mom called my mom a few days later to ask about the whole affair. I subsequently got grounded for the next two months. How should I have known it was my great grandmother's diamond engagement ring? But it was worth it: While she didn't give up her old beau, for months afterwards Debbie gave me a nice smile every once in a while during lunch period.

In sixth grade, I had managed to break my leg again. The Doc put me in a thigh-high walking cast after only a few weeks. The enhanced mobility I was afforded was of questionable benefit. I soon attracted the attention of the local police by making rum in the science lab after school. One of the town's three patrol cars drove up beside me as I was hobbling home with a small flask in my coat pocket. The policeman said he had a report that I was making liquor. I explained that it was all just an experiment, that the rum reeked of neoprene tubing, and that I was just going to use the ethanol to preserve some specimens in my caterpillar collection. The officer nodded knowingly, gave me a stern lecture on the evils of alcohol and the laws against bootlegging, and sent me on my way. He kept the flask.

The next years were not easy for me. Overweight, alternately arrogant and insecure – and occasionally insufferable – I made few friends. When sports teams were picked, I stared in escalating anguish as even the scrawniest of my classmates were chosen to stand smugly in groups before my name was all too frequently the last one called. My classmates had seen enough of my experiments and projects to conclude I was reasonably smart, but my lack of academic focus had produced unspectacular grades and a string of teachers who were only mildly enthusiastic about my college prospects. My advisors in school labeled me bright but poorly motivated. Since I had skipped a year in grade school, I was one of the last in my class to experience the joys of puberty. Nonetheless, when testosterone finally started flooding my system, the transformation was dramatic. My stature grew as my voice became a mellow rumble that I barely recognized.

In my junior year of high school I somehow talked my way into a position as a disk jockey on the only local radio station. I played a lot of Elton John, Carole King, vintage Beatles – and more than my share of practical jokes. I was lucky that most of the station's listeners liked my choice of music. Otherwise my job would have probably ended when I filed an April 1st news story that pranksters had contaminated the town's water supply with hundreds of pounds of magnesium citrate, a powerful laxative. The report noted that anyone who had consumed any water within the past 24 hours should not venture far from a toilet, as the effects of the chemical could be sudden and dramatic. Activity in the valley crawled to a standstill for several hours until the station manager tracked down the origin of the story. He gave me a stern but good natured tongue lashing before he went on the air to declare an end to the health alert.

The locals were generally more amused when I staged a series of calls the following December to the station's morning talk show. Jim, the host of "Talk Back", was sympathetic, compassionate, and just a little gullible. He was a recent transplant from Long Island and he frequently waxed rapturously about his new hometown. My calls were supposedly from several back country residents hysterical about a plague of vicious rodents that were attacking, and then eating, pets and small livestock. Jim didn't appear to have a clue that the situation was anything but real.

12

"Mah dawg Rex ran out in the deep snow by the crik. Then he started yelpin' real loud – like somethin' was hurtin' him bad – and then he was jest <u>gawn</u>!" I wailed into the phone from an unused rear studio, my voice choking back the tears. "All ah found wuz his collar, an' even that wuz half eaten up!" Adopting another voice, I placed a second call a few moments later to say I'd found the skeleton of my prize heifer in a snowy meadow with the bones picked clean. I waited a few minutes, then posed as a forest ranger who was calling to calm things down. This helpful ranger explained that these voracious "snow moles" were the North American equivalent of the piranha, and that they hibernated during the summer only to emerge with the first snowfall to dig thousands of almost undetectable tunnels through the drifts underfoot. Their swarms would eat anything they came across – but they rarely attacked humans.

Suddenly the phones were overwhelmed. Newcomers who hadn't seen their cat for the last twenty minutes went into a panic. Tourists demanded to know why they weren't informed of this before they'd bought their week-long ski passes. The joke was snowballing out of control when a biologist from the <u>real</u> Forest Service phoned into Jim. I was more than a little relieved to have his authoritative assistance in quelling the burgeoning uproar amongst the flatlanders in town for the holidays.

I could have used a little more guidance during my formative years, I guess.

My existence as a pudgy, self-centered nerd on crutches during my first years of high school began to give way to a life of enhanced popularity. In addition to working at the radio station, I got a job as a ski instructor, mobilized my classmates on behalf of various environmental and civic causes and was elected to head up our student government. Finally, as I saw my senior classmates flaunting their admissions letters, I decided to abandon broadcasting and try to get into college. It was March when I applied to several good schools. A small but well-regarded school in Sarasota, Florida – New College – offered me a place in the class matriculating the following fall.

My first night on the school's campus was celebrated with a raucous party to welcome the incoming freshmen. The Grateful Dead were pounding in a central courtyard landscaped with huge palm trees and decorated with smoky tiki torches. The music was deafening, the atmosphere tribal. It was only a few minutes before I realized the torches were not the only things smoking on campus. Professors, administrators and alumni openly joined the students in flagrant illicit drug use. A half-dozen plastic-lined trash cans around the courtyard were filled with Purple Passion, a tongue-numbing concoction of grape Kool Aid and grain alcohol. Students were in turn swimming nude in the Olympic-size outdoor pool, showing off the thousand-dollar stereo systems in their dorm rooms, and wandering back to grab hors d'oeuvres from five gallon buckets filled with potato chips, pretzels and Quaaludes. The school had attracted me with its reputation for offering a liberal, but high quality, education. My understanding of the definition of the word *liberal* changed very quickly upon my arrival.

Over the following months I devoted long hours to my studies, frequently staying up until three or four in the morning. Once again, however, the subjects I focused on failed to include the courses I was enrolled in – or for that matter almost anything related to schoolwork. I succeeded in programming the school's refrigerator-sized computer to play ersatz pinball and discovered that students could check out not only books, but sailboats, from the library. The perpetual motion machine I built had a few bugs, but the bicycle I invented looked promising. I even got a couple of part-time jobs washing dishes and building cabinets to help meet my entertainment expenses. While some of the other students seemed a bit eccentric, they were responsive enough to my friendly overtures to elect me as a class representative to the college's student governing body.

I campaigned a lot at the pool.

Grades were a problem. My enthusiasm for unsanctioned extracurricular activities was insufficient to convince my professors that I was pursuing a rigorous education. By the time I headed home that spring most were obviously growing tired of hearing about my special projects and excellent excuses. They may have appreciated my intentions and liked my inventions, but there was little doubt in my mind that I was facing some serious talks with Mom on how I was accounting for her tuition payments.

New College's academic term ended in early May. It seemed a good time to go into damage control mode. As soon as I returned home for the summer, I once again got a job on the air at the radio station and then talked myself into a stint as a news reporter. I had retained a measure of community respect gained through my service back in high school as the town's youth representative on the Aspen City Council.

My news reports were well received. After only a few weeks, one of the station's ad salesmen unexpectedly left town and the manager offered me the job. I had only the dimmest concept of how ads should be sold, but due to a fortuitous account list and some respectable work on my part I generated close to half of the station's revenues by the end of my second month.

In early July of 1974 I arrived home from a mid-day shift at the station to find a letter addressed to me placed carefully on the corner of the dining room table. It was set apart from the other mail, next to the newest magazines and a few envelopes for other members of the family. I didn't often receive mail. Magazines, yes. Letters, rarely. This letter wasn't thick – probably just a page or two – and the return address showed it was from New College. Had the envelope not been there, I would have snatched my <u>National Geographic</u> or <u>Popular Science</u> and studied it for the next couple of hours. But my enthusiasm for updates about advances along the frontiers of knowledge was stillborn, poisoned by the mere sight of the envelope. It almost certainly held my grades from my first year of college. Like most students, I had a rough idea what they were. It was unlikely to contain good news. From its position on the table, it was clear that my mom had noticed it when she picked up the mail from our Post Office box. I could expect her to inquire about its contents when I saw her at dinner. That meant we'd get to talk about my grades as we ate. The prospect didn't make the meal sound very appetizing.

The house was quiet. In the decade since my proposal to Debbie, my family had moved from our little brown bungalow to the house of my mother's dreams. It was perched halfway up the valley's hillside commanding a view of the Roaring Fork River as it threaded through Aspen. Our new home's ten foot high Thermo-pane glass walls afforded a panoramic southern exposure. In the east loomed the granite crags of 12,000 foot high Independence Pass. To the south we overlooked the verdant, alpine slopes of Ajax Mountain and the picturesque town at its base. To the west the sun was now well on its way toward Mount Sopris, a massive, extinct volcano. The early summer light shone brightly through the small, vibrantly green leaves on the aspen trees surrounding our high deck.

Aspen had changed over the previous years. Its magnificent scenery and unparalleled skiing had lured lots of other folks from cities around the nation, and they brought with them many of the country's big

15

city problems. The town's unbridled hedonism and materialism were apparent to a casual observer. But less obvious in our alpine ghetto was an underlying spiritual poverty which was manifest in rampant drug abuse and a host of other self-destructive behaviors.

The valley was still breathtakingly beautiful – as long as you didn't look too closely.

Mom's car was nowhere to be seen, so she was probably downtown running errands. My sister was away on a road trip with a girlfriend and my brother was out riding bikes with his high school buddies. I had some time to ponder how to handle the envelope on the table. I left it there untouched and wandered over to the stereo to cue up my favorite album of the day.

They'd understand, I reassured myself. I had developed quite a talent for making people see my point of view. If I just explained the problems I was facing and all my clever solutions, they worked with me. It had been that way since I was a kid. My sense of humor tended to get me both in and out of trouble, and led most people to look upon me as a decent guy with a lot of idealism and a couple of snowball's worth of mischief and rebelliousness thrown in. I had grown to accept my role as a classic underachiever, a kid with a lot of potential who hadn't gotten his act together yet. The envelope from Florida would just tell another chapter of the same story.

Bonnie Raitt's plaintively velvet voice called to me over the speakers:

> What is success?
> Is it do your own thing?
> Or to join the rest?
> Or do you truly believe,
> and keep trying over and over again?
> Living in hope . . .
>
> [*What Is Success? by Allen Toussaint;*
> *Copyright 1974 by Marsaint Music;*
> *used with permission*]

When that nervously anticipated envelope finally arrived from Sarasota, I had arranged things so I was pretty well situated. My less-than-stellar grades would be balanced by my more recent achievements. I figured I could rationalize to my hard working, long suffering mother why she should fork over another year's tuition. I'd even be willing to make a contribution from my own earnings, I thought charitably. As I took a deep breath and ripped the crisp white paper open, I was fairly sure I could talk my way through my predicament to enjoy another year on the beach – with, of course, a textbook at my side.

The envelope, however, didn't contain my grades. It contained a polite statement informing me that the Standards Committee had decided it was in the best interest of the school, as well as my own, that I not attend New College in the coming academic year. Should I desire at some point in the future to return as a student, I was invited to reapply for admission.

It didn't quite say it, but I had flunked out.

I frantically dialed the Dean's Office. I was relieved to find the Assistant Dean answering the phone. Yes, he remembered me. Yes, he was working late that evening. And yes, he was well acquainted with my situation. Although I detected some slight irritation in his voice, I plunged ahead. There had been a big mistake, I explained. I was sure I had completed enough work to continue for the next year. The standards committee must not have given me the appropriate credits, I suggested helpfully. I was very relieved to hear him agree that yes, there had indeed been a mistake. The edge in his voice became less well disguised, however, as he explained that it was clear to the members that the mistake had been made not by the committee, but by me. The matter was open neither to reconsideration nor to appeal. And if I would please excuse him, he had work to do.

Ouch.

Silence muffled by static filled the earpiece, so I carefully hung up the phone. A few moments before, I had everything mapped out. Now the months and years ahead were ill-defined and inconclusive. As I looked across the valley toward the surrounding pearlescent peaks, my vision of the future writhed before me.

It took me the better part of an hour sitting on the deck to analyze the situation. My life was at a crossroads and there were a couple of distinct paths ahead. One was fairly familiar. I had previously scouted it out. In many respects, it was pretty appealing. At nineteen, I was suddenly making more money that many people twice my age. I had just bought myself a sexy sports car and an Italian road racing motorcycle. The girls who would flirt with me on the request line at the radio station were all too delighted to keep me company after my shift ended. I could sell ads, teach skiing, and live in paradise for the foreseeable future.

Maybe. In reality, the path I was treading was somewhat more convoluted. Aspen was still a small town. While the Vietnam War-inspired laws of the day allowed me to drink legally, I hadn't demonstrated particular competence in mixing booze and women. There were already too many girls I'd dated a few times who I now just wanted to avoid. And there were some who were apparently trying to avoid me, too. As for money, I was spending it faster than I could cash my checks. My purchases were satisfying my companions and indulging my habits but draining my account.

When I was honest with myself, I recognized I was making other mistakes as well. You would think that a guy who'd lost his father to a drunk driver would never consider driving under the influence. But I was an unusually skillful driver. I knew how much I could handle. The lines on the roadway may have been blurred and the streets of our little town confusing, but I had always made it home without accident or being apprehended by the cops. Even if I continued to avoid a run-in with the police, I was spending a lot of time – way, way too much time – in a barely functional stupor. Only a few weeks earlier I had settled down to watch TV with a bottle of rum. Somewhere during the evening I got a craving for sardines. I ate the whole can. When I awoke the next morning – thankfully in my own bed – I was thrashing in a pool of rancid fish and vomit.

I shuddered involuntarily as I recalled showering the disgusting mess out of my hair and ears. Sooner or later, my poor judgment was going to trump my dumb luck. Most of my friends were headed the same direction. A dozen of my classmates in our small high school were already dead from "accidents" where booze or drugs were involved. They had skied into trees, skidded over embankments, or suckled at the blue steel of a gun. Most of them died with no higher goal in life than to have fun, get a season ski pass and find a cute girlfriend. For all that I'd been given, if I stayed on my course of the last many months I'd be continuing a journey deeper and deeper into a wasteland of self-indulgent ruination.

Even for a nearly invincible guy like me, the prospect was sobering.

There was an alternative, but at the time the second path was foreign and discomfiting. For me – and many of my peers – it was a road less traveled, marked mostly with signs I hadn't learned to read. I had little understanding where it would lead me, but I knew that the rules of this second road were fundamentally different. It involved building my future rather than consuming it and living so as to give more than I received. I had grown to celebrate my camaraderie, but this way would require I turn from the activities that had defined my relations with most of my friends. To progress along it would demand a level of work, commitment, and honesty that was unprecedented in my life. I was afraid – terrified at one level – that even if I had the guts to pursue this vision of my life, I'd fail. Then I'd have given up my comforts, my habits, my companions and my cool new self image to become some sort of quixotic geek – again. Memories of the social rejection I faced in junior high came flooding back.

But they weren't quite as bad as the sardines.

The sun was setting over Mt. Sopris as we finally sat down to dinner the day I got the letter from New College. As anticipated, Mom wanted to talk about what it contained, but she was pretty nice about the news. Perhaps she sensed that in many respects this was the best thing that had ever happened to me. For too long, my way had been greased by good fortune, privilege and my powers of persuasion. I suspect she could see where I was headed unless something interfered.

I lacked both the strength and the courage to immediately change my life in all the ways I might have, but I found enough backbone to make some new commitments. I resolved to do my best to lead a productive life. In the midst of my fear, doubt, and ignorance, I decided to reorient the compass of my soul.

I began to work on more worthwhile projects. I struggled to refine the bicycle I'd invented and talked my way into a sales management position with the radio station. To my astonishment, I was able to apply for a patent on the bike and I set new ad revenue records at the station. When I retook the college entrance exams, my scores were good – very good. I sent a long letter to several top universities which acknowledged that I had blown my first opportunity for a college education and begged them for one more chance.

It was in January after I received the envelope from New College that the receptionist at the station buzzed me in the studio. Linda had recently moved to town from Idaho. She was an enthusiastic supporter of my newly directed approach to life. Some guy was on the phone long distance, she said, and he claimed it was important. In those days, our DJ's ran the whole on-air show: I would spin the records, rip and read the news from the clattering teletype, and set my own play list of music. I asked her to have him hang on for just a minute while I got a long song cued up.

"Timber?" asked the man's voice through the noise on the line. "This is Christopher Murphy with the admissions office at Yale College. Did you get my letter? I sent it Special Delivery."

"Um, can you hang on a minute?" I frantically gestured to Linda through the big window that separated the studio from her cubicle in the station's lobby. I pointed to the day's mail still piled on the corner of her desk. It took her only a moment to notice the distinctive envelope addressed to me. She whisked it through the door and into my trembling hands.

"Uh, yes, sir. I just got it now – but I haven't read it yet."

"That's OK," Mr. Murphy responded. "It has a few forms that you'll need to fill out before we give you formal notice on your case. I just wanted to call you to let you know we went ahead and reviewed your file in a meeting this morning. As a committee, we're very pleased to have received your request for admission."

"Uh, gee, that's terrific!" I stammered, having lost all my broadcaster's poise.

Mr. Murphy continued. "The letter I sent you isn't really an approval of your application because we don't have all the information we need from you yet. However – " He paused for a moment to assure that I appreciated the full significance of his words, "As long as we get those forms back here promptly, the next letter I send you will be an invitation to attend Yale in the fall. Congratulations!"

Chapter 2

Twins?

At Dr. Porter's command, the radiology tech turned on the external speaker for the Doppler stethoscope. The steady, strong sound of the baby's heart ebbed and flowed across the darkened room like wavelets washing against the hull of a small boat. The tech and Dr. Porter stared at one another as they listened intently, but only for a moment. Then they refocused their concentration upon the images on the screen at Annette's side.

The otherworldly cadence of the heartbeat was a welcome distraction from the rising tide of tension in the examination room. Annette and I had listened to the hypnotic rhythm many times before. For years, we had taken a special comfort from the unique whoosh and thump that had characterized each baby's prenatal heartbeat. I knew my wife well enough to understand that we heard something markedly different in the sounds pulsing from the speakers. Our minds simply processed the information to give very disparate sets of associations. When I heard the dynamics of tiny muscles contracting on turbulent fluid to create amplified audio waves, she sensed a voice of life speaking to her through the skin and tissue that both united and separated her from the child she carried. We were like musicians who, upon seeing a new composition, imagined the melody as played on the instrument we knew best: piano versus violin; or a coronet instead of a harmonica – but we both cherished all that the sound of each tiny, beating heart represented. Annette held my left hand in hers as we both struggled to make sense of

21

the doctor's silence and the strange jumble of images glowing on the monitor.

There was little question remaining in my mind that something was seriously wrong. Before the test started, the technician had cheerfully told us he would provide a guided tour of the baby. "You'll be able to see the baby's arms, legs – you may even be able to tell whether you have a boy or girl," he explained. During Mercina's ultrasound, we could see her curled in a ball, sucking her thumb. They had given us a Polaroid to take home with us. Now Annette's expression told me she had given up trying to decipher the mishmash of screen imagery.

Annette hadn't always been the easiest patient. Too smart to automatically accept everything her doctors told her, she bridled at any sign of condescension or manipulation. Her reactions sparked occasional friction with some of her health care providers. From her perspective, medicine was a profession, not a black art. Good car mechanics or news reporters were usually capable of explaining their craft intelligibly when they did their job well. She expected the same quality of communication now. I could tell she was growing tired of Dr. Porter's reluctance to describe the significance of the machine's output. The equipment was telling her nothing, so she searched for clues and reassurance in the curiously strained expressions the doctor shared with the nurse and the tech. Conversely, I had concluded it was fruitless to pump them for information. Instead I tried to find my own answers in what I saw in front of me. I began to piece together a three dimensional image from the jigsaw puzzle of glimmering shapes floating on the dark screen. Except for the moments when I stroked Annette's cheek or kissed her hand, I became completely involved in the pictures flickering before me.

Few scenes could better highlight our differences against all that we shared. Annette was five foot two with eyes of blue, while my dark hair was usually found at twelve inches' higher altitude. Her bountiful curves somehow nested into my lanky frame like they were designed together. I was trained to be efficient and analytical; she blissfully took the longest distance between two points, whether in a commute or a conversation. She pondered the lessons of history and religion while I sought to develop my skills as an inventor and entrepreneur. Her parents were Hungarian Jews who had lived through the Holocaust. My father – who died when I was five – was nominally a Methodist. Our discrepant choice of married names reflected on the one hand her desire to honor her grandfather Tillemann's self-sacrificing effort to rescue his family

22

from the Nazis and on the other hand my wish to retain my deceased father's name.

Our differences were many, but we shared a passionate love for one another, a profound faith, and an uncommon commitment to forge a family. From the moment we'd detected the almost imperceptible pattering of our first son's prenatal heartbeat on an old-fashioned stethoscope a few months after our marriage, a huge wave of relief washed over us as we heard each ensuing baby's heart beating from within the womb. The pulsing of the speakers in the exam room served to both of us as tangible evidence that this pregnancy might still progress without problems.

We were well aware that the protein test results that prompted Linda to send us to Dr. Porter were not the only worrisome indicators. At Annette's age, there was roughly a 6% percent chance the baby would be born with Down Syndrome. Dr. Irwin had also noted the baby was growing unusually quickly. At twenty weeks, Annette looked almost ready to deliver. Driving downtown to the clinic earlier in the day, we had discussed the possibility of a Down's baby, or whether we might have twins in the works. I had refrained from voicing the thought that we might simultaneously be facing both. Now, as I looked at the doctor's strained face silhouetted against the glow of the test console, my thoughts revisited the possibility.

I stared more intently at the screen, methodically compiling its strange two-dimensional depictions into a human form. Suddenly a cold chill fractured what remained of my peace of mind.

I knew what they saw in the ghostly shapes.

Annette's patience expired. "Dr. Porter, what is going on?" she asked insistently. "Why aren't you telling us <u>anything</u>? I see twins – don't I see twins?"

The nurse behind me evidently shared Annette's frustration with the silence on the part of the men in the room. "Oh, yes, you definitely have a pair of twins," she said, and I watched a flush of excitement wash over Annette's confused face. Then a plaintive, tentative note crept into the nurse's voice. "Doesn't she, Dr. Porter?"

He cleared his throat, then took a long, deep breath.

"Yes – well..." His voice trailed off yet again as he grimly shook his head with disbelief.

"Doctor," I interrupted, dreading what I was about to say, "I see two heads – but I only see one torso. Is that right?"

For the first time in many long minutes, Dr. Porter turned away from the ultrasound screen. He looked toward me, but he didn't seem to see any of us. His eyes reflected the jumbled images and emotions that I had seen pass across his face since he had first studied the flickering console.

"Yes," he almost whispered, as if he were unsure how to continue. "Twins." He inhaled deeply again, then he cleared his throat once more and succeeded in mustering a more professional tone as he continued.

"This is extremely unusual. What you see are two torsos joined at the collarbone. These twins each have their own spines, and the conjoined section diverges right where the umbilicus comes in from the placenta. They each have their own legs and arms, and," he pointed with his pen at the glowing forms on the monitor, "as you can see right here, you've got two little boys."

Annette's eyes welled up as she choked back a sob. She turned away from the screen and the doctor to stare up at me. Silent, raw emotion filled her face. I had seen that look only once before and for years I had sought to blot out the memory. As a young, off-duty ski instructor, I was alone on a chairlift half-way up the mountain. It was an overcast afternoon. Cold. As I flexed my fingers and toes in a futile attempt to stimulate their circulation, I noticed the little girl riding solo in the chair ahead of me. She was perhaps eight or nine years old, with brown pigtails extending from her brightly knit hat. I saw her lean forward to adjust her ski boot. At that moment, her chair bounced over the guide pulleys of a lift tower. She lost her balance. She tumbled forward out of her seat, but with one hand she was able to hold on as she dangled three stories above the snowy hillside. She faced me, her left hand inexorably slipping out of her mitten as it gripped the frame of the chair, her right arm and skis flailing and failing to connect with anything solid, anything safe. She was too stunned to utter a sound, but the terror in her soul screamed out across the void between us. Her eyes locked into mine and in that instant we shared an eternity of dread and horror. She couldn't hold on for long. Tragedy consumed us inevitably and inexorably. I'll never forget what I saw in that little girl's pleading, silent face as she tried so hard to hang on. It was the same alchemy of fear, helplessness and, paradoxically, hope that flowed again between Annette and me as we grasped for comprehension in Dr. Porter's darkened examination room.

24

"I don't understand," she said, searching my face for an answer to a question that was beyond expression. I knew that Annette – like the little girl – did understand at one level. They could both see their lives twisting in a convulsion of change. Annette understood exactly what the doctor had said. What he had said was unimaginable. This mother of twin boys couldn't choose to believe her dreams were plummeting into a chasm of despair. But like the little girl, she couldn't escape what had already happened.

Dr. Porter pressed on with his explanation. "From what we can see, these twins share a liver, and their gastrointestinal tracts are at least commingled. There may be just one G.I. system, but I suppose we could deal with that. I don't claim to begin to understand what's going on with the heart, or hearts. I just can't tell whether there's one very abnormal heart pumping for both bodies, or perhaps two interlinked cardiovascular systems."

"There's some fluid buildup," the technician said in a low voice.

"Yes, that's right. This area here," Again he pointed to the screen's image with his pen, "Is a lymph-type fluid that has built up in the pericardium – the chest cavity. It's usually a sign of some degree of systemic cardiac stress or maybe genetic problems. You can also see that the fetuses are not developing evenly. The one on the right has significantly greater body mass and measurements."

"But," Annette asked, and her question didn't sound at all irrational at the time, "Are they OK?"

The doctor looked over from the computer console to her hopeful face shining with tears.

"No." His tone left no room for doubt about the gravity of the twins' prognosis. "I don't know of any way I can assure you that they are going to be okay. I've read of cases like this, but in almost forty years of high-risk obstetrical practice, I've never been personally involved with anything resembling this. Statistically, there's very little basis for any judgment. Siamese twins are among the rarest of all conceptual events. These have a very abnormal heart, the liver is shared, and there are quite likely to be genetic abnormalities, given some of the other things I see here. Their prognosis is almost certainly extremely poor."

Annette stifled several sobs. I looked back to my wife, but I saw a little girl with big eyes plummeting through the void to a bleak white slope. The silence of suspense cracked as her skis, poles, limbs and lungs were crushed into a broken heap. The drift-shrouded evergreens

25

ignored my impotent screams and the virgin snow drank the crimson traces blooming from her small, still body.

In desperation I turned to the nurse and the technician, as well as Dr. Porter.

"Doctor, we need some time alone."

Both out of respect for our situation and out of a transparent desire to obtain some relief from the tension and pain in the room, all three began to move toward the door.

"Of course," Dr. Porter said. "We'll turn off the ultrasound, but I want to leave you wired up. We should do a few more things. That is unless you want me to leave it on." He nodded at the ultrasound image casting its sickly blue glow over the room. As Annette's sobs grew louder, he slipped out the door without taking any action or awaiting further answer.

The doctor closed the door almost soundlessly behind them. With the quiet click of the door latch, we were both aware of the sound of the babies' hearts filling the room. What remained of our composure was drowned out by the unearthly rhythm from the speaker. Annette was racked with sobs as I held her close.

"Oh, Dear God, how can this be happening?" Annette buried her face in my chest, and I felt her quake and gasp with the pain. I stared once more at the shadowy forms on the CRT and felt my tears dripping off my jaw onto Annette's shoulder and back.

I have no clear idea how long I stood there. It might have been half an hour. Perhaps it was only a few minutes. We were together in that strange place where the pulse of time is imperceptible but its relentless transformative power courses onward. Her sobs became fainter, and my tears gradually stopped falling. Finally Annette relaxed her grip around my waist and took a deep breath. We were unable to speak. I pulled a wet lock of hair from her cheek, and we looked at each others' faces, drawn and stained, for a long moment.

Annette tried valiantly to regain command of her emotions. She grabbed a Kleenex from a box the tech used to clean up the electrolyte gel and wiped the tears from her cheeks.

"I can't believe we have twin boys."

Then her carefully reconstructed veneer crumpled, and she raised her arms limply to my shoulders as she once again collapsed into quaking sobs. I clung to her as I agonized over my utter inability to envision a solution for the trial before us. My right hand was intertwined in the gentle curls of her golden hair, my left was firmly supporting her as she leaned upon me. We were, for that moment, as closely joined as the two babies curled within her and now cradled between us both.

Usually I was pretty good at saying the right thing in a tough situation. Nothing came. Part of my mind had shut down, or withdrawn into a protective analytic cocoon. I mechanically cycled through my standard problem-solving procedures. I reassured myself that I was an inventor with a number of patents. It was my passion and my vocation to make things work better. As a father and as a businessman, I was confronted daily with difficult issues. But as a husband in this situation, I had no precedent, no relevant experience, and no vision of a solution. Nothing I had ever been taught provided a model I could work from. My mind was spinning in great uncontrolled circles, propelled like a powerful car careening about on smooth ice with the driver aimlessly flooring the accelerator but going nowhere. I couldn't face the questions or even try to formulate a mental list of issues to address with the doctor. It took a small slice of eternity for me to emerge into a netherworld of partial diagnosis and uncertain prognosis, of statistical likelihoods and fantastic surgical possibilities. It hurt less that way. I desperately tried to estimate how many pregnancies Dr. Porter handled each year, so I wouldn't be forced to ask whether I would ever hold my twins. I told myself that perhaps I could invent a device that would allow their hearts to function, because I couldn't face the fact that their – and now, our – lives together offered a relentless and uncertain flood of challenges and trials.

"Timber...?" Annette spent several moments searching my face before I acknowledged her attention by bringing my focus back to her mascara-stained eyes. For a second she was able to smile weakly up at me. Together we looked over at the grey-blue streaks, blotches, and shadows frozen on the screen. Now that we were oriented, we could more easily see the two heads in silhouette, facing each other, and the shoulders below. The babies' faces were almost touching. The smaller one had his hand raised up to his cheek in a tiny fist.

"Oh, baby," I said, "We're in for a doozie of a ride on this one."

"What do they do with babies like this?" Annette asked tentatively. "Will they try to separate them?"

She frequently asked questions that she knew were far outside my areas of expertise. Every once in a while I dredged up a well informed answer.

27

"I don't know," I began, and then I laboriously started to piece together what little we'd learned. "Dr. Porter's never seen anything like this. Maybe it's so rare that nobody knows what's going to happen. He couldn't see whether there were two hearts, and that tells me that it simply may not be possible to do anything surgically, at least not without sacrificing one of them." I looked into her eyes, and noted that she was gaining control of her emotions. "I remember hearing that they were trying to do some infant liver transplants, and that bleeding was almost impossible to control. The fact that they share a liver doesn't sound good to me, either."

"Maybe we'll just raise them like they are," Annette hypothesized with a note of hope. "We could do that. The kids'll help and we'll find a way to make things work." Her resolve was firming. We both leaned closer to study the console when the bright, yellow-white wedge of light once again streamed across the floor and ceiling as the door opened.

A woman's voice asked cautiously, compassionately, "May I join you?" It was Carol, the other Dr. Porter in our lives.

Dr. Carol Porter was in practice with her husband. Her office was across the hall and two doors down. She and Albert were both OB/GYN's specializing in perinatalogy, but by their mutual agreement she more often dealt with the "patient interfacing," as they called it. Annette and I had stopped by her office for a briefing on the test procedures less than an hour earlier. She was dark haired and trim, with soft brown eyes and a pleasant face. She appeared years younger than her husband but her easy smile may have contributed to an illusion of youthfulness. The walls of her office were literally covered with photos and letters from the parents of triplets and quads, and other babies that had been successfully treated as a result of the pioneering prenatal diagnostic work they had done.

"Annette – " Carol moved smoothly past me to gently embrace my wife. "Timber. I honestly can't imagine what you're going through. Are you OK?" She looked from Annette to me and back again. "This has got to be incredibly difficult and confusing. Timber, sit down for a minute." She pulled the rolling stool the tech had been using toward me.

"I know you must have a thousand questions, but I can see you're pretty wrung out, too." She handed Annette a fresh Kleenex. "I'm going to try to give you some context – a little background – on what's happening here. Feel free to interrupt me, but maybe I can answer some of your questions before you have to ask them. I've never had to deal with conjoined twins before and yours are particularly challenging because of the way they are joined. I'm going to try to explain this like I'd want things explained to me, if I were in you're shoes. So hang on – I'm not going to sugar-coat what I tell you."

Carol started by explaining that Albert had come directly to her door after leaving us in the exam room. She'd been on the phone when he peered into her office, but the troubled look on his face prompted her to cut the call short.

"I asked him what the problem was. Since we've been working together, we've dealt with most of the possible problems in conception and delivery and Albert almost never interrupts me that way. All he said was, 'Twins – conjoined at the heart...'"

Her succinct description had communicated volumes. Annette and I glanced at each other as Carol continued.

"First, I thought about you, Annette. I know you were excited that maybe you're carrying twins, and this has to be devastating. I'm so sorry." She stroked Annette's shoulder and was quiet for half a minute. "There are a lot of other thoughts and concerns that we should start to talk about. First there are the purely medical issues. We should run some more tests – genetic screens, probably an echocardiogram, maybe an MRI. The truth is that these guys may not be viable." She paused to let us absorb the sense of her remarks.

"If you decide that they can survive, what then?" Annette asked.

Carol seemed to choose her words carefully. "Pediatric surgeons had been developing new procedures and new confidence in separating conjoined twins in the past few years, but the mortality rate is still extremely high. If babies joined at the heart could be parted, one would almost certainly die. There's another concern. Annette, you're chronically – although not seriously – anemic and you've got a prolapsed uterus in your history. None of this bodes well for you. This situation doesn't offer much in the way of an easy way out. If you carry these babies to term, we'll have to subject you to the trauma of major surgery to deliver them. If they make it, their future will be marginal, at best."

Carol turned her attention to me. "If we can determine that these twins are viable, you two need to ask some very hard questions. Is this an appropriate risk to take with Annette's life, as a mother with nine other children at home? I can't answer that one for you."

29

We sat in silence for several long moments.

"Dr. Porter, do we really have all these choices?" I ventured. "At what point do you tell us what we can or can't do?"

"I think I know what you mean. Our practice functions wholly within our HMO, and Annette has to be treated according to the by-laws and rules governing your service agreement. That's mostly good for you. Your family will be spared the extraordinary expenses of treatment, whatever we choose to do. But you're also right – if I understand you correctly, Timber – in that you won't have unlimited options. Albert and I will be dealing with all sorts of administrative oversight committees, cost evaluation reviews, and interdepartmental treatment strategy teams. Most of it will be pretty much invisible to you, and they're intended to help assure the health of all our patients, but I should probably warn you that the politics of this case might get a little intense. If the twins are delivered, a lot of people are going to take an interest in your lives. The medical community will want to study your case, and who knows what the press would do if they got hold of this?" Carol paused. "I know this is a lot to handle at once, but you probably need all the data you can get at this point.

"Sometime soon you'll probably run into our Dr. Mahoney. He's the administrative director of the group. Don't let him worry you too much. He's very conservative – I mean medically and financially – and I'm sure he'll advise you accordingly. He's going to be the one around here who'll want you to take the lowest risk, lowest cost solution." She didn't expound any further, but I had an idea what she meant.

Carol reaffirmed her husband's preliminary assessment of the twins' condition.

"Albert says they don't look as healthy as we'd like. There's asymmetric development – one's bigger than the other. Steve," she nodded toward the unattended ultrasound console, "sees some things that may indicate genetic problems, too. It's just too early to tell whether either one of them is really able to make it even through delivery."

While Carol clearly did not enjoy this part of her job, she softly told us that it was actually a big reason she was drawn to the field. Early in her training, she said she had too often seen a woman confront the most searing medical drama of her life in the care of a doctor who discussed her condition like it was a plumbing problem, or perhaps a lawsuit. These doctors somehow thought that by being clinical and detached they could make it easier on both the patient and themselves.

She smiled as she told us that she had trained Albert to be a lot better than most, but she had also grown to appreciate that his greatest strengths were elsewhere.

"He's now in the library trying to find you anything we have on conjoined twins. I'll give him a few more minutes and then see if he can join us." She related that she thought she also had an article in her office that might help. She begged our pardon to go look for it, but promised to return promptly. We were only alone again for a minute or two.

Annette and I felt a measure of relief as the two Dr. Porters filed back into examination room, followed by Steve – the tech – and the staff nurse. Carol walked directly over and embraced us in a three-way hug. I felt she was trying not only to comfort us, but also to show the others by her example how to exercise compassion. Annette responded with a quiet flurry of tears, but quickly collected herself.

"I'm so sorry," Carol repeated while she stroked Annette's back and squeezed my hand. "After looking through my files for that article I came up empty-handed. Albert's told me what he's found, though, and we were able to talk a little bit about what we think we can do." She nodded toward Steve, who had taken his position at the console. "Annette, if you'll lay back down, maybe you and Steve can show me what these guys look like?" She glanced over at the technician.

"Sure," he said, and he picked up the ultrasonic transducer. "I'm sorry, I'm going to have to put some more of this goop on you," he said to Annette. "Maybe I can warm it up a bit." His gruffness was gone, and he was making a genuine effort to offer some support. He manipulated the sensor head on her tummy to paint new gray-blue figures on the screen.

"Depending on the view we get – let's try from over here, now – Yes. You can see that all their limbs appear to be in good shape. If you look carefully, you can even count their fingers. See? Five on that hand, and I checked them all out before. Four hands with five fingers each, and four feet with five toes." He was talking directly to us now, even as he was trying to bring Carol up to speed on the twins' condition. He glanced over to Albert. "In some respects, these little fellows are in pretty good shape."

Annette sniffed audibly, but we could all feel the stress ebbing from the room. Steve moved the transducer with practiced skill across Annette's swollen stomach, explaining with each swipe what was illustrated by the ultrasonic waves bouncing off the twins in her womb.

31

"This area – here – is the liver, and you can see it extends without a break across any reasonable dividing line between them. And this," he pointed to the screen with his pen, "is the heart, or hearts. As Dr. Porter may have explained, we're having a heck of a time figuring out the plumbing" (Carol winced at his choice of words...) "on both the circulatory system and the gastrointestinal tract. This black area over here is worrisome. Both fetuses are showing signs of this fluid buildup in their chests and on the backs of their necks. It can be an indicator of cardiac distress, or genetic abnormalities, or both. The other thing that's a concern is that the guy on the right is bigger than the guy on the left. Conjoined twins are always identical, and so we're not happy when one is clearly smaller."

Steve looked at the Porters for an indication whether he should continue, but I interrupted. "How can they be delivered?"

"Good question," Carol replied and then turned briefly to the woman in the white lab coat. "Regina, could you please turn up the lights? That's better. There are very few recorded conjoined twins in historical accounts. We don't have any reason to believe that there are more being conceived now, so researchers speculate that the incidence of conjoined twins was roughly the same in the past as it is now, but the mothers almost never survived childbirth. The medical term is 'failure to progress' and it used to be disastrous. Especially when twins were joined at the chest like these are, they're simply too big for the delivery to proceed. In the old days, that meant the mothers died. Since they didn't conduct routine autopsies, no one ever knew the babies were malformed. The same would hold true with Annette if we just let things go without intervention. Once they grow a little more, these twins could never be delivered normally. We'd have to do a C-section."

"How often does this happen?" This time it was Annette asking.

"Albert's got some information from a medical text that he'll copy for you. Apparently, about one in a hundred thousand conceptions may be conjoined, maybe a few more. Many are spontaneously aborted before the mother is even aware there's anything wrong. It is extremely uncommon that they are carried to term, and even more unusual the they survive much past birth."

"So what can we do to take care of them?" Annette asked.

Albert seemed increasingly concerned with the course the conversation was taking. "First, you need to remember that these fetuses have severe problems," he said, reverting to his clinically detached tones. "They are highly unlikely to survive to term. Second, if they were to make it through the birth trauma, they'd be very sick. They almost certainly wouldn't live long." In spite of his professional demeanor, the trapped look in his eyes made it clear he hated this part of his job. "And finally, carrying these fetuses will put Annette's welfare increasingly at risk. You could experience a host of complications that could endanger you, and you've got your kids at home."

Carol tried to cushion the impact of her husband's words. "You two have a lot to think about. In your situation, your first priority has to be to ensure Annette's well-being," she said softly. "We'll do everything we can to help you through this."

Albert could see on Annette's face the obvious emotional impact of his remarks, but I guess he figured he was better off to say everything up front. "We can't terminate the pregnancy here, because this is a Catholic hospital, but we can go right across the street to Denver Central. If we act within the next week or two, it'll probably be an uncomplicated procedure."

Tears welled up once more in Annette's eyes and ran down her cheeks. Almost unconsciously, I moved closer to her and stood between the doctor and the table where she was still reclined.

"I think we'd like to make sure we knew everything possible before we'd make that decision," I said protectively.

"Of course," Carol responded, trying with every syllable to be as comforting and reassuring as possible. She reached over and held Annette's hand. "I know you didn't want to have one before, but with what we've found on the ultrasound, we'd like to do an amniocentesis. It's possible that the babies" (Annette's expressions as Albert spoke apparently moved her to avoid using the word 'fetus') "may have a genetic problem that would give us a better sense of how we should proceed."

"It doesn't matter to us if they're Down's babies," Annette replied resolutely. "One of our best friends has Down Syndrome, and we love him."

"Is what you're saying that they may have some other problem that would make it impossible to live outside the womb?" I asked Carol Porter. I admit to feeling less inclined to talk with her husband.

"Exactly. There are only a few genetic abnormalities that threaten a baby's life, and we can test for almost all of them. If the twins are genetically normal, it may influence our treatment strategy. I think you know what's involved." Carol's tact helped shift the mood back toward the positive. She and Steve worked together over the next several minutes to insert a large hollow needle through Annette's abdominal wall into the uterus. It then took only a moment to draw a sample of the amniotic fluid. The procedure was not terribly painful, but the general effect was to make her more tired and more nauseous.

Finally they let Annette sit up. The tech disconnected the web of wires and belts entangling her to the apparatus by her side. Carol stayed nearby and helped clean the pale blue gel's residue from Annette's abdomen, but Albert Porter motioned me into the far corner of the room. He placed a large book and several Xerox copies on the counter.

"This is all I could find in the library we have here," he explained, opening the book to a two-page photographic spread. Some of the photos were clear and sharp, while others were of poor quality and obviously made many years ago. I recoiled involuntarily at the images. There were perhaps a dozen sets of twins shown on the pages. They were conjoined in ways I would have previously never imagined: head-to-head, by their chests, bottom-to-bottom, and other configurations that defy easy description. Most of the twins had every appearance of being dead, but a few had their eyes open. Dr. Porter turned the page to one additional photo that was eerily close to the image on the ultrasound monitor.

"I made a copy of this page," the doctor said, "and here's some additional material on genetic defects that might be relevant." He paused as if reviewing his options. He was clearly very uncomfortable.

"These fetuses have almost no chance of survival," he reiterated, "and Annette's risk goes up each additional day she carries them. If I were you, I'd terminate the pregnancy. If the twins were born, I'd take them away and let nature take its course. They're not viable." His phrasing was crude, but his meaning was unambiguous. He turned momentarily back to the pictures of the other twins, and then closed the book.

I felt dazed, rocked by waves of vertigo. There was an otherworldliness about the situation, as if the scene was being played out on the far side of a darkly tinted window. My ears were filled with a pounding like that of the heartbeats that had been pulsing over the speakers in the room, but louder, and hissing with static. For the moment, I was simply unable to respond. Then I managed to nod mutely to the doctor and I turned back to Annette. I quickly stuffed the copied pages into my jacket pocket as I tried to regain my concentration.

Carol and Steve were summarizing the twins' condition to Annette. They were oblivious to the conversation that had just taken place in the corner of the room.

"Clearly the heart is the biggest problem," Carol explained, but she was cut off by Annette.

"We know someone who specializes in diagnosing babies' heart problems. Timber, what is Dr. DeVore's first name?"

I blinked and struggled to think. "DeVore? You mean from Yale?" She nodded affirmatively. "Uhhh...Greg – Wasn't that it?"

Albert Porter turned to looked at Annette with renewed interest.

"Do you know Dr. Greg DeVore?" he inquired.

"Yes, of course. I mean, its been years since we've seen him, but he helped deliver our first son – well, actually, Timber delivered Tomicah, and Dr. DeVore took care of the placenta," Annette had recovered enough from the events of the preceding hour to regain her customary speech patterns, "And someone was telling me, maybe somebody back in New Haven, that he was in California now and he did this all the time, and he's an expert in diagnosing and correcting prenatal heart problems. We knew him well during his residency at Yale-New Haven. I used to teach his kids in church. Do you know him?" She glanced expectantly at each person in turn, but it was Albert who responded.

"Yes, certainly. I mean, I know of him professionally." The doctor was obviously impressed with this new development. "Dr. DeVore's pioneered the development of the echocardiogram as a fetal diagnostic procedure. I was just recently at a conference where he was the keynote speaker. If anyone could figure out whether something could be done with the cardiovascular system, it would be him."

Annette's speech tempo increased. "I'm sure we can get in touch with him. We can call the Igleharts, or the Chudleighs. I bet the Chudleighs know how to find them. It'd be nice to talk with them anyway. You remember Hal and Janice, don't you Timber?"

"I believe Dr. DeVore's in Salt Lake now," Albert reflected. "He's got a practice where he splits his time between Salt Lake and UCLA, if I remember correctly. I think I'd like to have him take a look at this. Maybe we <u>could</u> do something with the cardiac system."

After the doctor's recommendations to me a few moments earlier, I was pleased and a little shocked to hear Dr. Porter making comments that sounded as though there might be hope for the twins. He went on. "Maybe we can refer you to him. I'd have to get special approval, because I'm sure we don't have a service agreement with his practice, but I think we can justify it in this case."

Annette and I left a few minutes later. We had more questions than any doctor could answer, and except for the news that Dr. DeVore might be able to help, most of the answers we had received thus far sounded terrible. As we exited the examination room we walked past the bank of elevators to the end of the hall. There, next to some potted trees and a large window overlooking the city, we stood together with our heads bowed and our hands clasped as one.

People use different mechanisms to cope with the fears and trauma of life. Some folks drink themselves numb. Others build stony walls of bitterness and hate, or callous indifference. Some strive to find meaning in the pain. And the little, pigtailed girl on the ski lift had grimly held on in hope that by grace or gritty determination the Angel of Death might be moved – at least this one time – to pass over, so she could somehow continue along her life's smooth glide.

When I was five and my father was killed, I simply rejected the notion that he was gone. It took me years to stop looking for his white Chevy station wagon. About the time that the crunching of tires on our gravel driveway no longer prompted a flutter of excitement that he had returned, I started to ask the normal questions about where he might be. Mainstream religions offered answers that were initially unappealing. They seemed to require an abandonment of reason as they commanded archaic behaviors. As a teen of the Sixties, I had explored beliefs borne from the Far East and the far west. My search continued into college, where I found what I sought in a church. For the first time, I was comfortable with the demands and answers afforded by religion. Annette and I tried to live our faith and within a decade I was working – in addition to my paying job – as the lay minister for the congregation in our corner of town.

Then a few days before Father's Day in 1989 our three-month-old son died. SIDS, the doctors said. We found ourselves almost completely overwhelmed by responsibility, and anguish, and need. We responded in the only way we knew that might work for us: We relied on our faith through prayer.

I learned a powerful lesson: I had a choice. As far as my life was concerned, I had to do more than lay a claim to faith. I couldn't just be diligent and assume we would be protected from the hard, ugly side of life. Instead, I must dig deep and choose to believe – as well as live – in faith. There was still no assurance that we'd be spared the sufferings experienced by all people since time immemorial. But there was a promise that the most important part of my being would be shielded, and that I could in turn offer strength to those I love.

As I had held my beautiful little Lincoln's body, I consciously decided to hope. As I then relied on the promises of faith, I was able to keep the wolves of despair at bay. Annette and I found that not all our burdens were lifted, but neither were we crushed by the avalanche of anxiety and grief descending upon us. We found reasons to be grateful for Lincoln's brief life and to value his role in our family in a way that made the pain of his loss bearable. Our faith wasn't shattered – but perhaps only because we had chosen to actively and affirmatively protect it, strengthen it, and rely upon it.

Now, in the same way, Annette and I stopped in that quiet corner of the clinic to thank God for our twin boys and the ray of hope that we'd been given to build our lives with them.

II. Improbable Answers

October 1976
New Haven, Connecticut

A month or so into my third semester at Yale, I found myself sitting alone on the floor of my dorm room, surrounded by texts. I knew I'd reached a critical turning point. Academically I'd had a decent first term followed by a fairly impressive spring semester, and shortly after I returned from summer break the Dean had called me in for a conference.

"Timber, we don't have to review the academic record you brought to Yale," Dean Davie began, and my stomach swirled with anxiety. For all my resolve to redirect my life productively, I still found myself occasionally getting drunk and rowdy with the guys. I

37

rationalized that I was one of the best behaved of a group comprised primarily of football and hockey players. Non-competitive skiing didn't quite fit into their hierarchy of sport, but they accepted me. When they periodically got at cross purposes with the authorities or other, less athletically inclined members of the student community, they needed a cultural liaison. My role became a bit like that of the chief diplomatic officer for Attila's Happy Huns. In spite of – or perhaps as a result of – this dubious distinction, I was concerned that I had unwittingly managed to get into big trouble.

"I've talked with a couple of your professors, and they're impressed."

I let out a silent sigh of relief.

"You're attitude's good," the dean continued, "and the quality of your work is steadily improving. If you'll stay focused, I think you can do very well here."

I had walked out of the meeting flattered and a little frustrated. My pursuit of academic acclaim was proving reasonably successful, but I knew I had precious little chance to excel in scholastic competition with the geniuses on every floor of the dorms. In the following weeks, I had nonetheless tried to immerse myself in my studies. I found I could do the work well – at least, most of it – but the strain had been tearing me up. As I sat on our cheap, dusty carpet, I was forced to shrug my shoulders in disgust. I had everything I reasonably dared to hope for, but I felt like I had nothing. I was becoming the man I dreaded. I was so fixated on grades and recognition that I had no time for true companionship, and precious little for common civility. In an effort to stay focused and avoid repeating the mistakes of my first college try, I had decided to forswear the company of the fairer sex. I rarely played any more with my room mates, or even punctuated our study periods with intellectual explorations into the history and nature of man. In spite of being surrounded by people I counted as friends, I was wretchedly lonely.

My soul was desolate and parched, my vision of the future barren. I buried my face in the pillows of our old worn sofa in an attempt to muffle my pain. On the floor that dim New Haven afternoon, I sought an answer.

"Oh, God – I don't <u>care</u> about being a great student. I want to do a good job," I begged, "but can't I please just have someone to love?"

My faith was simple, almost childish. It was born in the absence of any formal religious upbringing. In my whole life, I had only attended church a few times with friends or for an infrequent funeral. My passing acquaintance with the scriptures came about during visits to my paternal grandparents, where we read the Bible after dinner. But after my dad died the visits to Grandma and Granddad Dick tapered off to one or two brief encounters a year.

Paradoxically, my belief in God was an unintended result of my effort to find scientific explanations for observations of the world around me. Over the years, I studied voraciously to learn how things worked. I found that behind every question there was, if I was honest, yet another question. In a universe filled with glorious order and magnificent chaos, science offered as answers only restatements of my fundamental questions. Yes, the answers each time became more specific, and the theories more precise – but I tried and failed miserably to explain the beauty and symmetry, the uniqueness and consistency of a fragrant, succulent orange I sliced open one sunny afternoon.

It was enough to prompt me to test the hypothesis that God existed. As I sought to exercise my juvenile faith I discerned miracles and wonders in the great and small. At Yale, I began to study statistics and probability theory. From my new vantage point, the cold, irrefutable power of logical mathematics left no doubt in my mind that the universe was not random. It could not be the result of unintelligent development. A wholly unfamiliar vision of this life was beginning to take shape. If God lived, I wanted to know Him as others have known Him. To work with God, I had to work with people. If I had a soul of worth to Him, I could better explain why I felt something extraordinary and sweet and true when I touched the spirit of other good people. My conclusion was that all we have done – invention, art, construction, service, theory – only had worth if we used it to positively affect the lives of those we love.

This train of thought made my acoustical engineering class seem a little irrelevant.

So I did my best to talk with God. I told Him that there must be a more important reason for me to be at Yale than to savage my spirit in a quest for good grades. As I sat alone on the floor of my room with a tear-stained pillow in my hands, I resolved to do enough schoolwork to get by, and to devote the best of my self to building lasting, positive relationships with those around me – and with God Himself.

"Timber! Look what Dick's dad got us!" Doug caressed the case of Michelob with a confusing expression best described as a blend of reverence and lust. He was my roommate – one of three – and although he wasn't a wild drinker, he was clearly delighted at the prospect of sharing a whole case of this premium brew.

A low-level debate raged among the incoming freshmen classes at Yale as to the mysterious inner workings of the student housing department. While the school voiced no official pronouncements on the issue, some newcomers were convinced that the initial rooming assignments were carefully calculated to provide the optimal balance of stimulus and support for the students. Others argued the assignments were as well thought out and carefully planned as a train wreck. Our room served as a prime example for both camps.

Doug was, in many respects, typical of a substantial segment of the applicant pool. He was from Massachusetts, a whiz at science and math, friendly, gregarious, and just a bit of a nerd. Bob, on the other hand, was atypical. He was from Virginia and carried himself like a Marine – which, not surprisingly, was his father's career. His objective was to secure the most rigorous education imaginable. He was as sociable as a Sherman tank, and he blasted through classes like Medieval German Literature and Neo-Marxist Economic Structures before the rest of us were up for breakfast. Bob and Doug were Exhibit #1 for the advocates of the train wreck theory.

Exhibit #2 was supportive of the rational theory. Dick and I came from small, mountain towns – he was from New Hampshire, and I was from Colorado. We were both 6'2", with brown hair and similar builds. We both taught skiing, had been class presidents in high school, and had similar academic interests. As if these were not enough to convince an open-minded observer that someone had sorted through the 1200 incoming freshmen to find compatible soulmates and had carefully evaluated our backgrounds and interests in making the room assignments, there was the bizarre fact of our names: Timber Dick was placed in the same room as Dick Swett.

It's hard to believe <u>that</u> was a random assignment.

We all got along great. We were one of the few quads around that chose to stay together, not just through our freshman year, but through the following year as well. We found ways to resolve our differences and use our diverse strengths to compliment our abilities. In the end, I sided with those who attributed some higher wisdom to those who placed us together.

Dick's dad was down from New Hampshire for a meeting of the alumni association, and the liberal drinking laws of the day permitted him to offer us the case of beer. Dick and Doug conferred for all of a microsecond before gleefully accepting his generosity. By the time I walked in from dinner a half-hour later, they had already begun the hard work of quality-checking the contents of several cans – each.

They had also decided on the agenda for the evening. Although it was officially frowned upon, adventurous Yalies were sometimes inspired to go where no man had gone before – that is, to explore the labyrinth of halls, towers, steam tunnels, and the occasionally unlocked labs and facilities of the campus. Dick, Doug and I were quite intrepid in this pursuit. At the close of the previous year, we had barely escaped apprehension by Campus Security in our successful effort to fly my shirt from a pole atop the massive Payne Whitney Gymnasium. Only rarely were we thwarted in our attempts to gain access to a building. Bob usually declined our invitations to participate, in part because he was a strict teetotaler, and in part because he got his kicks on Friday nights doing experiments deep in the basements of Science Hill. We were never quite sure what he was up to, but it seemed to make the lights all over campus intermittently go dim.

"We want to see if we can get out on the roof of Sterling," Dick said with an interminable belch as he polished off a Mic. "Nobody ever goes up there."

I agreed that the school's main library would serve as a meaningful goal for the evening's expedition, and I grabbed my cowhide jacket and a Michelob of my own. Actually, I grabbed two cans, and nearly made myself sick by draining the first in one, long draught. The resultant carbonation inflation of my upper gastrointestinal tract gave me an instant replay of the night's main course at the dining hall – except that the second time around, my meatloaf was considerably less savory. Why I chose to immediately open the second can is one of those little mysteries of life. I trotted down the stairs and out into the street after Doug and Dick, spilling beer on my jeans as I went.

We chose a slightly indirect path to Sterling Library because Dick wanted to hit the men's room at Woolsey Hall on the way. One would think that we could make the full three block transit from our room to the library without a pit stop, but such was the effect of fine beer on the bladders of we young men. In his defense, Dick also wanted to thank his dad – who was dining at Commons – for the beer, and the public restrooms were immediately adjacent.

As we drew near the towering stone columns of Woolsey, it was apparent that major festivities were in progress. Woolsey Hall and Commons were huge, ornate edifices that met at a right angle to one another in a large rotunda. If you stood in the center of the sculpted marble friezes surrounding the rotunda, you could choose to go back out to the street, forward to Sterling and the Law School, left into Woolsey with its grand pipe organ, or right toward the main entrance of Commons. (Speaking of grand organs, from the same spot you could see where a mischievous sculptor years ago played an anatomical joke on the University. One of the life-sized Greek soldiers carved into the wall is forever preserved holding his sword – at least, the university tour guides steadfastly maintain it is his sword that he's holding – in a highly suggestive position. But I shouldn't digress.)

Once we entered the tall, brass doors, our illustrious expedition was surrounded by mature, elegantly dressed couples loitering about. Many were smoking cigars and most were sipping champagne. I hadn't seen so much fur since the annual livestock show back in Denver. Campus security guards stood at the doors to Commons. Signs were posted about: "YALE : 1701 - 1976"

"Oh, great! We're never gonna get to see my dad," Dick exclaimed as he half-walked, half-ran, towards the men's room. "They've got this big bash going on in Commons to celebrate Yale's anniversary. They'll never let us in." Bearing mutually pained expressions, Dick and Doug disappeared down the stairs to the lavatories.

The beer I'd consumed was still manipulating my meatloaf to torment my tastebuds but had not moved on to cause me to feel my roommates' urgency. I could afford to take the time to gawk at the glittering alums. As a precaution, though, I was still sauntering toward the same stairway when I saw something quite remarkable: A lovely young woman, in a long, black velvet gown was sitting alone with a book near the doorway to Commons. Yale's student body was still predominantly male and attractive blondes were virtually never unaccompanied, or otherwise unattended by at least a few anxious, would-be suitors. Yet there she was, stunning in her solitude amidst the throng, reading quietly.

42

The gentleman I nearly knocked down was very nice about it. And I was actually fortunate to have blundered into him, because his slightly corpulent frame was probably a lot more forgiving than the corner of the polished stone wall right behind him. I sheepishly begged his pardon and took one more long glance at her before redirecting my steps along the path of my roommates.

Doug and Dick were still standing, laughing, at the bank of urinals at the base of the stairs as I clumped down. Doug had apparently just been shaken by a vicious sneeze. Since he was simultaneously engaged in serious business with the plumbing, this was not without its consequences. Dick somehow found Doug's spastically redirected aim hilarious – but on the other side, a gentleman in a tux was openly disgusted as he stepped back to examine the possible impact on his velvet-trimmed trouser cuff. Doug apologized profusely as he fought to control his laughter and continue to hit the target drain before him.

After the requisite stop at the mirror to adjust our collars and rake our terrific hair into place, we headed back up the marble steps. We emerged from the stairwell, beer cans in hand, ready for our heroic assault on the library.

Her eyes were very, very blue.

Long, gently curled blonde hair framed her exquisite, oval face. Her perfectly proportioned nose was pertly posed atop positively mouth-watering lips. She held my gaze for only an instant before she returned her attentions to the black, leather-bound book in her lap. The full-length black dress she wore was cut conservatively, but it flowed over her body like honey. Her scooped neckline was, for the moment, not particularly puritanical – it was low enough to prompt a large shot of adrenaline to surge into my slightly intoxicated veins. I was spellbound until she straightened her shoulders and reached behind her back to adjust her collar. The motion veiled most of her lush, soft curves, and the apparition before me assumed a more prim and proper appearance.

It was then that I realized that she wasn't reading a textbook, but what looked to be a Bible. I managed to start walking again and I steered my way through the minks and topcoats toward the door to Commons. I noted that Dick and Doug were obliviously tracing a tortured path in the general direction of the door nearest Sterling, but they were making little headway. It no longer mattered to me if I lost them.

They <u>were</u> scriptures – I was almost sure of it. <u>Nobody</u> read a Bible at Yale – at least no one I knew. Religion was not particularly fashionable at the time, and I had never noticed anyone publicly reading the Scriptures since my arrival in New Haven 14 months previously. I had learned an enormous amount in my studies and conversations at Yale, but I was still seeking to fill a huge gap in my knowledge regarding God, and faith, and prayer. I hadn't believed in angels when I walked through the doors of Woolsey Hall's rotunda, but now I had reason to wonder.

"Excuse me."

The deep voice filling my ears was my own. I couldn't believe I was trying to talk with her – yet this fool ventured in.

"I walked by a few minutes ago and saw you here, and it just doesn't seem right that you're still sitting all by yourself."

Not too shabby. I'd certainly done worse with an opening line.

"I'm waiting for my date. He should be here any minute," she replied matter-of-factly.

Her voice was smooth and feminine, and my audacity afforded me the thrill of looking into her enchanting face from only an arm's length away. Her skin was flawless. I could scarcely resist the urge to touch her, to stroke and caress her exquisitely sculpted cheek – but I did wish she had avoided the reference to her date. I suddenly became more than a little self-conscious. Here I was talking to someone who just might be an angel, and I was presenting myself in beer-stained jeans and a cowhide jacket. I maneuvered the can in my hand out of her view and banished my doubts. Come on, Timber, get in there and <u>try</u>!

"If you'll forgive me for saying so, I'm kind of glad he's late. Is that a Bible?" I asked warmly, as I looked once again at the book in her hands. "No one reads the Bible around here."

"I'm up at the Divinity School, and I thought I'd get some studying done." She offered just the hint of a smile.

I felt fabulous.

The Div School was located atop a hill in a corner of the campus. In spite of its national prominence, most Yalies barely knew of its existence. It was serenely beautiful, but as far as I could tell it was uninhabited by living human beings.

"Really?" This was honestly better than I had dared hope. "I've been wanting to meet someone who went to school up there. I'm fascinated by the place, but I've never found anyone who was a Divinity student. Would you mind – just for a minute, as long as your date's late – could you tell me just a little bit about the curriculum and what

44

subjects people typically study there? I don't know when I'll get a chance to ask another student."

She took a deep breath and looked straight into my soul before she answered – then we talked. I don't remember everything she said, but on a campus swamped in cynicism and antireligious sentiment, it felt wonderful to talk to someone who was really searching for spiritual truth. We talked about the Div School's degrees, and what she was studying, and what she hoped to do with her knowledge. I ventured a few comments on my evolving views of science as an investigation into God's art. It took only a few sentences for me to realize that either science wasn't her strongest suit or I was perilously close to making a fool of myself as I tried to sound profound. Nonetheless, I peppered her with questions over the next few minutes and was repeatedly afforded the exquisite pleasure of her smile, warm and encouraging.

What in the world?

I turned to find Dick tugging petulantly at my coat. I had forgotten completely about him and Doug.

"Hey, like, I'm sorry to interrupt, but I've been trying to get your attention for a long time," he said under his breath. "Don't you want to come with us?" He gave me the woebegone look of a third grader who's best friend is being dragged off by the ear to the principal's office.

So profound was her influence upon me that I wasn't even irritated with him for interfering. I knew her date was overdue and I'd been lucky to keep my foot out of my mouth thus far in the conversation.

"I'm sorry," I told her. "Those guys are my roommates, and they're gonna barbeque me if I don't get out of here. I'm having a great time, but I promised them we'd do somethin' tonight."

"Sure," she replied, and again graced me with that dazzling smile. "I need to let my sister know why I'm taking so long, anyway." She began to gather her purse and shawl as if she, too, was about to leave.

"Thanks for talking to me. I didn't mean to wreck your studying, but I just couldn't walk off after seeing you sitting there alone." I did my best to give her <u>my</u> most dazzling smile. "And I'm really glad I spoke with you. You answered a lot of questions for me. I've gotta go. Maybe I'll see you again sometime."

I spun around and trotted across the hall toward the guys. For some inexplicable reason, they had changed course and were now headed away from Sterling through the doors toward the street. They probably wanted a refill back at our room. I could see they were a little bummed that they had been abandoned.

I was accelerating to rejoin them when the whole world around me crawled to a halt. Almost instantly, the hubbub and chatter faded away. It was as if I was completely alone in the very center of the gleaming, silent dome of the rotunda. The scene unfolded in slow motion. Overhead, hundreds of little lights installed for the evening's events glittered and sparkled like celestial fireworks. I felt weightless – except for a strong, warm hand on my shoulder, gently holding me in my place.

"Timber," said a calm, authoritative voice that I felt as much as heard, "If you walk away from this woman, you're walking away from the best thing that could ever happen to you."

That was all.

My soul was flooded with light, and warmth, and extraordinary excitement. Then the people around me began to move once again, and the volume of their laughter and conversation was restored. I turned back to see her sitting as she had been, her Bible in her lap.

Her sapphire blue eyes were focused on my own.

I couldn't explain what was happening, but there was no doubt as to what I was being called to do. Her gaze widened slightly with surprise as I retraced my steps.

"Look, I don't mean to bother you," I said even before I reached her. "It's just that I don't know when I've enjoyed a conversation so much, and – well, I figured I'd be a fool if I didn't at least try to introduce myself. My name's Timber – Timber Dick, and I'm very pleased to have met you." I held out my hand to her.

For a moment I wasn't sure she'd respond. I felt my life pivoting on a hinge of history, and it seemed just possible that it might swing the wrong way. The situation was getting a little complex. She somewhat cautiously took my hand in a polite greeting, but then she glanced downward as first her cheeks and then her bodice blushed markedly against her crisp white collar.

"I usually don't introduce myself to strangers," she stammered, and for the first time in our conversation she showed some uncertainty.

Her statement had the ring of truth. I realized that a little anonymity could be a useful thing for a girl at a school with a 3-to-1 ratio of men to women. Still, she couldn't find it in her heart to refuse

46

such a straightforward and sincere overture – could she? As if in answer, I felt her hand clasp mine more firmly. It was warm.

"I'm Annette Lantos. It's been nice to meet you, too."

Or was it "Atlantis"? Maybe "Tandoz"? When I walked into Woolsey Hall that night, I was looking to have a fun evening with the guys and to find a bathroom somewhere along the way. When I walked out fifteen minutes later, I could barely see straight. My hearing was obviously affected, and my feelings were awash in a fountain of joy.

The hinge had turned: I was staggeringly, out-of-my-mind, kiss the ground and praise the heavens, smitten like a fool – I was in love.

"I'm trying to locate a student," I explained over the phone to the Div School receptionist. "Her name's Annette Tondoss, or Atlantis, or something like that. Can you help me?"

"Do you know how to spell her last name?" she responded mechanically. "Our students are listed by last name."

This shouldn't be that hard, I told myself.

"Yes, of course. You see, I've looked in the campus directory under all the spellings for the last name that I can think of, and I can't find anyone named 'Annette'. I thought you might know her."

"Uhnh-hunh, okay. Perhaps she's a student in the Graduate School, or she could just live in New Haven. We occasionally have people who claim to be students at the Divinity School, but they aren't, really. Did you look in the city phone book?"

I was trying to have a positive impact on people and build uplifting relationships, I affirmed under my breath. This was probably a very nice person.

"It won't help me to look in the city book, because I'm not even sure about the first letter of her last name," I explained. "I was hoping you'd know her. How many students are at the Divinity School?"

"Two hundred and thirty-seven." Precisely.

"I'm almost certain her first name is Annette. How many Annette's do you know up there?"

"Our whole system is organized by last name. Are you sure you don't know her last name?"

I bit my tongue. This was proving to be far more challenging than I anticipated.

47

"Look, maybe I can describe her. She's blonde, quite pretty, has blue eyes."

"OH! I know who you're looking for – You want to find Annette, right?"

"Yes, thank you so much," I gushed. "Can you tell me her last name?"

"Of course! She's such a sweetheart. She's a new student – she just got here this semester. She even volunteers here in the office. She's a lovely girl – beautiful eyes, don't you think? Do you want me to give you her number?"

"That would be great – and if you could tell me her last name, too?"

"Sure. Next time, if you will try to have her last name ready, I can help you more quickly. She's at Centrex 62427. You have a nice day, now." She hung up the phone.

Chalk up half a victory, I thought as I scrambled to write down the number.

I reached her late the following Monday afternoon. After reintroducing myself over the phone, I asked if I might meet with her again sometime to resume our conversation. It was going to be tough, she explained. A couple of late midterms and then a trip to Washington to meet her father. She finally agreed to let me join her Tuesday evening, at the dining hall – Tuesday two weeks hence.

I moped for the next fourteen days.

Monday afternoon rolled around, and I heard the phone ringing as I struggled to unlock the dorm room door while carrying a day's worth of textbooks.

"Timber? This is Annette. Were you still planning to come up here tomorrow night?"

I was thrilled to hear her voice, delighted that she had obviously not forgotten our date, and deeply concerned with the tone of her query.

She continued without awaiting my reply. "Tomorrow's election night, and I think I told you I've been volunteering for the mayor's campaign? Anyway, they need me to help with poll watching, so I'm afraid I won't be able to make it..."

How can you be in love, you idiot, if you've talked to her for less than ten minutes? I slumped back in the sofa, completely crushed. I was so sure about the significance of that first meeting. She clearly didn't share my enthusiasm. I was about to offer some sort of a polite reply when I realized that she had not yet stopped talking.

"And I was wondering if there was any chance we could still get together for dinner tonight?"

From plummeting emotional free fall to roaring romantic rocket launch in less than one sentence – but I wasn't ready for dinner! No clean clothes. I needed a shower. There was a quiz in acoustics tomorrow.

"That'd be wonderful! Do you still want to meet at five thirty?"

Was that my voice talking? It was four-thirty, and the Div School was a twenty minute walk away.

We met outside the dining hall and spent more than an hour eating and talking amidst the cacophony of two hundred other students similarly engaged. If Annette was an angel, she was a very talkative one. I was surprised that she offered some very personal insights into her life. She was older than she looked – a few years older than I was. After first coming to Yale as an undergrad and a grueling stint earning a Masters in Communications at Stanford (along with an ill-fated and short-lived engagement), she had returned to New Haven determined to earn her Masters of Divinity – and to avoid all men.

Sure, she acknowledged wryly, Yale was a great place to do that.

Still, she loved the Div School, and the guys in graduate school were a little less predatory than those she'd grown accustomed to as one of the first women to attend Yale College as a full-time enrollee.

We ran into Rufus, the date she been waiting for that night at Woolsey. She told me he had never shown up after I left. She explained that he was a bit of a character, but he wasn't a wolf. They certainly made a striking pair as they chatted in the serving line of the dining hall. In spite of her Jewish heritage, Annette looked like a typical WASP. Well – not quite typical. She dressed with a subtle flourish of continental peasantry, but was modest in her demeanor. Rufus, on the other hand, had been transplanted to the Div School from the inner city of Philadelphia. He apparently made it a habit to walk around campus with a tribal drum, a beret capping his untamed afro haircut and a large gold ring in his ear. Annette said that bib overalls, sandals, and no shirt comprised his favorite uniform.

Rufus's attire was one reason Annette had been sitting in the lobby of Woolsey that night, rather than with her sister in the poshly decorated dining hall behind her. The University's 275th anniversary celebration was open only to those who had tickets. Her sister was serving as an alumni representative and was therefore able to swing four seats at the formal dinner. Annette figured it would be just like Rufus to show up with his drum and jeans, and she knew there was no way he'd be able to talk his way in without the ticket she had tucked in her Bible as a bookmark.

She had known him only for the past six weeks, and although they genuinely liked each other, she explained that the relationship wasn't really romantic – at least from her side. I wasn't so sure. He seemed a little too interested in her for my comfort. Still, the tale she told made their relationship sound oddly expedient for both of them. Both had been drawn to the Div School for the best of reasons: They wanted to learn all they could about the Scriptures, and through them, about the Lord as he has revealed Himself over the ages. Yet both of them felt out of place. Rufus was a smart black kid from the ghetto who'd made good in school and now was surrounded by an overwhelmingly white, upper middle class peer group. Annette was a Jew by birth and a practicing Mormon in a school where many viewed both faiths as nearly heretical. When they hung out together, they were able to affirm the legitimacy of their respective places in an institution that welcomed them, as well as in a social structure that hesitated to accept either one of them. It made sense, in a strange sort of way. I also quietly appreciated her effort to dispel the notion that their relationship represented any kind of entanglement. Before we could move on to subjects that were of substantially greater interest to me, Annette explained she was late for some sort of election-day coordinating meeting, and she departed.

That first date ended up like one of those liquid diet meals: Pleasant, smooth, and even tasty – but I remained unsatisfied. I craved more. When I reached her by phone late Tuesday evening, she agreed to lunch on Thursday, just two days later.

The day arrived bright, crisp, and clear. We met at her job as a coordinator for the media center. As I opened the door to the office she occupied, I was again transformed into a blithering fool in love. She looked spectacular. This time, in the quiet of the small, off-campus cafe where I took her, I could actually hear everything she was saying. The conversation soon shifted away from classes and families. I had been trying hard to understand God's relations with us as people, and I found myself interrogating her about her efforts to communicate with Him.

50

"How do you pray? I mean, what do you actually do?" I asked as I watched her toying with a bowl of clam chowder. "It seems everybody has their own idea, and a lot of'em seem inconsistent."

"Me personally? Lots of ways. Sometimes it's a big, formal deal where I have what I'm going to say all pretty much planned out. In those cases, I first address Him as my Heavenly Father, and then I thank Him for my blessings, and then I ask Him for whatever else I think I need. Other times, we just talk."

"Like we are now?"

"Kind of. Not really, though. I talk, but it's not so easy to hear the answers."

"What if you have a real important question?" I pressed. "Does He answer you then?"

She was wonderfully easy to talk to, but the lace panels of the embroidered blouse she was wearing constituted a dangerous distraction. This was a complex young woman.

"Specific answers to prayer come as a special gift. It takes some work to earn them, but it's really not very mysterious," she offered. "First, you study the problem as best you can. We're here on earth to learn, and so Heavenly Father wants us to try our best to figure things out by ourselves. That's step one: Answer the question using our own knowledge and experience. The next step requires faith. After you go to all the trouble of deciding what's best, you present your conclusion prayerfully to God. You tell Him that you're prepared to proceed in the best way you know how. But – and this is critical – you also tell Him you want His affirmation before you proceed. In the scriptures, they talk about submitting your will to that of the Father. It's what Christ did when He atoned for our sins in the Garden of Gethsemane. Do you remember when He said, 'Nevertheless, Father, not my will, but Thine be done.'?"

"I think so." I hoped that my almost total lack of scriptural knowledge wasn't too apparent. I felt painfully ignorant, yet excited by what I was learning.

"Jesus knew what He had to do. He'd studied it all out, and in this case, it was apparently a horrific prospect. He begged His Father not to have to drink from the bitter cup before Him. So, He knew what He was supposed to do, and He knew He didn't want to do it, and as the Son of God He still submitted His will to His Father." She paused reflectively. "That's one thing I love about Divinity School. You get to

51

talk about things, like the double meaning of the word 'submit'. Both meanings work beautifully here. You submit your plan, like you submit a paper to a professor. You also submit your will completely, like you submit to the judgment of a higher authority. Does this all make sense?"

I thought back to my time alone in my dorm room several weeks earlier. Maybe I was beginning to understand.

Later we walked past the century old homes of New Haven's streets, kicking the windrows of oak leaves into fluttering clouds like brown butterflies. She glowed in the diagonal sunbeams of the afternoon. Actually, she sparkled. Something – some magic dust on her cheeks – caught and reflected the bright sun as hundreds of transient, momentary microflashes of light. I was utterly transfixed. No spell could have exercised greater power over me.

I struggled to stay focused as she spoke of Kierkegaard.

"He called it, 'The Leap of Faith.'" She sculpted her speech with her small, graceful hands. "It's an incredible image. Kierkegaard said, in order for us to be truly converted, we have to scale the peak of human knowledge about God. Then, after we've exhausted ourselves by learning all that we can, we're still not going to be converted. He says that will only happen when we spiritually leap from the highest cliffs of our own understanding, and have the faith that God will not only save us – He will lift us higher than we ever dreamed possible. It can only happen if we are humble enough to make the leap with the certain knowledge that without God, we will surely crash down on the rocks of our worldly understanding." She stopped to pick up a leaf that retained a radiant scarlet hue. "I know I'm not expressing it well, but it's a concept that I feel in my heart is true." She stared up at me, her bright blue eyes again probing deep into my soul.

"It sounds to me like it's a matter of the most profound kind of trust," I ventured. I really thought I knew what she meant – at least partly. Nonetheless, I found myself fumbling for words to express these new theological constructs, while my mind was almost overwhelmed by the sensuous experience of her companionship.

"Yes!" she exclaimed jubilantly. "I've got a wonderful class this semester studying the Psalms, and we just finished number thirty-six. It's so beautiful. Part of it goes, 'Trust in the Lord and do good; so shalt thou dwell in the land, and verily thou shalt be fed. Delight thyself in the Lord; and he shall give thee the desires of thine heart.'"

She gave me an entrancing smile and slipped her hand into mine. Her fingers intertwined, commingled with my own, and we walked together back up the sunlit hill to the Divinity School.

Chapter 3

The Watchful Eye

Wednesday Night, 17 May 1995
Denver, Colorado

The twitch wasn't noticeable, I decided as I stared into the big mirror on the wall above the sink in the men's room. If I got up close, I could see the muscles under my right eye flinching intermittently, but from a distance it would be almost imperceptible. The twitch had started earlier in the morning and had added yet another element of confusion and stress to the day. At least other people were unlikely to see the muscle spasm, I reassured myself. From the way it felt, I came to the mirror concerned that I looked like some bizarre character from a bad movie.

Weird.

I stepped back from the glass. It didn't matter whether people noticed the twitch – I still looked awful. My face was lined and drawn, and my red-rimmed eyes were only three-quarters open. I couldn't open them any further without distorting my whole face. It shocked me to see how I was hunched over, stooped almost like an old man. I attempted to pull myself together to make the tired guy in the reflection look more like the one in the photo with Annette on my desk. I shoved my lifeless hair into place and made a determined effort to stand erect, with my shoulders square and head level.

I paused for a moment before the mirror to evaluate the results, and then gave up in disgust and pulled open the door leading to the hall.

There was no one in the office to impress, anyway. It was late. Everyone else had left for home a couple hours earlier. For the thousandth time in the last few years I was working alone, trying to keep the company afloat for another day. I must have done a pretty good job of hiding my emotions during office hours. No one had taken particular notice of me. None of my coworkers had asked prying questions about Annette's tests of the day before or had even wise-cracked that I looked like a ghoul. Justin, my brother and partner, had been unusually focused on his duties. On the other hand, maybe if I'd talked more with him – or someone – about what was going on, I wouldn't have been facing this annoying twitch. But I didn't feel ready to talk with anybody.

Everyone here has enough to worry about, I concluded. I headed back into the office and hesitated just for an instant to inspect the sign on the door: Safeline Children's Products Company. Justin had bought the engraved plastic plaque several months before and it looked good. Too bad the business behind it was having such a rough time.

Ten years earlier, I had invented and applied for a patent on a baby stroller that could be converted in seconds to a safety carseat. Annette had been thoroughly frustrated with her daily travels. By the time she got to the grocery store, the baby would be sleeping in his seat. When she extracted him to go inside, he'd complain – noisily. I devised a compact stroller with retractable wheels linked to a mechanism that converted it to carseat and back again in moments.

Justin was enthusiastic about the product and we teamed up to commercialize the design. We spent the frosty nights of November and December cutting tubing and drilling aluminum bar stock in a rented, unheated garage as we handcrafted prototype models. Annette helped to refine aesthetics. The finished units were gorgeous: jewel-like metal surfaces, soft and attractive fabric, and a smooth mechanical function. When we finally sent videotapes of the prototypes in action to several of the nation's largest carseat makers, we thought that the world would beat a path to our door and that licensing discussions would begin immediately.

We elicited a fair amount of interest, but none of it developed into detailed negotiations. The big companies would invite me out to make a presentation to their designers, who would in turn pick my brain and then stall for months. I spent much of the next five years trying to find a licensee or investor to launch the product. With 20/20 hindsight, I recognized that I scarcely could have chosen a more difficult product to serve as the centerpiece of a new business. Carseats were regulated by the National Highway Traffic Safety Administration, the Consumer Product Safety Commission, the Federal Aviation Administration, and a host of other entities. We had to comply with hundreds of pages of arcane regulations governing everything from the performance of the seat in a crash test to the size of the lettering on the warranty cards and the type of paper used in the decorative decals. It was not a product and market that beckoned to the entrepreneur or offered easy rewards to the adventurous.

We persevered, and in 1989 Justin and I found an individual financial backer willing to put up a half million dollars to start Safeline. It was only about half the money that my fancy business plan called for, but we all agreed it was worth the gamble – there was no one else standing in line with the rest of the money needed to start the company properly. We didn't want the opportunity to slip away because we were too slow to act. The backer, an ex-chief financial officer from the oil industry, christened the product the "Sit'n'Stroll" and we set up Safeline to finalize the tooling and secure the required regulatory approvals.

It had taken over a year to test, redesign and refine the product to our satisfaction. Since then, we had been embroiled in the exhausting struggles typical of an undercapitalized company – with some added, agonizing twists. The huge injection molds for the plastic parts weighed as much as a bus and alone cost $500,000. The product liability insurance premium for the first year amounted to thirty dollars for each unit we sold. Safeline grew quickly, but I scrambled to have enough money to pay for parts for the next production run. The company checking account was like Elijah's barrel of meal: always virtually empty, yet containing just enough for the day's needs. We managed to meet the payroll and stay in production, but the balance sheet steadily weakened.

The strain made everyone pretty miserable at times. I was working consistently twelve – and often twenty – hours a day. Annette and the kids liked the idea that I was soon to be a successful inventor. They were a lot less enthusiastic about living with the overworked, overstressed manager of a struggling little business. There were other pressures. Each time he would visit, Annette's father asked me with grave concern when it would be necessary to file for bankruptcy. Many times, all of us would have loved to sell out or just shut down and move back to the security of a more conventional job.

One compelling fact kept us from calling it quits: The Sit'n'Stroll turned out to be a great product. Almost every day's mail contained witty and endearing letters from mothers who extolled the carseat/stroller's virtues. It was conceived to make it easier for parents to keep their child with them, and it exceeded almost everyone's expectations. It was reasonably simple to use, compact, and very comfortable for the baby. Most people who owned the Sit'n'Stroll assumed we were wildly successful. Unfortunately, the company's shortage of cash was most evident in the marketing budget: There was virtually none. As a result, stores didn't want to carry the product without advertising, and even the consumers who knew about it couldn't find the Sit'n'Stroll in retailers. Sales languished far below the level required to make a profit.

Annette put her formidable talent to work on securing free press coverage. We persuaded an old college friend to come aboard as sales manager, and they managed to get the company written up favorably in Newsweek, Fortune, and The Wall Street Journal. Movie stars bought them, and so paparazzi photos of the Sit'n'Stroll appeared in tabloid newspapers. The nationally syndicated consumer editor for the Los Angeles Times picked the Sit'n'Stroll to lead the paper's annual list of the Ten Best New Consumer Products. I was even afforded the satisfaction of seeing our carseat featured in Popular Science.

Most importantly, the endless effort we spent on designing in a new level of safety was paying off. Each year, even as sales grew, our product liability insurance premiums plummeted. In an industry plagued by multimillion dollar lawsuit settlements, Safeline Children's Products Company never faced a claim. The Sit'n'Stroll compiled an unblemished carseat safety record: Not once had a baby in one been hurt in a crash, no matter how severe. Parent after parent wrote us from the hospital as they were recovering from life-threatening injuries, expressing profound gratitude that their infants had emerged from the accidents unscathed.

Much of the product's success was obviously beyond my control. We did our best to assure the carseats' quality, but it was nearly miraculous to have a safety product that had always worked under such horrific circumstances. As for the publicity coups we scored, they would be for naught unless I could find a way to secure the company's financial position. My old issues of Popular Science were filled with clever products from businesses that failed before they could ever catch on in the marketplace.

Safeline was perilously close to joining their ranks. A few months earlier, we had been approached by a real estate speculator who wanted to invest in the company. I opened candid discussions with the man and his wife. After several meetings, in a spirit of full disclosure, I duly informed them of Safeline's cash-strapped position. A few days later I grasped their real intent. These supposedly friendly investors were systematically sabotaging our supplier relationships as they maneuvered to take over the company and move production to China. To them, business was a game where the highest score went to the guys who grabbed all the chips under any pretense. They played by different rules than I did. There were no umpires.

It was the ugly side of capitalism.

Usually I could work better in the calm hours of the night. The phones were quieter, and I was able to get a clearer perspective on the ceaseless barrage of problems pounding across my desk. This night, I could barely work at all. The spreadsheet on my computer was acting like the modern equivalent of a stubborn mule. I knew it could do the job, but I was having a heck of a time leading it to the right conclusions. The flickering rows and columns did make one thing clear: I had no money to pay the plant this week. My mind was simply overwhelmed with issues that demanded resolution but defied my best efforts. The snake of a real estate developer was coiling, preparing to strike. And now, the twins. I abandoned my effort to whip the spreadsheet into compliance and wandered out into the empty reception area. The twitch in my cheek seemed to be getting worse.

A cookie might help, I concluded.

The big black eye of the television in the lobby stared blankly at me as I crossed over toward the cookie jar. Over the years, I had developed a love/hate relationship with the tube. At home, I almost never watched it. Convinced that the vast proportion of TV programming was junk, I usually regretted the little time I spent viewing it. It made me feel just a little – as I used to say in college – wasted. Still, the electronic pacifier was seductive. Every once in a while it called to me, and lured me with its glow to be lulled into that semi-oblivious state that afflicts those subject to its addiction.

I punched it to life with my forefinger.

Channel 2: Geraldo. Junk. The cookie dissolved into bland, greasy mush as I mindlessly chewed it. I switched.

Channel 4: Nightly News. War footage from someplace. Wonderful. More stress... I poked once again at the channel controller.

Channel 6: Medical show. The last time I got suckered into watching one of these gory new documentaries, I nearly threw up. I stabbed at the control.

Wait!

A surge of adrenaline flushed the driftwood from my mind. Twins! Little girl Siamese twins! I crouched down until the screen filled my vision.

Twins. Conjoined at the hips, like some of those shown in Dr. Porter's book, but these were walking, and talking, and laughing! They were not only alive, they were happy little kids! I was incredulous. The show was a documentary on the 1994 surgical effort to separate the two year old girls. Up to that point, I had never seen anything more than a few brief articles about conjoined twins. Years before, I remembered seeing an article in <u>Newsweek</u> on the surgical separation of twins, and after Annette and I had left the Porters' office we stopped at Denver's huge new civic library to try to learn all we could. We thumbed through medical texts and poured over encyclopedias and old midwifery guides. The library had a sophisticated electronic catalogue that allowed us to exhaustively search any subject remotely related to the topic.

We had found exactly three brief articles, along with an historical biography of the lives of Eng and Chang Bunker, the Thai conjoined twins who gave rise to the appellation "Siamese Twins." The articles told us little we didn't already know, but book was intriguing. Chang and Eng were joined at the chest, but they had separate ribcages. From what we knew already, if the original Siamese Twins had been born after the advent of medical X-rays, they probably would have been surgically split shortly after birth. As it was, they led productive lives. They worked, married sisters, and each had children – a total of 21 children between them. They died within days of each other at age sixty-nine. The most poignant aspect of their lives was that they spent their later years searching all over the globe for a surgeon who would separate them. None would, for fear that he would become known as the doctor who killed the Siamese Twins. Annette checked the book out from the library, but it actually taught us very little about our children. Our hours of research had uncovered almost no new information.

Now, here on the television I disdained was a complete, detailed discussion of the medical, social, and emotional implications of raising conjoined twins.

I tore myself away from the screen and called Annette. She was orchestrating dinner, conducting the evening's events like the determined choreographer of a less-than-talented dance ensemble. She much preferred it when I was home. Kimber, our soon-to-be fifteen year old, answered the phone.

"Can I help you?" she offered. "Mommy's frying falafel." Kimi was an able assistant to both of us. She could almost always be relied upon to help out in either the office or the kitchen, as long as the task didn't involve the vacuum cleaner. There were some things she just wouldn't do.

Kimi knew I always took my wife's calls, and Annette, mine. When I said I needed to talk to her mom she immediately handed the cordless handset to her mother.

"Honey," I asked intently, "Can you turn on the TV?"

"Turn <u>on</u> the TV?" she asked with disbelief. "I'm right in the middle of trying to feed everyone. Why?"

"Turn it to PBS. Don't make a big deal about it. Tell the kids they get to watch 'Nova' tonight."

We had a small portable television that was used mostly by the little guys to watch "Sesame Street" while Annette worked in the kitchen. She stopped poking in the hot oil and did as I requested. When the electrons painted the first moving pictures on the phosphors of the glass screen, I could hear a small gasp from my wife.

"What <u>is</u> this?" she asked tremulously.

"They're twins, and they're in the process of separating them."

We'd told the kids nothing yet about the condition of the babies Annette was carrying. Both of us felt we needed more information before we could answer the inevitable stream of questions that would ensue.

Annette was transfixed by the story and images of the program. The children, too, were captivated by the human and medical drama. Although we virtually ceased to converse, I could hear many of the kids' remarks in the background as they watched. Annette carefully crafted her comments to the children to promote an open-minded acceptance of the twins' situation. As the story progressed, the doctors explained to the twins' adoptive mother that the proposed operation posed a life-threatening risk to each of the little girls. As I watched intently, I realized Annette was crying quietly.

"Are you okay, Honey?"

She sniffed as she pulled herself together. "Sure. I'm in the pantry," she explained. "I didn't want the kids to see me so involved, but this is amazing, Timber. How did you know it was on?"

"I didn't. I just turned it on."

For a while longer, we watched together, linked by the phone. The program was well researched and intelligently presented. We learned that most conjoined twins are girls. Most are miscarried. Annette was fascinated by the numerous photos of Eng and Chang Bunker. More interesting to me was the extremely detailed description of the surgery. The doctors discussed why they believed the surgery was feasible and how the separated twins would have to be reconstructed. The little girls had a commingled lower gastrointestinal tract, and their legs were skeletally linked. Except for a small section of the extreme lower spine, they shared no critical nervous system structure or organs. The girls were joined in a manner that was much more involved than the Bunker twins, but I also realized the commingling of their vital organs was not nearly so complex as the twins Annette was carrying.

At some point, Annette had to get back to the now-overcooked dinner, but I continued to watch after she'd hung up the phone. The operation was a medical success. Perhaps more significant, both twins appeared to thrive after an initial period of emotional adjustment. It was a story with a happy ending.

I turned off the tube and sat back in the folding chair I'd dragged over near the set. There was no rational explanation for the events that had just unfolded before me. The largest public library in the Rocky Mountains was devoid of meaningful data on conjoined twins, but I'd just been given a wealth of information – including the names and locations of surgeons experienced in the separating operation. Out of the hundreds of nights I'd worked late, I'd turned on the television only a handful of times. The odds of the evening's events occurring by chance were infinitesimally small. As I saw myself reflected in the now darkened tube, some of my anxiety ebbed away and was replaced with awe and wonder.

III. Silencing the Joker

November 1976
New Haven, Connecticut

As a kid growing up in Aspen, I was often introduced to celebrities. Even back then the resort had a reputation as a playground for the rich and famous. The guy sitting next to you on the chairlift might have starred in the western you watched on television the night before. On occasion, network news anchors like Peter Jennings and Eric Sevareid came to dinner. Working at the supermarket after school, I sacked groceries for Lucille Ball. At one of the town's fancier restaurants, I watched in fascination as Batman drank himself into a stupor and then urinated into the decorative plants at the edge of the dance floor. As a news reporter, I interviewed John Denver and shook hands with a slew of senators. I liked to claim I knew these people – at least some of them, anyway – but I suspected they weren't making the same boast about me to their friends.

Once I got to New Haven, my perspective shifted. Some of the professors there could legitimately claim to have changed the world. Some of my peers were likely to do so in the future. My classes were held in ornate granite mausoleums of knowledge named to honor alumni magnates and benefactors. The campus was electric with intellectual energy, but in the Seventies it was strangely alienated from the spiritual commitment of those who gave their books and blood to build it. Most of the college's founders were not captains of industry inspired to teach physics and commerce, but more often were men of faith. Elihu Yale, Timothy Dwight, George Berkeley and many others whose names adorn the stained stone towers of the school sought an alternative to Harvard's single-minded pursuit of knowledge. The Cambridge school's crimson flag bears the motto, "*Lux*" – or Light. Those in New Haven ascribed a greater vision to their true blue pennant: "*Lux et Veritas*" – Light and Truth. One without the other was insufficient to justify their sacrifice.

In the years prior to my arrival at Yale, I'd learned a lot – maybe too much for my own good in a couple of areas. Knowledge without wisdom was as useful as a ship without a rudder. Too many times, I had run aground on the shoals of my own ambitions and understanding. I was now trying to set a new course, but I first had to learn the fundamentals of a new school of navigation.

How could I get to know God? My dictionary described Him as the creator and ruler of the universe, regarded as eternal, infinite, all-powerful, and all-knowing.

He was obviously very different from the influential people I'd met thus far in my life.

The question became the most important concern of my education. It presupposed the existence of a Supreme Being, and I was sympathetic with those who were still uncertain about whether He lives. Nonetheless, I was increasingly sure He was there. And I was becoming convinced that He knew me and cared about me enough to teach me – if I would cooperate with Him.

Cooperation seemed to involve learning His etiquette. It didn't take me long to understand that the Lord appreciated appreciation. "Praise the Lord!" some Baptist friends had told me. As a child, my mom taught me to be polite. Now I was learning that God expected that and a lot more. It gradually dawned on me that He had a personality. If I was distant and solitary I couldn't expect Him to lavish His attention upon me. Yet there were many times I came to know His pleasure. Sometimes He would even tease me – play little jokes on me – but I had to watch and listen carefully, or these subtle gestures of His affection were easily lost in the clatter and clutter of everyday life. I would read an article from a random book pulled off the shelf and find the topic to be the focus of discussion in a class the following day. Or I would realize I had forgotten an important phone number, but then look at the clock at precisely the moment corresponding to the missing four digits I needed. Or I would think about someone that I hadn't seen in a long time, and they would soon after appear in my life. None of these coincidences proved anything and none was alone particularly significant, but over the years I filed them in a mental notebook filled with wondrous observations.

One evening while I was still at New College, a friend and I had been discussing these inexplicable phenomena. After years of studying science and observing people, it had become clear to me that there were many occurrences that science was compelled to ignore because they were simply not subject to conventional analysis. They happened once, but were not repeatable. Since no one could devise an experiment to replicate these important but arguably random events, scientists generally refused to include them in their descriptions of the rules by which the world worked. What they failed to see, I had explained to my friend, was that these "random" developments determined the course of our lives as much as the scientifically predictable outcomes.

We were both enrolled in a psychology seminar on Carl Jung, the groundbreaking investigator of cross-cultural dreams and myths. I was powerfully impressed by a reply Jung had given an interviewer from Life magazine when asked whether, as a psychologist and student of science, he could claim to believe in God.

"I don't have to believe," Jung had said. "I know."

"I'm beginning to believe," I had told my friend, "that God isn't some imaginary creation sitting up on a cloud. He is behind everything that we are experiencing. All these so-called random events are His work."

As the final syllable left my lips, the quiet stillness of our room was rent by a crack like a pistol shot. We were startled physically and emotionally by the intensity of the sound as we reflexively looked around the small, concrete-walled room for the source. But there was no source. None. The closest explanation we could devise was that a piece of bamboo standing in the corner had dried to the point where internal stresses built up and suddenly released themselves to make a substantial physical and audible crack. A close examination of the bamboo pole, however, had indicated no visible split.

I filed this random event in my mental notebook under "Practical Jokes."

I didn't like my dentist much when I was a kid, but he had some excellent magazines in his waiting room. One of them, Highlights for Children, had a monthly feature consisting of a full- page, detailed line drawing that was usually relatively nondescript. It might have been a scene from a forest, or a cityscape. It was more than it first appeared, however. It was a puzzle – a kind of test of one's powers of observation. Incorporated within the lines of the picture were a dozen or more sketches of common articles or animals: a hat, a frog, a spoon, or a chair. Only as you studied the image very carefully could you see how cleverly the artist had hidden the solutions to the puzzle in plain sight.

Evidence of God's hands at work was similarly hidden all around me, I concluded. If I searched for them, I saw his fingerprints everywhere. There may not have been demonstrable proof of His existence, but circumstantial evidence abounded. I began to have increasing respect for the countless generations of people who had made their acquaintance with God and devoted their lives to His service. Their faith preceded miracles and inspired masterpieces.

As Einstein put it, "I seek to know the mind of God. The rest are just detail."

It was as if God was little by little giving me the opportunity to know Him. He seemed to appreciate my ignorant sincerity and to be patient with my lapses of judgment and foresight. In my first year at Yale I think He put me on supervised probation. I nearly blew it a few

64

times. While I sought with only spotty success to rein in my appetites, my search for better ways to understand His will never abated. In retrospect, I both tested and proved the Lord's patience.

Inventors presume the powers of creation. We claim the vision and command the elements to create something – a mousetrap, perhaps? – that is both different and better than any preceding. The arrogance of our profession fuels the quest to find improved solutions to the problems surrounding us. It's a glorious part of the process of providing mankind with mousetraps – when we're successful. Most of the time, however, we fail. Usually someone else thinks of our brilliant idea first. Perhaps we can't build it. Lots of times the fruit of our creative genius stinks. The design doesn't work. Or maybe it works just fine, but does nothing of use – it doesn't solve a real problem. Edison claimed that the process of invention is 1% inspiration and 99% perspiration. When budding inventors came to me for advice on a fabulous new idea they had, I routinely told them the first thing to do was learn about how people in the past had tried to solve the problem before them. Only then could they determine whether they had, in fact, invented something new.

When I sought to learn more about God, however, I was quick to abandon my own teachings. I had observed with awe His works and wonders and filled more mental notebooks than I could ever review. I eventually came to know He was there with greater certainty than I knew that Columbus sailed the seas or that I had been born with a liver. Like Jung, I knew – but I remained painfully ignorant about how one grows to know Him better and serve Him. More than anything else in my life, I wanted to advance my knowledge of God's work. I was no longer satisfied to be an interested bystander. I aspired to be a cooperative participant. I should have had the humility to respectfully study how the wise and learned people before me had harmonized their lives with the will of the Lord. Instead, I decided to invent a new solution.

Like most unschooled inventions, my concept was simple. It was based on three principles. First was faith. Faith was apparently an essential prerequisite to gain true knowledge of God. Faith was belief without proof. Second was power. My observations indicated and acknowledged that the Lord was the master of enormous and subtle power. And third was love. As I sought to know Him and appreciate the wonder of His works, I came to the inescapable conclusion that he loved me personally – and by extension, everyone. I had come to believe in a wonderful and omnipotent God who cared for me. But the scientist in

65

my soul still wanted proof – even though I had learned that the Lord's etiquette would not permit the design of anything resembling proof.

The solution I devised was laughably naive. What if I in uncompromising faith asked my all-powerful God to manipulate some completely random event? The outcome would by definition prove nothing – it would have been, after all, just another random event. But by a solemn contract I would offer to Him in faith prior to the event, I could gain that personal knowledge which supercedes belief.

If proof of God's existence and intent would obviate the need for faith, I needed to search for knowledge of Him where there could never be objective proof of the results: in randomness. If God wanted to teach me, He could show me order out of chaos. In the development of theology, this was a Stone Age insight. I'm sure there were Neanderthals who exercised more faith than this Yale student – but the Lord nonetheless proved willing to demonstrate both His power and His love.

It was late during my second semester in New Haven when these deliberations came into focus. I was taking an utterly fascinating course in Statistics and Probability. Suddenly it became clear that even random events behaved according to a strict set of rules. Breaking the rules of probability was as unthinkable to a statistician as defying the law of gravity would be to a physicist. As I devoured descriptions of Poisson distributions and standard deviations, my brilliant professor challenged us.

"C'mon people – Have you ever wondered why the world works this way?" he asked bluntly.

Arthur Swersey was gruff in his demeanor, but his command of his subject matter was astounding. Tall, bearded and just a tad unkempt, he took particular delight in playfully proving his prowess to the class. At the beginning of the period, he would give some eager math wiz ten, one dollar bills. The money was theirs to keep – if they could. Over the next fifty minutes, he would challenge them to wager on a series of statistical outcomes. If they won, they could increase their take. By the end of class, he always had his ten dollars securely back in his wallet.

"What makes a Normal Distribution normal?" Professor Swersey relentlessly pressed his point. "Why does it follow this perfect bell-shaped curve, and why can we predict so confidently what percentage of the outcomes will fall within one, or two, or three standard deviations? We can prove that these rules work, and I can even tell you precisely how confident I am in predicting the probability of an outcome. But do you guys know <u>why</u>?"

The room sat in silence as thousands of IQ points failed to even posit an answer to his queries.

"I hope you'll think about this stuff," he continued, "because it's probably at least as important as learning the rules themselves. Here's one for you: Einstein brilliantly deduced that the relationship between energy and matter can be expressed as a formula. How many times have you heard it: Energy equals mass times the speed of light squared. By one school of thought, that's a statistical certainty. 'E <u>equals</u> em cee squared', right? Well, <u>why</u> is it the speed of light squared? That's a specific, precise and extremely large number that has been repeatedly verified by experiment over the past half century. Do you guys just take all this stuff for granted? Or do you ever stop and wonder, 'Wow, that's really kind of odd and amazing, isn't it?'"

We sat shaking and nodding our heads, looking to one another in dazed silence. In the boxer's ring of the classroom he had just scored an intellectual TKO against sixty of us simultaneously. He was the only professor that I saw receive a standing ovation from his class.

The logical conclusion of Art Swersey's interrogation was initially obscure. Then it hit me: From his perspective atop a pinnacle of knowledge and experience, he saw an intelligent design in the world's haphazard unfolding. Professor Swersey was begging us to see past the probabilities to the indefinable order that structures our known universe.

My hands were shaking slightly as I later sat alone at my desk. I had come back from the dining hall to find no one home. Dick, Doug and Bob were all busy elsewhere on campus that night. The flap on the box of playing cards fought me for a moment, but I won soon enough. One of Prof. Swersey's problem sets involving a deck of cards was before me, but I was confronting a bigger issue. I surmised, just perhaps, that I might have figured out a way that God could talk to me. I had been talking to Him for quite a while. I felt in my heart that He heard me, but I had been struggling with the problem of hearing what He wanted to say back to me.

I was determined to have a solemn conversation with the Lord. I spoke to Him out loud.

"Dear God, thank you so much for giving me a sense that you're there. Thank you for listening to me, and showing me the wonders of this life. Thank you for letting me come to Yale, and thank you for all the help you've given me with my work. I'm really, really grateful.

"Dear God, I'm kind of embarrassed to even bring this up, but I'm having a rough time figuring out who you are. It seems like people have all sorts of different ideas about you, and I really want – or maybe I need – to know for myself. I know this is kind of insulting, and I'm really sorry – I don't mean to insult you. I just need to know."

I had never been more serious about anything. If He would deign to let me know what I sought, I would be held accountable for that knowledge for the rest of my life. If He would work with me, I was willing to commit to work for Him – forever.

"Who are you? Forgive me – I don't mean to ask a stupid question. What I mean is, are you the God of the Bible? Can you please just let me know?"

My hands were noticeably shaking now as I carefully shuffled the deck of cards.

"Dear God, if you <u>are</u> the God of the Bible, let me draw an ace when I cut the deck. I know you're there – Now, please, let me learn more about you."

My whole body was tingling. I had lain my faith upon the table as a willing sacrifice. He had to know how important this was to me.

It was time. Fifty-two cards. Four aces.

The compact brick of cards split effortlessly.

The ace of spades nested in my trembling hand.

"Whoa . . ." I gasped involuntarily. The card beckoned me to examine it more closely. The deck was from some obscure maker. The symbol in my grasp pointed up like a sculpted ebony arrowhead. Its black face was decorated with tiny stars floating in constellations. If it wasn't a window into heaven, it still afforded me a moment's glimpse into eternity.

As I pondered in awe what I had just experienced, an irritating whisper of scepticism rasped at the edge of my thoughts. The sweet peace that had flooded my soul when I saw the upturned card ebbed away as I chose to listen.

"So it's an ace," it observed dryly. "One chance in thirteen. There was a seven and a half percent chance you'd get an ace. Things like this happen all the time. Don't let it get to you. The Bible is irrelevant these days. God's around – somewhere – but church people are stodgy and small-minded," it argued sinuously. "You don't want that kind of life. People who believe in the God of the Bible are either hypocrites or fanatics. You're neither. Are you gonna let your life be ruled by a seven and a half percent random outcome?"

The voice belonged to me – to the most cynical part of my spirit. As I attended to its wiles I felt ashamed and grieved. I was appalled at my willingness to abandon the deal I had made only moments before. I had asked for an ace. I was given an ace. I had only disdain for the defect in my character that would entertain feelings of doubt now.

My fingers tapped on the calculator next to the problem set.
7.69%

That's even a little more than seven and a half percent, I noticed – and then was all the more embarrassed.

"Look, God," I heard myself saying, "I want to believe. But I'm obviously a lot weaker than I thought. I know you've already given me more that I deserve. You've let me feel your love and approval, and you haven't punished me when I really deserved it."

Panic seized my thoughts as I realized I was turning my back on the gift of knowledge and wisdom I'd just been offered. Like a spirited horse I'd once ridden into a wide and beautiful meadow only to have it bolt for the comfort and security of its stable, my nervous thoughts were running ahead of my conscious control. But if I was going to be true and honest, there was no longer security to be found in retracing my steps. By my own instruction the stable gate had been locked. There was no going back. I had made a commitment to the Lord that I could choose only to honor, or dishonor.

My fingers clicked the calculator keys once again. A mixture of fear, shame, and hope inspired me.

"Dear God, I'm so sorry. I thought I could do this. I thought I had enough strength to hold to the knowledge I was asking for. I can't – I'm too weak to ignore the doubts I'm feeling. I know this is unreasonable, but I have to ask."

The cool glow of the calculator's display told me the statistical probability: 0.0059171 The chances of getting two aces in a row were one in 169. There was virtually no chance.

"Please God, help me to banish my doubts. Let me draw another ace. Please let me know for sure."

I shuffled the deck three times, feeling all the while like I used to when I'd cheat on my brother when we'd play cards together. I had failed to keep my word to the Lord that I would listen honestly to Him –

and now I was asking Him to repeat when I knew exactly what he had said.

I wanted to get the process over with and stop thinking about the whole mess. I cut the deck quickly.

It was an ace.

It was the ace of spades.

My head dropped heavily to the desktop as I clenched the half-deck in my right hand. My heart pounded with joy and relief and excitement and wonder. The ace of spades. Twice. Not even the ace of clubs and the ace of diamonds.

The little voice whimpered from a dank recess of my being, still insolent and insistent – grasping for any conceivable shred of vindication. "Big deal. So what are the odds of that particular card, twice?"

Let's see. My fingers fluttered at the calculator again. The Lord obviously didn't just give me any ol' ace when I had asked the first time. He gave me the ace of spades to make a specific point. So the odds there weren't one in 13, but rather one in 52. That got multiplied by itself to give the odds of the same event happening twice.

One chance in 2,704. I had to smile as I checked my math. The cynical little voice had nothing to say. The Lord had spoken. I could never prove to anyone else what had just happened, but I <u>knew</u> – and I knew He knew. We had a deal. This time, I was bound to keep my part.

Doors opening and muffled voices down the hall let me know that Dick and Doug had returned. I debated whether to tell them about what had just happened. The evening's events had left me exhausted and elated, but still a little confused. What had I really determined? And how in the world could I ever explain to anyone that the Lord had answered my prayers through a deck of cards? What had transpired was at once ludicrous and sacred. My room mates might never understand.

I decided to tell them as long as they seemed like they were in a mood to listen respectfully. Impulsively, I scooped up the cards and fanned them out face-up. There sure seemed to be fifty-two different cards there. Nope – There was even a joker tucked in the deck. I turned them over and shuffled them preparatory to sliding them back in the box.

One in twenty-seven hundred, I mused with a smile, and bricked up the deck.

"Do it again!" sneered the grating little voice. It was now mean, ugly, and startlingly forceful.

"Hunh? That's ridiculous. God will never want to listen to me again," I muttered. I no longer cared about the pitiful rants and nebulous doubts the voice was promoting. I had received all I had asked for – and much more.

"C'mon, do it! Are you chicken? You think He can't make it three in a row, don't you?" It clamored from somewhere deep within me, taunting me until I wanted to turn away – but somehow I couldn't.

"Face it," the voice snarled. "You know it was a fluke. Just cut the deck, sucker!"

Motivated by no conscious choice on my part, the ace of spades flashed in my right hand. I stared incredulously at celestial symbol I held, my mind unable to fully comprehend what He had just done.

Order out of chaos. Impossible odds. From that moment forward, I may have doubted myself, or those around me, or even many things other people held to be self-evident truths of the world. I have never since, however, doubted the existence, power, or love of the Lord.

"You're right, Timber," Doug affirmed a few minutes later as he verified my math on his fancy Hewlett Packard. "The odds are one in fifty-two cubed. That's one in 140,608. Are you sure you didn't fold the card somehow so it kept naturally splitting the deck at the ace? Those numbers are impossible!"

Dick carefully studied the stack of cards. He was serving as our experimental quality control technician. He extracted the ace of spades and examined it for any irregularities. Then he reinserted it and methodically cut and re-cut the deck eight or ten times as we watched him intently.

"I'm not getting any card twice, and I haven't gotten an ace even once. Hey, look – the odds are even higher." He grinned as he flashed the Joker at us. "There are fifty-three cards in here."

Through the summer and into my third semester at Yale, I continued to explore and develop my relationship with God. Occasionally I would pull out the deck of cards to shuffle and cut them. Sometimes I would attempt to use them to get an answer or direction. There were times when I felt that I had received what I sought, and many other times when nothing notable resulted. It seemed as though I was being taught by example that the episode with the cards was a unique situation, and not a pattern that I could employ to discern the Lord's will whenever I wanted.

It took me a while to realize that I wasn't so special that I could expect a dialogue with Him at my convenience. It was neither His way nor His will to talk with me on my terms whenever I felt like having an informal chat. I had also glossed over the specific question that the Lord was responding to in my room that spring night. In my excitement at getting His answer, I neglected to pay attention to just what the answer might mean for me.

"Are you the God of the Bible?"

At the time it seemed an intelligent question to ask, and I guess it was. I just wasn't wise enough to grasp the wealth of knowledge the answer carried with it. Over the years, I had tried to read the Bible – The King James Translation, the Revised Standard Version, the Good News Bible, and many others. I would pick them up in bookstores and hotel rooms and give them my full attention for perhaps ninety seconds. In general I found the scriptures either impenetrable or inauthentic. When years before my grandparents had read to me from the Bible I was often bored – but also inexplicably comforted and mystified. In the years intervening I had paid increasing attention to what other people said about the scriptures and decreasing heed to what was really written in them. The Bible had gradually become to me a symbol of rigidity, self-righteousness and hypocrisy. Religion didn't solve problems. It promoted divisiveness and self-deceit. I was too intelligent to partake of what Marx called "the opiate of the masses" – even as I continued to blithely numb my senses chemically.

After the Lord answered my question about His identity, I might have immediately devoted time and effort to studying the Bible. I didn't – not much, anyway. I was too enthralled with the experience I had been through to appreciate where my newfound knowledge could take me. The arrogant inventor in me was disinterested in learning how the Lord had revealed His truths over the eons. I gave only passing attention to what those truths were and how they applied to me in the present. Instead, I bought an inexpensive, pocket-sized copy of the New Testament, haphazardly read a few chapters, and spent a lot of time fiddling with the deck of cards.

Then I met Annette. The message I heard in Woolsey's rotunda was as unambiguous and important as the one I had discerned with the cards six months earlier: "If you walk away from this woman, you're walking away from the best thing that will ever happen to you." As if I would have wanted to leave her. She was dazzlingly intelligent, succulently sweet-spirited, heart-breakingly attractive – and she seemed to like me, too.

She was also a Mormon. Annette said it was a little more proper to say she was a member of the Church of Jesus Christ of Latter Day Saints, but that was the same as a Mormon to me. Aspen was not a big Mormon hangout, but I'd heard about them. My friends and I agreed that they were strange folks. Ascetics. The few I'd met were okay, though. For a brief period in high school I dated a wonderful girl from a nearby town who I suspected was a Mormon. About the same time, she was selected as the homecoming queen and all the guys in town were after her. There was definitely something different about her, something unusually nice. She grew tired of my antics before I could find out for sure what it was. We never talked about religion but she told me she was planning to attend Brigham Young University in Utah. She was one of the few people I could place as a likely Mormon from my youth.

Yale wasn't a big Mormon hangout, either. Annette said she was the only one then attending Yale's Divinity School. Yale undergrads rarely demonstrated religious commitment, but it turned out that a couple of my friends went to church with her. Henry Chou and Frank Martinez were both gregarious, unassuming guys I'd come to know during my first year. They liked to kid around and were fun to sit with at dinner. Frank and Henry gave me a blue paperback copy of the Book of Mormon and Annette presented me with a leather-bound edition of the King James translation of the Bible – the Old and New Testaments.

At her prompting, I began to read both the Bible and the Book of Mormon. I also tried to reconcile my preconceptions about religion in general and Mormons in particular with what I was learning. Religious people in general were closed-minded, and Mormons in particular were reputed to be bigots. But those who eschewed formal religion – including me, until I honestly started looking – often seemed highly resistant to the idea that a loving God was at work in our lives. Conversely, I could openly explore all sorts of possibilities with Henry and Frank over a pleasant dinner. And Annette was viewed as almost an insider within the Afro-American community at the Div School. So much for bigotry. Politically, Mormons were also supposed to be notoriously conservative, but Annette and Frank were Democrats – active Democrats. I was getting a little confused.

No doubt remained that Annette was potentially a Very Important Person in my life. It remained to be seen what that meant. Was she to be my teacher? My friend? My mate? I couldn't tell, but I soon concluded that I had a beneficial purpose in Annette's life. She needed a manager. She was bubbling over with worthy ideas and ambitious undertakings. She was continually overextended. Our needs were complementary: She could teach me, and I could keep her sixteen simultaneous virtuous commitments from overwhelming her.

As I came to church with her, I also came to see more of her faults. She could at times be spoiled and stubborn, but try as I might, I couldn't claim her flaws were the results of her religion. They were instead the same human foibles I frequently saw in the mirror. And she had somehow managed to steer clear of my more pernicious vices. Her religion afforded her some limits to the behavioral excesses that were threatening me. Perhaps the first thing she taught me was to approach a life of faithful observance with a little more humility than I was previously prepared to offer.

We didn't "date." Instead, I did my best to reconcile the conflicting demands Annette made upon her own schedule. She repeatedly prevailed on her best friend Suzie to loan us her '66 Plymouth Valiant. She always had a good reason. She would volunteer to take an elderly lady from the Jewish Home to get a new dress, or she'd want to bring some books to a patient in the Veteran's Hospital. And since she hated to drive New Haven's winter streets, I became the eager chauffeur on her "Mitzvah Missions." It was an unusual way to get to know each other, but it was immensely satisfying to both of us. I was seeking truth and love. She was happy to let me drive. If for some reason our relationship fizzled, we both knew we had accomplished a lot of good in the process.

We were sitting in the car, perhaps three weeks after we met, when Annette informed me that I had best banish any thoughts of romance with her. She was happy to spend time together and teach me whatever she could about God, but I had no chance with her. As I looked deeply into the sapphire starbursts of her eyes, she firmly explained she would only get serious with someone who shared her faith, and she wasn't the least bit interested in a non-serious romance. Since I was not a member of her church – or any church, for that matter – I must simply avoid any notion of a conventional date, I had to abandon any hope of a long-term commitment, and I must never, ever even think of kissing her.

74

Oh, the agony I felt! I wondered once again if she were an angel come down to test me. I had never known anyone so spiritually compelling and so exquisitely tempting. She was someone who deserved to be held, closely and passionately. When I was able to arrange a dinner with her, I would watch her at the dining hall's salad bar and marvel at her delicate waist and her sumptuous decolletage. When the time would come to say goodnight, we would stand together at the doorway to her dorm. I held her hand, but I ached to take her into my arms and run my hands through her golden tresses. Her lips begged me to kiss her. It seemed wrong to me that she should deny herself the affection I craved to give her.

But I knew she meant every word she said.

Little in my experience prepared me for the situation I was confronting. Through the beginning of high school I had been clumsy, overweight and generally oblivious to the need for social graces. If I went to a school dance, I went alone or with the guys. At night's end I usually came home without ever having held anyone, much less the girls of my dreams. But by the time I left high school, testosterone had transformed me from an ugly duck into a studly buck – at least in the eyes of the girls who vied for my attention. At the outset of adolescence I had minimal opportunity to exercise self-restraint. Later, none was asked of me.

Now it was mandatory.

In spite of the intense attraction I felt and her apparent affection for me, Annette had decreed that our relationship could be only platonic – at best – for the foreseeable future. Some of the spiritual yearnings of my soul were satisfied, and even pleased, with the prospect of simply learning and serving with her. I had begged the Lord to send me someone to love. If, in His wisdom, that love was constrained to be non-romantic, I guess I could understand. I'd grit my teeth and bear it. I was tough enough. I certainly couldn't claim to deserve more. But while I didn't see myself ever joining her church, my determination to craft a permanent, intimate and affectionate love was almost unmanageable.

As far as I was concerned, we were bound together in the face of irreconcilable differences. It was a profoundly frustrated young man who sat down at his desk on a November night in 1976. Alone in the cramped dorm room, I was facing a mountain of class work and a molehill of motivation. Confusion reigned in my soul. Should I serve or study? Should I invent my own religion and seek to convert her, or assume that the Lord had led me to her church? Was Annette a teacher of truth or my true love?

The last question bothered me the most. If she was to be my beloved – in fact, she had consumed all my affectionate attentions since the moment she had first graced my sight – then I was duty-bound to respect her expressed desire to only pursue a romantic relationship with a man who shared her faith. Yet my uncompromising independence was at odds with even the thought of joining her – or any – religion.

The compact brick nested in my pencil box caught my eye. Somewhere along the way the box had disintegrated, and the deck was secured with an aging blue rubber band. I rarely tried to talk to God with the cards any more. It seemed as though He didn't want me to – the results of my inquiries had become, for all intents and purposes, random. I grabbed the deck and began to shuffle it, moved mostly by boredom. I did, however, allow myself just a moment of wistful hope that I might better understand the path I was being called to tread.

"Heavenly Father," I began (that's what the Mormons called Him, and it seemed to work), "I know I can't do this any more. I guess I understand that you don't want me to look for tools and tricks to help us talk to you. You just want us to pray in faith.

"I do have faith," I assured Him, "and I'm incredibly grateful to you for that. But I can't seem to understand who Annette is. I'm in love with her, and I don't even know if I should be."

My voice stalled. Unlike my earlier affirmation with the cards, now I had no idea how to ask the right question, or what would constitute a meaningful answer. When I had approached the Lord the previous April, I thought I had devised a mechanism to communicate with Him. Now I was just begging for help.

Almost without thinking, I clasped the top two dozen cards of the pile and took a glance at the card exposed underneath.

The queen of spades.

"Whoa..." I blinked, hard.

I found myself marveling yet again. In my eyes, it was the only card that could have served as an unambiguous answer. The Lord's design became apparent, like one of the little drawings in the <u>Highlights</u> magazine at the dentist's office. If He was symbolized by the ace of spades, then I had an obligation to strive as his closest, most reliable, and most faithful ally. And next to His king there should be His queen.

"Oh, Heavenly Father, I hope and pray you know that I'll do my best to do what you want me to do." Faith was not an issue now. I simply wanted there to be no misunderstanding on my part of His will. I vigorously reshuffled the deck.

"One more time, please, so I can proceed with certainty. Should I try to make Annette my queen?"

She smiled up at me from the half-deck in my right hand.

One in 2,704, I recalled. I whooped with joy.

I knew I could still blow it. If I didn't strive with all my heart to be teachable and faithfully obedient, she could certainly find her king in the form of someone else. But now I more clearly saw the path I should try to take, and I better understood the kind of person I should try to be.

And there was a chance – one in how many? – that she would be at my side.

I rose to the challenge. I disciplined my thoughts, studied my scriptures, and exerted myself in every way I could imagine to focus my energy on learning the right lessons before me. I knew, through a voice that I recognized as Divine, that she was the best thing to ever happen to me. I had no clear concept of exactly what that meant, but I knew this woman was made of different material than those I had met at school dances and off-campus keggers. I couldn't bear to imagine losing her as a result of an offensive word or deed – or even a licentious thought. My mind became a daily battleground between the soldiers of spirituality and the armies of adolescent hormones. Most of the time, the soldiers won.

Several weeks later we were in Suzie's car. It was late, and we were returning from the VA hospital. We had been taking care of Ed, a fellow student of Annette's at the Div School. He was blind and diabetic, and his leg had just been removed due to circulatory complications. His wife had abandoned him when he lost his sight three years earlier. Ed was older than most students at the Div School. His experience growing up in New Haven's ghetto and his service in Vietnam had combined to afford him a unique and powerful spiritual outlook. He was both liked and respected at school, but on the day after his surgery Annette was the one who stepped in to make sure his kids were at his side when he woke up.

I agreed to drive.

The evening had been emotionally wrenching and physically demanding. Nurses and orderlies were nowhere to be found. We located Ed's two children and brought them with us to the hospital, but under the circumstances they were suffering almost as much as he was. Finally his pain medication stabilized, the kids settled down, and we were able to leave him with tears of appreciation filling his sightless eyes.

We dropped Ed's kids off at their home. Before we climbed back in the car for the ten-minute drive to the Div School, we stood and talked for a while in the fresh night air. It had been a tough but rewarding day. Annette had shown uncommon strength of character, I reflected, and remarkable compassion. And she looked fabulous. Just like a young queen, I thought with a smile. I opened the car door for her to get in.

We were tired but happy to be heading home. As we halted at a stop sign in the quiet residential neighborhood I looked over to see her hair radiant in the streetlight, her eyes sparkling, her cheeks blushing even in the dim light – and those lips!

"Ohhh..." I moaned, almost inaudibly, and quite unintentionally.

"What?" she inquired innocently, her eyes flashing.

I certainly didn't plan to kiss her. The right time would eventually come – I sincerely hoped – but I felt I must first prove conclusively that I was worthy of her love. I had developed enormous resolve to wait for the appropriate moment. I figured I could hold out for as long as it took. In a torturous exercise of willpower, I had just about gotten to the point where I never, ever even thought of kissing her.

I watched with rising panic as my body was seemingly moved by forces that were beyond my control. My heart pounded as I saw my right hand lifted by some mischievous, invisible puppeteer playing Cupid. It floated up from the steering wheel. My arm proceeded to casually drape itself along the back of her headrest. She sat at least a foot away on the shiny vinyl of the Valiant's bench seat. It was cool outside, but I felt a sheen of sweat breaking out on my forehead as she looked at me expectantly.

"Yes?" she asked, with just a touch of concern creeping into her voice.

Her unbuttoned jacket, V-neck sweater and plain skirt ill disguised a figure that had on more than one occasion caused me to swoon. If the Yale Divinity School had a football team, she would have been the homecoming queen. Her jacket fell open further as her lively

78

eyes searched the cross street for an explanation as to why we were stalled at the intersection. Her bosom heaved gently as she pivoted to face me, curious and alert. I desperately tried not to notice her knee – it slid a couple of inches toward mine as she turned.

Adrenaline flooded my guts. My hand – my own, treacherous right hand! – reached up purposefully and caressed the back of her neck. Her skin was so smooth. It was just as I'd imagined it to be. In one short moment, my fingers slipped into her loose blonde curls and I cradled the back of her head. Her sparkling eyes widened as I calmly pulled her, without resistance, until our lips met.

The softness of her touch was stunning. My senses were flooded with the intoxicating scent of her breath and the soothing warmth of her lips. I realized with shock that, in a fleeting lapse of self control, I had probably blown the sweetest, most positive relationship I'd ever known.

It was over.

An instant later, I realized with even greater astonishment that I was still kissing her – and for that matter, her restraint seemed to have dissolved with my own.

Behind us, a car tapped its horn impatiently.

It was just a few days later that I threw the cards away. They had lain untouched since the queen of spades had beguiled me. I realized that they been my training wheels as I sought to balance my will with that of the Lord. Like Gideon's fleece, they had afforded me the confidence I needed to march on as His servant. My prayers had been answered, not by a deck of cards, but by the power of the Lord.

As my third semester at Yale concluded, I had graduated. Not from college, but from His primary school of faith. I had come to understand that a sincere prayer can be answered in a man's heart with eloquence and precision that made my exercise with the cards look like what it was: Child's play. Useful, yes. Evidently even necessary for my weak and uneducated soul. But upon graduating the Lord let me know he expected me to listen to Him and study His ways just as countless generations have since He first spoke to His children. I was to explore issues of service and faith through the Scriptures and by respectful discussion with those I loved and trusted around me.

"OK, Lord, it's trash time," I said sentimentally as I grabbed the deck from the pencil box. The cracked rubber band that held the cards had long ago lost its elasticity. As I turned the deck over in my hands the band broke and slithered down to my lap. I fanned the cards and pulled out the ace of spades.

"I'll keep this one," I said and tucked it as a bookmark into my Scriptures. "Thanks, Heavenly Father. I really appreciated having these. And thank you for Annette."

"Aren't you going to cut them? Maybe the Lord has something *important* to tell you."

I was surprised to hear the snide, rasping little whisper. I thought I'd banished it completely. The voice was still irritating but had lost almost all its influence.

"I don't need these any more," I responded calmly. "They wouldn't work anyway. They're going in the trash."

"Don't! You can't throw them away! Doesn't the Lord ever change his mind? What if they're the only way for you to get answers to your prayers?" It was shrill, almost panicky. "You might need them some day!"

"Nope. I don't need them now, and I can't use them in the future. And I don't think the Lord changes His mind about much. So sure, I'll cut the deck – and we'll both see that it's just a bunch of cards." Nostalgically I gave the deck one last shuffle and split the brick.

My Queen smiled up at me from my right hand.

Maybe it was a kind of graduation present, an affectionate report card. I was beyond being surprised. I raised it to my lips to give her a brief, chaste kiss. Then I slipped the card off the stack and tucked her next to the ace in my Bible.

"See? He doesn't change His mind very often."

Chapter 4

The Fax

Thursday Noon, 18 May 1995
Denver, Colorado

"Timber, there's a Regina on line three, from Dr. Porter's office."
Shelley's voice floated in over the intercom. I picked up the handset.

"Is this Mr. Dick?" Regina inquired politely. "I'm with Dr.
Porter's office. I just called your wife at home, and she said I should fax
this material to your office. Is that OK?"

"Uh, sure, I guess so," I said. I was tired. "What're you going to
send?"

"It's the results of the amniocentesis you had done on Tuesday,
plus some other material Dr. Porter thought you should have."

I was getting confused about which Dr. Porter she was referring
to.

"He already gave me some Xeroxes," I ventured.

"I know," she said, offering a warmth and understanding that felt
almost like a reassuring hand on my forearm. "I was there."

"You're the nurse?" I asked. "Of course. I'm sorry – I didn't get
your name on Tuesday -- or I didn't remember it. Did you say Regina?"

"That's right. I'm actually not a nurse. I'm a medical assistant,"
she explained, although I didn't have the slightest idea what the
distinction meant.

"I was just telling Annette, and I wanted to tell you – " She
hesitated, and then her words started tumbling out with breathless
urgency. "I'm so sorry about the babies. My heart ached for you when I
realized what you were facing. Maybe I shouldn't say this, but I heard
what Dr. Porter told you and I was really offended. Some of us were
talking after you left, and, well, I just want you to know that we're

81

praying for you and the twins. A lot of us don't feel he should have even suggested what he did. I mean, he has to tell you what's going on and all, but to make a recommendation like he did, well, we think that was just wrong." She paused and audibly took a breath.

In spite of my fatigue, I was touched and a little surprised she had gotten so emotionally involved. I guess I thought she'd seen so many high risk cases, ours wouldn't be that different.

"Thank you," I said. "I'm still kind of dazed. I guess Dr. Porter felt he had to say some of that stuff."

"I guess he did. He <u>had</u> to because of Dr. Mahoney." She lowered her voice. "He's the guy who's always pushing for abortions of high risk babies. It's cheaper, you know, and he figures he's got to make sure they keep to their budget. It makes me sick!" she said vehemently, and then her tone softened again.

"I know you and Annette will do the right thing. She's kind of legendary around here, you know. Nobody can believe she's had all those kids, and she still looks so good, and she's just so nice to everyone."

"I'll tell her you said so. She kind of likes to hear that stuff." I found myself smiling for a moment in anticipation of telling my wife about the nurse's compliments.

"Anyway, I've got the fax number," Regina explained. "But I didn't know whether you wanted me to just send this without any warning. It seems pretty personal to me."

"Uh, yeah." I still hadn't told anyone in the office – or anyone else, for that matter – about the twins, and I appreciated her discretion.

"Thanks. And Regina – thanks for telling me that other stuff. Prayers mean a lot to us, and this is kind of a rough time."

"I know. I'm not sure, but I think these test results may make you feel a little better. I'll fax them in just a couple of minutes. Okay?"

"Sure. Yeah. Thanks."

As I hung up the phone, I pondered her last remark. Earlier in the morning, Annette had called me to say she had succeeded in tracking down Dr. DeVore. He had been wonderful, she said, and wanted us to come to his office in Salt Lake for an echocardiogram as soon as possible. He also said that we didn't need to bring anything with us except the results of the genetic screen. The amnio results, combined with the echocardiogram, would tell him about as much as he could know about the condition of the twins.

82

The hardest part about this whole thing, I realized, was that nothing was really black or white. If the amnio results were clean, then the twins had a better chance of survival – but the longer Annette carried them, the greater the risk to her. Paradoxically, from Dr. Mahoney's position the best result would be if they had serious genetic defects. Then he'd probably push hard to have them aborted as soon as possible, to make sure Annette's life was preserved. And in the courts of heaven, would he be wrong?

I was startled out of my deliberations by the distinctive ring of the fax machine. From many perspectives, I didn't have any desire to keep any of this from my coworkers. Justin, Shelley, and the others had weathered tremendous trials with me at Safeline, and we formed a resilient and supportive group. But there was so little that I could control I wanted to choose the time and place to discuss the twins with them.

By the time I walked over to the fax, the cover sheet was in the receiving tray. Like most cover sheets, it was a waste of paper, I thought. The second page was much more interesting. It looked to be the actual test results from the genetics lab in Santa Fe. I was a little surprised to realize that Dr. Porter must have sent Annette's amniotic fluid test sample down by overnight express. Before I could make sense of the results, the fax ejected a third page. It was from Volume 49, Number 9 of the "Obstetrical and Gynecological Survey," the first page of an article entitled, "Prenatal Ultrasound Diagnosis of Conjoined Twins." I took a deep breath and scanned the page filled with words that I'd never seen before, like polyhydramino and omphalopagus. I stood at the fax and collected a total of twelve pages.

The lab report took a few minutes to understand, but when the results became apparent, I realized what Regina was trying to say. Buried in the fine print of the pages from the genetics lab was the following –

Results: No evidence of quantitative
                    abnormality for chromosomes
Sex: Male

Annette was carrying two little boys who had no observable genetic problems. The twins were healthy. They were not Down's babies, nor were they afflicted with any of the other obvious chromosomal defects that Dr. Porter had described. At least genetically, these boys would be no different from Tomicah or Levi, Corban or Shiloh. If they lived, Annette and I could teach them, play with them, and expect them to contribute, in turn, to the family and the world just like their siblings. They would be able to think and learn and love.

The ten page article following the test results was not nearly as encouraging. It was a detailed technical summary of the different types of conjoined twins, and the prognosis for each physical configuration. Once again, I was looking at grainy photos and diagrams of little bodies that were unlike any I had ever seen. The text was the type of article we had hoped to find when we searched the Denver library after our first visit to the clinic downtown. It was packed with answers to questions I had only begun to formulate.

Researchers had apparently found no explanation for the medical phenomenon of conjoined twins. Annette's age had nothing to do with the twins' condition; it was as likely to occur in the pregnancy of a twenty-year-old as in that of a woman of forty. The article noted that,

> ...X-rays have proven almost useless in identifying conjoined twins at an early gestational age, and ultrasound technology is a very recent development. It was only in 1981 that the first modern sonographic techniques were developed for use in the diagnosis of conjoined twins. Prior to that time, the diagnosis of the condition was usually made only during labor, with grave consequences for the mother and babies alike. Even today, the fact that the twins are joined is frequently not determined until delivery problems arise.

Although the majority of identical twins are boys, the article continued, seventy to ninety-five percent of conjoined twins are female. The twins are always identical, and even with prenatal diagnosis and subsequent critical care procedures, "seventy-five percent of those delivered either are stillborn or die within 24 hours."

Especially given that some people remove them from their mother and "let nature take its course," I thought soberly.

It was possible to surgically separate the twins in some cases, but "the prognosis for twins with a shared heart or liver is poor." This type of joining was called thoracopagus, which simply means twins joined at the chest. There were very few recorded incidents of twins who shared a heart living beyond three months. The chance for one twin to survive did not increase statistically if the sibling was sacrificed in an effort to minimize organ trauma.

My head ached. I stared up at the tiles of the ceiling.

The article concluded,

> "Delivery of viable conjoined twins should be at a tertiary center for optimal neonatal intensive care and pediatric surgical support... Occurrence of conjoined twins is a very rare, random event. The risk of recurrence is negligible."

Random. At one point I had looked up the word in my dictionary. It defined random as haphazard. Purposeless. Without method or meaning.

SIDS deaths were supposed to be random. I wondered: Is there such a thing as a meaningless death?

In the five years I served as the bishop of our congregation, I had helped three dozen families cope with the death of a loved one. That number included my own wife and children. Most bishops I met dealt with only a handful of funerals in the same amount of time. Through my calling I had become well acquainted with people at – and beyond – the edge of life. I had held dear friends as they cried and as they died. Some of the bereaved families grew closer to God through the experiences accompanying death. A few were just happy to hear that in our church we don't charge anything for our services. Even for the most calloused, however, death wasn't completely without meaning.

Life was filled with meaning. What about death? I couldn't bring myself to even give voice to the thought, but it was becoming clear that death was again planning to visit my home. Within the next weeks or months our twins would probably die. The doctors were saying there was at least a possibility Annette might accompany them.

The simplest of men, as well as the most faithful, tend to profess a belief that blessings await the deserving who pass away. Faith assures a great reconciling of our eternal accounts. Justice would be satisfied. I found the corollary more challenging: If our existence is ultimately just

85

and fair, then there was a purpose and benefit which can be derived from pain, hardship and grief.

The Apostle Paul voiced exquisite faith when he wrote in Romans that, "We know that all things work together for good to them that love God, to them who are the called according to His purpose."

All things, he said.

"Timber, Dr. Porter's on line one," Shelley interrupted.

"Which one? I mean, is it a man or a woman?" I asked.

"Sounds like a man to me."

Dr. Albert Porter's voice was strained. He extended a somewhat awkward greeting and then proceeded directly to the point of the call. His tone was thoroughly professional – it was just like listening to legal counsel. He explained that the HMO's Treatment Advisory Committee had convened a special meeting to discuss Annette's case. Although they would respect the parents' wishes, the majority of the committee members felt the fetuses were not viable, regardless of the results of the genetic screen. If she were to continue to carry them, Annette faced the risk of toxemia, hypertension and hemorrhaging, in addition to the risks of the mandatory surgical delivery. After an extended discussion, Dr. Mahoney, the chairman, had instructed Dr. Porter to tell us that the committee strongly advised immediate termination of the pregnancy.

IV.   A Challenger on the Bridge

December 1976 – 21 March 1978
New Haven, CT – Washington, DC

Annette's enthusiastic response to our first embrace in the car left me excited and confused. Her previous commitment to a chaste friendship seemed to portend relatively sterile relations in our future. Maybe even ascetic. This possibility had saddened me greatly. I liked affection. I really liked the thought of someday being affectionate with her. Just when I was resigned to playing by her rules, I had committed what should have been a major infraction – and no one had called a penalty. I wasn't ejected from the field. She hadn't declared the game over.

Had the rules changed? If they had, I had no clue about what the new limits might be.

That night, we drove back to the Divinity School in near silence. Annette was pensive but not withdrawn. In the glimpses of her face I was afforded by passing streetlights and headlamps, she seemed not offended, but – dare I hope? – perhaps even a little pleased. I offered my right hand. She clasped it first in her left, then both, before releasing me with her right hand to carefully rest our still interlinked fingers on her lap. The warmth of her thigh radiated through her skirt.

My pounding heart was interfering with my ability to pilot the car.

As we disembarked and walked speechlessly to her dorm, I briefly contemplated apologizing. Instead I carefully inquired whether I had violated the terms of our agreement.

"No, I guess not," she said quietly as she glanced down toward my boots and gently shoved at a bit of nothing with the toe of her shoe. "Not really." We stood together at her door. Then without another word, it was her turn to reach up to entwine her hands in my hair and administer a kiss that permanently disrupted my bodily chemistry.

"We'll go back to the hospital tomorrow," she whispered through glistening lips. "G'nite," she smiled.

I had lost my ability to talk. I nodded, waved at her weakly, and stumbled out into the crisp night air and down the hill. Any concerns about Annette's desires for affection were melted in the warmth of that kiss. Now I was worried about keeping the fire raging in my heart under control.

We subsequently managed to maintain a reasonable level of decorum while we were in the dining hall and library. We learned that it was perilous to spend time together in our dorm rooms without our room mates about. We were generally safe as we drove about on various errands. We went to church twice on Sundays and sometimes again on Wednesdays. And thus, in the weeks that followed, Suzie's car became our semi-private refuge, our planning center, our conference room. While she was most generous with her wheels, Suzie wasn't the only one to support our efforts with the loan of a car. As we gained experience with different makes and models, I abandoned my previous fascination with high-output engines, bucket seats and stick shifts in favor of a more mature appreciation of the finer points of automotive design. I decided the single most underrated feature of a modern American motorcar was the humble front bench seat. In fact, I felt sure I could trace the majority of our society's ills back to some unidentified Communist infiltrators on Madison Avenue who successfully persuaded the youth of America that a center console and a Hurst shifter were sexier and more romantic than the opportunity to have our sweethearts snuggled up next to us. There was little doubt in my mind this insidious plot led directly to the demise of the drive-in movie and the burgeoning popularity in the 60's and 70's of no-contact dancing. It was no wonder the divorce rate was skyrocketing and folks were being driven to buy pickup trucks!

The American family was under assault, but I was determined to do my part to win the battle. More than once neighbors, passers-by, even police on patrol stopped to inquire about our activities and well-being as we conversed together behind the wheel. Occasionally, as if by some mutual but unspoken agreement, we chose the relative privacy of a vehicle as the place to argue whatever issue was boiling that day. On the other hand, our activities were frequently far more congenial and neither of us would pretend that our first kiss in the car was our last.

The combination of virtuous intent, willful (if imperfect) self-restraint, and sincere affection nurtured our love. The rules of the game had indeed changed. My goal had become perfectly clear. With Christmas break upon us, I pulled Annette into her dorm room as we prepared to part late after our evening's activities. Her face registered bemused alarm as I pushed the door closed until it almost – but not quite – latched. I took her cheeks between my palms and inhaled deeply as I gazed for a moment into her lovely eyes. Then I let my hands fall to grasp hers and dropped to one knee. Somewhere I had learned that's how it was supposed to be done. ·

"Annette, I love you," I began haltingly. There was no script for my performance – this was all impromptu. "You have taught me so much, and it seems like everything we're doing is right. I know I'm blessed to be with you – and I want to be with you forever."

Annette's eyes refocused as she realized I was on a mission far more serious than an attempt to sneak a passionately playful embrace. They narrowed as I clasped both her hands together in mine.

"I'm asking you to marry me," I continued as she cocked her head just barely to the side and took a breath. "Wait! Don't say anything now – I know this is really too fast, but I mean every word I'm saying. Think about it, and then let me know whenever you're ready to talk. But I mean it: I don't ever want to walk away from you and all that we can do together. Please marry me."

She exhaled slowly and said nothing, but stared deeply into my soul as only she could. I wasn't going to get the answer I hoped for that night, I realized. I scrambled to my feet to give her a chaste kiss and make a strategic retreat. She interrupted my choreography.

"Of course this is too fast," she replied, smiling as she lifted her hand from mine to run it through her hair. "I love you, too, Timber. We'll talk about this – but now, it's late." She raised up on her toes to kiss me warmly, but briefly. Then she pivoted about and opened the door. My mind was blank. I squeezed her hand and headed out.

"Timber?" She caught my forearm. As I halted my momentum through the door she pressed herself against me. Once again we kissed, and I was again stunned by the overwhelming sensations that accompanied her embrace – the softness of her lips, the scent of her skin, the texture of her hair, the fit of her body into mine. Then she pulled away, smiled at me for a heartbeat, and shut the door. With a quiet click, it latched.

What had I done? No flowers, no restaurant, no ring. She deserved a proposal worthy of a queen. I had tossed it off like it was little more than heartfelt goodbye to my grandmother. Worse, it was a goodbye: Annette was leaving the next day to California, and I was headed away to Mexico for the holidays with my family. In my rush to propose, we'd made no arrangements to meet prior to leaving.

So much for impromptu performances, I told myself. I had done a better job ten years before with my first proposal through the mail.

The mail! Maybe my live performance was lacking, but I could still try to reach her heart with a meaningful expression of my commitment – and she'd have it in her hands as she sat on the plane. On the long walk down the hill and back to my room, I paused in one of the grassy expanses of the campus to have an extended chat with my Heavenly Father. The clear night sky was deep with stars. I clearly had some work to do before dawn. The best parts of the letter were composed before I unlocked the door to my room, but it was 5 AM before I lay down to a fitful nap.

The raucous buzz of my alarm at seven prompted a double surge of adrenalin as I remembered I had a semester final in an hour. It would be administered in an auditorium on Science Hill – halfway up the hill to the Div School. I skimmed the pages I'd written in the long hours of the early morning, said a quick but fervent prayer, pulled on my boots and started running.

I left for Puerto Vallarta without knowing whether Annette had received the envelope I slipped under her door. Phone service was primitive and exorbitant at our Mexican hotel, but I made a daily trip to the rustic post office to send additional affirmations of my love. The vacation was emotionally grueling. The suspense and vulnerability of my circumstances left me intensely frustrated.

Justin thought I was crazy.

"She doesn't drink? She didn't even want to let you kiss her, and now you're talking about spending your whole life with her? What has gotten into you?"

I proudly proffered a photo of Annette in a wispy summer dress. He whistled quietly and nodded appreciatively – but balked when I told him we had an essentially spiritual relationship.

"Right, Timber – I'm sure you're thinking all sorts of religious thoughts every time you lay eyes on her. C'mon – She's a dish, but I can't believe you've asked a Mormon to marry you. What are you gonna do if she says yes? Change your whole life?"

Leave it to my brother to get to the heart of the matter. He was asking some very important questions. I was unable to answer many of them. From his point of view – even from my own – the woman I described came as a complicated package. He found some major elements without much appeal. I loved Annette, but more importantly I knew I was supposed to do all I could to learn and grow with her. I honestly don't know what I would have done if my scintillating, spiritual and scrumptious Annette had instead been dull and drab. There was no question that the electricity she sent surging through my soul stimulated my spiritual search. Nonetheless, she had joined me on a journey that I had originally undertaken long before I met her. If she'd had all the appeal of a Soviet truck, the obligation I felt to travel onward with her would have remained – and it wasn't worth it to me to speculate whether matrimony would have been a part of that hypothetical trip. I wanted her by my side, but not because she was cute. There were certainly times I'd pursued attractive women as a satisfying refutation of my own insecurities. But physical attraction wasn't enough to sustain a life

90

together. Annette offered to help me search for wisdom – and I was very happy to appreciate the scenery along the way.

"Just have a beer. Enjoy the sunset. Look at the girls. You'll get over it," Justin advised.

Mom was similarly cautious, but for different reasons.

"Remember, Timber: You don't just marry the girl, you marry the family," she counseled soberly as we sat watching the sun nestling among the palm frond-topped fish stands along the beach. "It sounds like her dad is a an important person in her life, and he doesn't seem to like you very much."

These familial observations were not enhancing my vacation.

As was often the case, Mom was right. Annette's father, Dr. Thomas Lantos, was proving to be a fascinating and challenging man: A university professor, he was a Hungarian survivor of the Holocaust who was active in political affairs. He'd established the California State University Study Abroad Program and served as an economist with the state teacher's union. Aristocratic and intellectual, he regularly appeared as a commentator on San Francisco television. The family lived on a hill overlooking the bay with a pair of Mercedes in the garage. He lavished attention on his beautiful and precocious daughters – Annette was the first of two – but he appeared to rule his family with an iron fist.

And so far, he didn't seem to like me very much.

Annette spoke to her parents by phone almost every day. On several occasions I had listened to her tout my accomplishments and character as she chatted with her dad before we departed for an evening's outing. His contempt for me seethed into their conversation. She couldn't help but be defensive given the intensity of his responses. I had met him only once during a brief visit he made to New Haven and I was accorded little more status and recognition than a baggage porter. Annette's mom, known as Mimo, was attractive, vivacious and pleasant. Her sister Katrina seemed genuinely fond of me. Nonetheless, her dad's response to the prospect of my joining his clan was decidedly problematic. It wasn't at all clear how his reaction might in turn affect my relations with the rest of the family.

Upon my return from Mexico to New Haven we picked up where we left off – or perhaps, more accurately, from a bit before where we left off. Annette proceeded as if neither my spoken nor my written offers of marriage had ever been broached. She was entrancing, affectionate, and enthusiastic when we spent time together. Annette was

91

effusive about my correspondence from Mexico and she evidently cherished the trinkets I presented as tokens of my esteem. When I received straight A's for the fall semester, I was stunned, but she wasn't fazed a bit.

"But I've never gotten straight A's in my life," I said incredulously. "I'm just not that smart. Look – I even aced the exam I took with almost no sleep the morning we left!"

"Of course you did," Annette explained. "Timber, you've been working hard, and even with the time we're spending together I suspect you're being more productive than you used to be. But also consider the possibility that you've been doing what the Lord wanted you to do. I'm not surprised."

It was so inexplicable to me, so straightforward to her. Then it hit me: I'd aced my courses. The playing card still served as a bookmark in my scriptures. The bond between us was growing daily ever more strong and sure – but she never offered a response to my proposals.

Three hundred and sixty dollars. After tuition, it was all I had. Eighteen twenties were neatly folded in my pocket as I hunched over the display case of the jewelry store. The clerk was giving me an extended lecture on how to assess the quality of diamonds. Keep your eye on the three "C's," he kept repeating. The best diamonds have near-flawless clarity, cut, and color, he intoned. He seemed oblivious to the salience of the fourth C: cost. After the better part of an hour I left with a small velvet box and a certificate from the resident gemologist attesting to the stunning quality of the sesame seed-sized stone on the ring within, plus eleven dollars in my pocket.

This time, it was all or nothing.

Annette had invited me to accompany her to Jimmy Carter's Presidential inauguration. I borrowed enough cash for train tickets and a tuxedo. Jimmy Carter wanted a "People's Inauguration" – there were to be seven Grand Balls to accommodate the thousands of attendees – and the city of Washington throbbed to the tempo of new hope and populist participation. We stayed with different acquaintances but spent our waking hours together. Annette showed herself to be at home in Washington, but I was about as comfortable as a cowpoke in a lingerie store. That doesn't mean I didn't enjoy myself – I did, thoroughly. I was just a bit out of my territory.

For three days I waited for that magic moment when everything would be perfectly memorable and romantic. A quiet pause in the tumult when the excitement and festivities would seem to be happening just for her. A time when we could both look around and feel that the joyful events of this national celebration were an expression of the promise of our love. A time when –

It was time to go. We were both dead tired from the series of exotic nights, effervescent days and unfamiliar mattresses. We dragged ourselves onto the train and collapsed. The mechanical genius in me figured out that the armrest between our seats could be folded well out of the way, and we snuggled together into a semi-conscious blur of sensation, vibration, and exhaustion.

We were on our way out of New York City when it hit me that the primary mission of my trip remained unaccomplished. The realization was a powerful tonic. The fog of my fatigue evaporated almost immediately. As we nested together in the rocking railcar, my mind raced to seek a solution. I breathed deeply the complex perfumes of the woman in my arms. It was quiet. We were almost alone. We were returning from a wonderful, completely memorable celebration. I pressed my left arm against my side and felt the reassuring bulge of the velvet box nudging my ribs. If I didn't act then, another opportunity might not arise.

"Annette?" I shifted my shoulders slightly to move her along toward consciousness.

"Mmmmm." She murmured without opening her eyes. "Are we there already?"

"Not quite. Can I talk with you for a minute?" I squirmed my torso to face her. Thus deprived of her support, she had little choice but to sit up and flash her stunning – if slightly bloodshot – blue eyes around the darkened railcar to finally focus on me.

"MmmmHumm? Where are we?" She blinked repeatedly as she sought to orient herself.

"A ways outside New Haven," I explained, and we spent the next few moments in small talk about the events of the past 72 hours. She was by then fully awake.

"I had an absolutely incredible time," I summarized. "I want to thank you, not so much for the tickets, but for your company."

It was time to get serious. I kissed her briefly.

93

"Annette, I love you very, very much. I hope I've made it clear how much you mean to me." We had spoken weeks before about my experiences with the deck of cards. Although she didn't hesitate to tell me that the Lord was unlikely to continue to use a game of chance to answer my prayers, she appreciated the significance that the experience had to me.

"I didn't do this right before," I confessed. "If I could, I would have found the perfect time and place to pledge my love to you forever. I may have said things kinda' clumsily, but you need to know I meant every word. If you'll let me, I'll love you, and protect you, and cherish you, and provide for you with every breath I ever take. You are the most important teacher I've ever had, and I know that if I can work with you forever we'll both be blessed beyond measure." Annette was giving me her undistracted attention as I shifted my position to kneel in the aisle of the gently swaying train.

"This is the third time that I'm asking you, and you need to understand that I won't ask again. Not in a week, not in a year. I won't have both of us face this issue again for a long, long time. If you can't say yes, that's OK – I understand. No matter what your answer is I hope and pray that we'll know and love each other for the rest of our lives. But I also pray with all my heart that your answer will be 'Yes.'" I reached for the velvet box and fumbled for a moment to open it and extract the ring within.

"Annette, please marry me." She let me place it on her, but the ring was too large – it slipped effortlessly and insecurely over her diminutive finger.

She looked at me until time became irrelevant. Were her exquisite eyes filled with tears? Had I blown it again? I could see so much in them, but I was assured of nothing. Finally she glanced down and drew a long breath. When her eyes again met mine and she began to speak, her voice was calm.

"Timber, I love you so much." She stared soberly for moment at the gliding lights and shadows beyond the window. "You've completely captivated me. I think of you every day and every night. I pray for you and I know I'm really praying for myself. I want to love you completely." Resignation had crept into her voice, and suddenly I wasn't at all sure I wanted to hear what she would say next. "But I can't say yes – not now. I know you mean it when you say you won't ask me again. You've proven to be a man of your word. But I need to know this is the right thing. You have to let me have a few days. Let me fast and pray, and then I'll give you an answer that I know is right."

Once again she had rendered this smooth talking disk jockey speechless. At least she didn't say no. I kissed her hand and gingerly repositioned myself up on the bench seat next to her.

"Thursday," she whispered, and she kissed me chastely. "Give me until Thursday evening. Then I can answer you." She melded herself to me, seeking once again the comfort and security I had afforded in the hours of the ride before I had broached the topic of marriage.

There would be no more discussion of the matter that night.

How many minutes are there in three days? How many times did I look at my watch or double-check the calendar? How many heartbeats pulsed in my ears as I lay sleepless awaiting her answer?

I arranged to see her for dinner Thursday. We met at her room and she asked me to kneel with her to pray before we headed off to the dining hall. It was soon apparent she was following her own agenda.

I chose to follow her.

We talked small talk through dinner. She ate sparingly. I asked her if she was OK. She responded that she was fine, but she'd been fasting and she didn't yet feel like a full meal. I searched for any clue about her answer. She seemed in good spirits. I couldn't tell whether she was trying to find the right opportunity to say yes or showing me that we could still be friends even though her answer was negative. It was for me a memorable, but not an especially comfortable meal.

"Let's go for a walk," she suggested. January in New Haven is not the most accommodating month for a pleasant stroll. That evening was true to form. Within moments a cold mist had sprinkled my glasses and my vision was festooned with starbursts of refracted light. The effect sounds poetic, but I was half-blinded as we trekked along Yale's aging slate and cobblestone sidewalks. Annette didn't seem to mind me quite firmly holding her arm as we navigated the hilly streets. She soon arrived at the topic of my hope and consternation.

"When we met, I told you to abandon any thought of romance with me," she began. "This is hard for me to admit to you, but I wasn't trying to protect you – I was trying to protect myself. Not long after we had that lunch together I had this kind of a waking dream – more than a fantasy, but not really a vision – where I saw you quite literally as a knight in shining armor. I told myself that you were going to make some lucky girl very, very happy. And then I couldn't help myself – I started crying. Really crying. It hurt – and you hadn't done anything wrong at all." She paused to look at me. "Timber, I wanted to be that girl."

I started to feel a little better about the evening's prospects. I found myself nodding encouragingly. She continued.

"My faith is as important to me as my life, Timber. You know that. My family was nearly exterminated by Hitler because we were Jewish. If you look at history, Mormons have borne the brunt of a lot of persecution, too – but I can't change what I know to be true. I understand you find a lot of what you've learned about my religion hard to swallow. One minute I'm talking about the Torah and how God's word has impacted the fate of my people throughout the ages. The next I'm telling you that Christ is my Savior. A lot of people won't even try to comprehend my perspective. You've listened, and it's been wonderful to talk about it with you."

We had spent hours over the past months exploring the teachings and contentions of the Christians and Jews. She made clear to me her conviction that the Book of Mormon's restored – or newly discovered – scriptures confirmed both the Old and New Testaments and allowed her to respect the teachings of her heritage while acknowledging Christ.

"I can't abandon my faith. And to me, marriage is a commitment within my faith. I want my husband to share my beliefs. I want to be married not just 'til death do you part,' but in the temple, forever."

She had also told me about the Church's doctrine of eternal marriage. As long as it would involve her with me, I rather liked the idea.

"But right after we met you said you couldn't imagine ever becoming a member of the Church of Jesus Christ of Latter Day Saints – or any formal church, as I recall. So I figured the best way to protect myself while still respecting your desire to learn was to tell you to just quit thinking of me that way – romantically, I mean. I thought we were both doing pretty well until you kissed me that night." She laughed quietly as she looked up at me. The droplets on my glasses made it all but impossible to read her expression. Then she moved closer to me and raised her face expectantly. I may have been half blind, but I wasn't stupid. I wrapped my arms around her and kissed her with every bit of passion and respect and hope that my body could express.

"Oh, Timber! We've gotta stop that!" Her tone was playful, but at one level she was serious. A kiss meant more to her than it did with the other girls I'd known. I wanted that kiss to be the most meaningful of my life.

She stepped back a pace, brushed some invisible wrinkles from the front of her overcoat and shook her hair to the side. Then she began to speak very earnestly.

"If you believe that God led you to me, you have to understand that my faith is inseparable from my affection. I love you because I really believe you want to know the truth – God's eternal truth – and you want to do His will. You can't accept me as your wife unless you accept the beliefs that are at the core of who I am." Her voice dropped off, and with it some of the elation that had flooded over me during our embrace. She must have sensed my difficulty in seeing her. She carefully raised her hand and used her fingertip to wipe my glasses clear. Her eyes were delving into mine as she resumed speaking in little more than a whisper.

"I asked you to wait so I could pray about this. When I did, I didn't quite get the answer I expected." Her face was painted in hues of hope and vulnerability. Her voice caught for just a heartbeat as she continued.

"I love you. I know that you love me. And I believe that you love the Lord and want to serve Him." Never had I seen her eyes so round and blue as they glistened in the light of the streetlamp overhead.

"If you can accept me – all of me – then I want to be your wife." She raised her arms hesitatingly in an offer of herself to me. My vision was clear enough to see that it wasn't only the New Haven mist that was streaking down her cheeks. I held her again, tightly, and felt my own tears of joy welling through my soul.

"I really, really want to be your wife," she whispered into my shoulder.

When I finally got back to my room that night, I sat at my desk contemplating the new curves in the path before me. I understood what Annette had told me – but I was concerned that her words may have meant one thing to her and another to me. I tried to remember all that she said.

Hers wasn't an expression of unconditional love. The princess wasn't offering herself to this knight in shining armor unless I willingly met the challenge implicit in her acceptance. She was mine, forever – if I accepted the whole package. Not just those intoxicating eyes, not just her beguiling smile, not just that embrace that fogged up my glasses and buckled my knees. Her offer included not just her faith, but her religion; not just her company, but her family; not just her counsel, but also her criticism.

She was mine only if she was all mine.

I took a deep breath and began to use the knowledge I had so recently gained. I prayed to the God that had brought me to that juncture, to the God of Abraham, Isaac, and Jacob. I was on the right path.

A few days later we revisited the jewelry shop. Since the ring didn't fit, I wanted her to choose a design to her liking.

"How come these over here are the same price as the one you got, but they're a lot bigger?" Annette asked innocently.

"Yours has a certificate attesting to the diamond's nearly flawless color, cut and, um, clarity," I answered proudly.

"But it's so little! Look at this one," she advised. "If I'm out shopping for groceries and some old beau comes up to say hello, which ring would you rather I be wearing?"

We left with the biggest $350 solitaire in the store.

I asked to learn more about the Restored Gospel, as Annette called it. Two guys my age came by several times over the next weeks to teach me the essential doctrines of the Church of Jesus Christ. Elder Tinney and Elder Miller were missionaries serving full time at their own expense to teach the Gospel to people like me. They taught that Jesus was truly God's son, and that He had lived to teach us by His words and example how we should live. When we got to the part in Matthew where Jesus was baptized, they explained that each of us had the opportunity to be washed of our sins by following the Savior into the water.

"Do you have any sins that you wish to be cleansed from your life?" Elder Tinney asked me. My mind was flooded with images of events from high school, New College – even some from my early months in New Haven.

It was probably the most important – and easiest to answer – question of my Yale career. Ten days later, he and Elder Miller witnessed me being baptized. A few weeks later, again in keeping with the example of the Savior as he established his lay ministry, I was ordained into the priesthood by a resident at the Med School, Dr. Greg DeVore.

Not everything proceeded smoothly. Annette and I wanted to get married as soon as we could make the appropriate arrangements. It became evident that our blissful wishes and rollicking hormones were on a collision course with some immovable constraints. First, the bishop of the New Haven congregation told us that there weren't very many inflexible rules of the Church that didn't have a Scriptural reference, but one of them was that I had to be a baptized member for a full calendar year before we could be married in the Temple. We could be married civilly at any time – he would be happy to perform the ceremony himself at the chapel – but a temple marriage would have to wait.

Some of Annette's friends enthusiastically promoted the alternative of a wedding at the Div School's stately chapel on the campus. We could marry during spring break. The daffodils would be blooming in profusion and we would enjoy an end to our agonizing effort to maintain an appropriately chaste premarital relationship.

I admit to being rather attracted to this plan.

Nonetheless, a temple marriage promises unique blessings. Most important is a commitment that the bride and groom make, which is then sealed with ecclesiastical authority, to remain in the bonds of wedlock for all eternity. If we were married first under civil authority in the Div School's chapel, we could still be married in the temple a year later. This seemed a workable approach. We decided to each fast and pray to affirm that we had chosen the right way.

"So – How did you feel?" Annette inquired cautiously two days later. She had been happily engaged discussions with friends in and out of the church detailing a lovely ceremony and reception at the Div School. A temple wedding would be by its nature not only delayed a year, but also a much less festive event and, instead, sacred.

"I kind of don't want to tell you, but I felt pretty strongly that the Lord wants us to be married first by His authority, in His temple," I responded carefully. It was a daunting prospect and I knew she would probably be very disappointed. I could only hope that she had felt the same answer. "We need to wait."

"I know," she said dejectedly. I breathed a sigh of relief. "It would have been so lovely to be married at Marquand Chapel – but I got the same answer." She looked at me just a little petulantly and then she flashed a mischievous grin. "We're going to have to work harder to behave ourselves. You'd better keep your hands in your pockets!"

It was probably the most consequential choice of our early relationship. We demonstrated a commitment to each other – and to the Lord – to put aside our natural desires in pursuit of a goal we knew to be eternally important. While we were sorely tested over the ensuing months, we were living in fundamental harmony with one another and His principles.

We set a wedding date for the first day of spring: March 21, 1978.

Our love flourished, but so did the complications. When we called in January and inquired at the Washington, D.C. Temple, we found there remained a single opening for a wedding on the 21st of March. It fell on a Tuesday, during the second week of Spring Break, and evidently a lot of other couples thought it was a good time to marry. Annette had been proudly wearing her engagement ring, but her father pointedly ignored it and firmly quashed any discussion about our relationship. As a consequence, Annette's mother and sister were supportive of our intent, but nervous.

"Elope!" Katrina suggested. "He'll never support your wedding, so don't even try to cooperate with him. He'll just be hurt and offended that you went ahead against his wishes. What's that old joke?" She looked from her mother to Annette. "'Sometimes it's better to ask forgiveness than permission' – That's it."

Annette's mother, Mimo, nodded cautiously but approvingly.

"It might be a good idea," she tentatively concurred in her charming Hungarian accent.

"Elope to the temple?" Annette asked. "Well, I guess it could simplify a lot of things."

In fact, eloping to the temple proved an excellent strategy. We were both completely overcommitted in the other areas of our lives. Annette was finishing her studies for her Master's at the Div School. She had decided to stage a major theatrical production of *Godspell* with the support of the university, and the illness of one of the key actresses meant that Annette both directed and starred in the play. I volunteered as set designer and stage manager. I found that active members of the Church were kept busy with other responsibilities, as well. I taught classes, helped to maintain the chapel, and prepared for a group trip to the Washington Temple that was scheduled to occur in early summer.

In the face of the additions to my schedule, something had to give. I tried to keep my priorities ordered, but often school work received substantially less attention that it probably deserved. My grades should have suffered. Instead they soared. Soon after I met Annette I received approval to accelerate my studies and receive my B.A. in seven semesters instead of the usual eight. Then I was accepted into an elite program which allowed me to take graduate courses at the nascent School of Organization and Management while still technically an undergraduate. I was one of a handful of students elected to Phi Beta Kappa while a Junior. As our wedding date approached I was slated to simultaneously receive both my B.A. and M.A. at the end of the following semester – after just three and a half years of study.

It seemed to me this list of academic accolades should have made me more attractive to Annette's father – yet the chemistry between us remained almost toxic. Generally when I was with Annette, I seemed to say just the right thing. When I commented at dinner with her father, my remarks seemed to certify me as the assistant village idiot. The gap between Professor Lantos and me was more than cultural. It was galactic. We were like different life forms. We both tried – Dr. Lantos would occasionally indulge his daughter in a significant accommodation, like providing a plane ticket to allow her to spend time with me during a holiday or giving Annette one of the family's Mercedes to take school. But there was still no hiding the fact that he just didn't like me.

As the wedding date approached we were thus spared the task of coordinating a grand wedding reception. In the face of Dr. Lantos' antagonism, Annette and I planned a temple ceremony that was modest in the extreme. We didn't anticipate any family members would attend. Afterward – as a surprise – I planned to take her to Disney World for a few days honeymoon prior to finishing the semester.

Annette went home to California as was her custom for the first week of spring break. She explained to her father that she was going to go on a road trip with her room mate for the second week. He assumed Annette was referring to her former room mate at the Div School, Pam. Did he suspect she was instead referring to me as her future room mate? He may have, but he gave no sign whatsoever. Instead he acknowledged that since he had business in Washington at the time, he'd be happy to take the whole family back East for a brief holiday.

Annette had earlier noted that she found me to be a man of my word. As the date approached, I felt increasingly uncomfortable with the subterfuge surrounding our wedding. Just as a proposal was supposed to be offered on bended knee, I had been taught that the groom should at least ask the father of the bride for permission to marry his daughter. If no permission was then granted – well, I would have to cross that bridge when I came to it.

Once again, the U.S. Mail empowered me. I had been convinced by Mimo and Katrina that any attempt to talk directly with Dr. Lantos was predestined to end explosively. Even a phone call was likely to precipitate unhappy and unpredictable consequences. They grudgingly accepted the notion that a well-drafted letter had the best chance of according Annette's father the respectful treatment I felt his position warranted.

The letter detailed everything about our marriage except the date. I told Dr. Lantos of my love and commitment to his daughter, of my plans for gainful employment, and how we planned to live nearby so he and Mimo could enjoy any grandchildren. I even provided a listing of my assets – my car, motorcycle, bank accounts, and so on – to assure him that she would be well provided for. After this somewhat sober presentation, I lightheartedly quipped that if he still found my arguments unpersuasive, he should bear in mind the following: I was holding his white Mercedes hostage in Connecticut. If he failed to deliver Annette to Washington in a plain brown wrapper by no later than the 20th of March, I would feel forced to shoot the car – right in the carburetor. I figured if he couldn't smile when he got the letter, perhaps he'd save it and laugh with us later. I sent it off Special Delivery to arrive while Annette was still in California.

On the phone Annette told me he got the letter and took it immediately into his bedroom. He shut the door and remained there for almost half an hour. When he emerged, he made no comment whatsoever.

Dr. Lantos, or Didi – as he was known in his family – proceeded to make good on his offer to fly with Annette, Katrina and Mimo back to Washington on Thursday the 16th of March. They took a suite at a hotel right downtown. After spending all week writing research papers in Annette's absence, I clambered aboard a Greyhound from New Haven on Friday evening. I was met at the D.C. bus station by my somewhat chastened fiancee.

"Timber, nobody in my family thinks we're going to go through with it," she explained when I asked why she had such a long face.

102

"Mimo wants us to get married, but she's sure Didi will find some way to stop us. Are you sure it was the right thing to send that letter?"

I didn't know. We spent the next day talking and planning, checking details and confirming what few arrangements we had made. Late Saturday, I climbed back aboard the Greyhound so I could be in New Haven to teach my class Sunday morning.

Through three years of studies and shenanigans, Bob Whalen had remained my roommate at Yale. Sunday after church, Bob climbed in with Suzie in her Valiant and I pulled in behind them in the Lantos Mercedes. Our two car caravan traveled south uneventfully to Washington where Bob switched cars. Suzie proceeded to a rendevous with Annette while Bob and I went to his family home in nearby Springfield, Virginia.

"Sweetheart, I have to talk with him," I told Annette late that evening on the phone. "There's no way I want to, but I've thought and prayed about it until my head aches. I guess it comes down to this: If my daughter were getting married to a guy I didn't like, and he didn't even have the decency to talk with me about it face to face, I'm not sure I could ever trust him again. I want there to be at least a foundation for a good relationship with your dad. I figure our wedding is going to do a lot to make our lives with him either better or worse, and talking to him now is the best way I can think of to make things better in the future."

"I trust you, Timber," she responded cautiously. "But you have to remember: He's not like you. Just because you'd like to be treated a certain way doesn't mean he would. If you're sure it's the right thing to do – well, he'll be busy on The Hill in the morning, but I think he's free all afternoon."

It was almost 2 PM when Dr. Lantos strode into the huge atrium lobby of the downtown Washington Hyatt. He was near enough six feet tall with striking white hair and a matching moustache. His crisp, $900 suit was immaculate, his eelskin shoes gleamed softly. Piercing blue eyes scrutinized my open shirt and slacks before he was prompted to grimace slightly at the sight of my scuffed boots. I escorted him to the table I had waiting.

It seemed to me that Dr. Lantos had mastered the art of cordial intimidation. The rules of the conversation were implicitly established before we sat down. He was comfortable and in control. I was not. As long as we played our roles, the conversation could proceed.

We started out discussing his activities on The Hill, but he quickly lost patience with my inquiries and asked that we attend to the matter at hand. Since I had explained the reason for the meeting when we spoke by phone earlier in the day, we shared a common agenda.

I thought I knew how to work with people. I had some experience persuading all sorts of people – from crusty Aspen shopkeepers to arrogant Yale professors – to trust me to take care of their interests. I enjoyed the challenge of identifying a mutually important principle or goal and leveraging off it to secure benefits for both parties. People generally liked me. I liked them and we almost always found a way to work constructively.

Nothing in my repertoire moved him a millimeter. Nothing in my arsenal even nicked his armor.

"Of course I understand why you want to marry my daughter, young man," he explained in his tailored Hungarian accent. "But you're not ready. You need more experience. You should grow a little more – perhaps get a stable job."

When in his opinion would I be ready?

"Well, I'll make you a proposition. You still have to successfully complete a semester after this one before you'll have earned your degree," he posited.

Degrees, sir, I said to myself. Plural.

"If you graduate, you should be able to get a reasonable job. Work for a year," Dr. Lantos counseled as he toyed absentmindedly with his tie clasp – a Phi Beta Kappa key. (Rats – mine was back in New Haven. On second thought, I wasn't wearing a tie.) "And then I think you should travel. A boy like you should see a little of the world before he settles down. Travel for six months or so, and then come back and talk with me. Maybe then we can discuss whether you should consider asking to marry my daughter."

Our discussion continued in this vein for over an hour. We were getting nowhere. I gradually realized part of the problem was mine. In an attempt to find some grounds for agreement, I had continually referred to our impending vows without specificity. Clearly, the premise for whole conversation was only an abstract possibility to him. In his mind there was no way Annette was going to get married anytime soon – and certainly not to me.

"This has been a very productive meeting, Timber. I'm glad we've been able to come to an agreement here," he said, standing up suddenly. Without further courtesies he began to walk briskly toward the big glass doors of the lobby.

"Dr. Lantos, please give me just a few more minutes," I stammered. "There are a couple of misconceptions I need to clear up."

"That's fine," he replied as he waved his hand generally in my direction. "You can walk with me to the car. I really need to be going." We were already heading through the sliding doors into the warm humidity of the afternoon.

"Dr. Lantos, I understand you may not want to hear this today, but if I were in your place, I'd want my future son-in-law to be honest with me."

He stopped abruptly in his place on the sidewalk. The sun was in his eyes as he slowly turned to scowl at me. "You're not my future son-in-law, so by all rights this conversation need not continue." His voice had all the pleasant character of a saber scraping its way from its scabbard. "Let's just terminate this conversation now. It's been a long day."

"Dr. Lantos, I came here to ask you for Annette's hand in marriage. Part of me hoped for your blessing, but at least I wanted to show you the respect I felt was due to the father of my wife – "

"What is this insanity?" He interrupted me. His face was red with anger. "Nothing is happening between you and Annette. You're in a fantasy world if you insist on talking about her as your wife – and I don't have time for your fantasies."

Wow. This was careening out of control. I said a quick, silent prayer as he stormed on down the sidewalk.

"Look, Dr. Lantos," I said as I caught up with him. "If she will still have me, Annette and I <u>are</u> getting married. We've discussed it –"

"Well, maybe you should discuss it one more time," he interrupted me again. He was livid with rage. "And make sure you tell her that if she chooses to proceed with this insanity, I want absolutely nothing to do with either of you for the rest of my life. I will turn my back on you if I see you. I'll throw away her letters without reading them. I will refuse to talk with her on the phone, and if – God forbid! – if you have children, I will treat them with less respect than a stranger's. So maybe you should talk this all over again. And maybe you – you punk! – should ask whether you want to inflict this on the girl that you claim to – to – " He couldn't bring himself to finish the sentence.

"I do love her," I answered quietly, filling in the end of his words. "You've made yourself perfectly clear, Dr. Lantos. I'll do my best to tell her what you said."

I had no idea how to reintroduce any semblance of civility into the conversation. I didn't have much of a chance.

"Punk!" He almost spat the epithet at me, and then defiantly turned away from me and marched down the street.

Until we had walked from the hotel, Bob and Suzie were watching the meeting from the cover of the abundant foliage in the Hyatt's atrium. They could hear little or nothing, but Suzie still updated Annette by phone several times. When I returned to the lobby they were waiting for me. I felt like a battered boxer returning to my corner of the ring – except I couldn't tell whether the fight was over, or whether I'd already lost.

Suzie led me to a private phone off the lobby. Annette was in the loving care of Pam, her former Div School roommate, at her sister's apartment. She was near the hotel, but we had previously agreed to honor the custom of the groom not seeing the bride the night before the wedding. I wasn't sure Annette would still want to be a bride when I told her about her father's fury.

"Timber, you should understand that this is part of Jewish culture," Annette said softly on the other end of the line. Pam had dragged the phone in so Annette could talk to me from the tub, but I was too exhausted to be titillated. "When a member of the family marries out of the faith, the other people in the family traditionally act almost like they'd died. In the old days they even used to 'sit shiva' for them. That's a ritual of mourning." She sounded pensive. "Didi's grieving, I guess."

This was so blasted complicated, I thought.

"In a backhanded way, it's quite a compliment that he loves you so much that it'll be like you've died," I offered sympathetically.

"As I said, it's part of the culture. I know he's really upset, but maybe some of what you saw was just the acting out of a ritual."

"If that's all it was, he's one heck of an actor." I paused to choose my words carefully. "Annette, he said some pretty harsh stuff. Are you sure that you want to do something that's going to hurt him so much? It's going to end up hurting you, too."

She was silent for perhaps a minute, perhaps longer. My hand ached from clenching the receiver.

"I know my father. I know my Heavenly Father. I know you. What do you feel we should do, Timber?"

"Well, I guess we know now where your father stands. We've waited a year, and I kind of thought we'd be able to smooth things over with him. I don't know that your dad'll ever be happy with the thought of you marrying me – or anybody else, for that matter. I really believe our Heavenly Father wants us married tomorrow. Obviously, I'll support whatever you feel is right."

I realized my last remark was pretty meaningless. If our plans were derailed, I certainly couldn't put this train back on the track by myself. But as long as she'd asked me the question, I'd answer.

"As far as what I want, I really want to see you at the temple tomorrow at seven."

"I was hoping you'd say that." Her voice was smiling over the phone. "Don't be late."

"You think after all this I'm gonna be late?" I grinned. She was always the late one. I'd be there. "I love you so much. Now get a good night's sleep."

Bob and I took the elevator into the bowels of the Hyatt where I'd parked Annette's car. She would be primped and pampered by Suzie and Pam that night and then driven to the Temple in the morning. They were her faithful and loving bridesmaids while Bob was my impromptu Best Man. Their love and attention was all the more impressive given that they couldn't attend the actual ceremony. The sanctity of the ordinances was guarded by a requirement that only Church members in good standing were to attend.

Bob and I drove out of the garage and to his home in relative silence. We told his mom of the afternoon's pyrotechnics, ate a dozen of her extraordinary chocolate chip cookies, set three separate alarms and went to our beds.

I slept, but found myself wide awake moments before the first alarm sounded at five AM. The shower was brief but refreshing. I found my tie after only a couple of minute's search, we wolfed down some toast and milk, and we were off. Bob took his brother's Chrysler Hemi – a bright red, fat tired, throbbing animal of a car – to allow him a way home after the wedding. I followed him in the meek, mild Mercedes sedan as we headed across town, not directly to the Temple, but to first pick up a friend.

Bob's dad had retired from the Marines and was now a Driver's Ed teacher. Had he been along, he would have been proud: Bob drove perfectly – but perfectly slowly. That wasn't a problem. We had time to spare. The sun was rising as we were both enjoying a positively lovely morning. He made it to our friend Ellen's address ahead of schedule. I calmly watched him get out of the Hemi and look up and down the street several times. He trotted over to talk with me through the car's open window.

"Sorry – We've got a minor snafu," he explained humbly. "I know I wrote down the correct address because I had her tell me three times. I even had her tell me what the building looks like – but that address doesn't even exist here. She told me it was Northwest, when it must really be Northeast." Ellen was from Wyoming and only in the city for spring break. It was a reasonable mistake. "Don't worry, we've got plenty of time. We'll find her in a jiffy."

Six-oh-four. We had almost an hour. Bob pulled a U-turn, motioned for me to do the same, and we were off. We had to cross the heart of town – again – but I was relieved to deduce that both addresses were on the north side of town, and the temple was, too. Shouldn't be a problem. Still, Bob was driving so – – so *precisely*. I drummed my fingers on the steering wheel.

"Good ol' Bob," I thought as I waved to Ellen. She was waiting patiently on the steps of a pleasant row house. She quickly hopped into the front seat of Bob's car. We were running a little late. It was six-twenty-nine, but we couldn't have been that far from the temple. Bob was soon driving due north.

He was a very careful driver, I noticed. If he had driven just a little bit faster, we probably wouldn't have had to stop for the last five yellow stoplights. I knew he was just making sure we'd all get there in one piece. And we still had almost nineteen minutes.

Those yellow lights were about to drive me crazy.

Six-forty-seven. Bob patiently braked for another intersection.

I couldn't take it any more.

"Call me a nervous groom, but do you mind if I go on?" I shouted over to Bob as I pulled abreast of him at the next light. "I just go straight ahead to the Beltway, right?" He nodded helpfully, and I floored it at the green. The sedate sedan raced ahead like a filly given free rein.

Rats! I reflected as I threaded my way through the commuters. I had really wanted to be early. I wanted to enjoy seeing Annette dressed as my bride, and to talk with her to make sure she was still OK. Maybe she'd be late. Except Suzie was driving with her, and Suzie was never late.

I made it through two green lights, two yellow and one that we won't talk about before I had to stop again. In my rear view mirror I thought I saw Bob descending a hill a couple of blocks back.

Green. I pressed the gas firmly toward the floor, then cocked my ear slightly toward the firewall. The engine had made a strange noise – just for a moment – a quick, sharp, knock-knock-knock from deep within.

I backed off the gas, but the noise was gone. Still, the reduced acceleration made me hit another yellow – and I was too far away to gun it through. I hit the brakes.

I quit swearing when I met Annette. It was one of the first vices I jettisoned. But rarely had I been so tempted as I was by that – ahem – amber light. I clenched my teeth 'til I was afraid the enamel was going to flake off.

Six-fifty-one. I could drive miles in nine minutes. Maybe I'd still make it.

Green. I gave the Mercedes a healthy shot of gas.

KNOCK-KNOCK-KNOCK-KNOCK-KNOCK. . . . I let out a scream of frustration as cacophonous clatter from the engine compartment flooded over me. I let off the gas, but the horrible thrashing in the bowels of the car only diminished. It didn't stop. In disgust, I pulled into a fortuitous parking alcove, shut off the ignition and popped the hood of the car. It took me only a few seconds to check the oil and see if any belts or perhaps the fan was loose. Everything checked out fine.

Bob pulled cautiously into the space behind me. He was smart enough to know I hadn't stopped for donuts.

"How bad is it?"

"I dunno," I yelled back as I jumped back in the Mercedes to see if maybe – just maybe – the noise would be gone when I restarted the car.

KNOCK-KNOCK-KNOCK-KNOCK-KNOCK. . . .

Bob was out of his car.

"Let me help you get your stuff," he offered with remarkable clarity of thought. "Leave your luggage. We can come back for that. Let's get out of here!"

I grabbed what I could as Ellen climbed in the back seat of the Hemi. I jumped in the passenger seat as Bob got in on his side. The crimson beast rocked and lurched as he shifted into gear.

Good ol' Bob, I thought with a pained smile. Then he carefully pulled onto the street and almost immediately braked for the yellow light ahead.

"Bob," I pleaded. "It's six-fifty-eight. You're an exceptional driver. Annette's gotta be sitting there thinking I've stood her up. <u>Please</u> can we get a move on?"

"Oh, sure! I guess I'm not in the habit of driving aggressively." He increased the tempo of his driving appreciably, but it did little to reduce my agony. There was nothing more to be done.

Moments later we saw the overpass of the Beltway ahead. I was elated.

"Oh, CRAP!" Bob cried. I was shocked – to say the least. That was very strong language for the Bob I knew. "Timber, think: We're at Exit 31," he explained urgently. "We want Exit 33, but I can't remember whether the numbers increase clockwise or counterclockwise! It's your choice – do we go east or west?" He looked at me expectantly. Ellen shrugged sympathetically. You could have slammed my hand in the car door and I don't think I would have noticed: I was in too much pain already.

"OK. It's gotta be logical – They've gotta increase clockwise!" I calculated. "Go east!"

The exit was upon us.

"Wait! I think I remember it's the other way!"

"JUST GO EAST!" I bellowed. If we were going to make a mistake, this time it was going to be my mistake. Bob accelerated up the on-ramp. The three of us silently scanned the roadway ahead for any clues as to the success of my tactic.

Exit #30a – 1 Mile

Three grieved sighs filled the rumbling Chrysler.

"Sorry, Bob. My mistake."

I couldn't help looking over at the speedometer. The speed limit was 55 MPH. He was going sixty. Oh, well, I muttered to myself. If we'd gone his way, we'd have been there by now. I shouldn't complain.

"Timber, I don't think we can turn around here." I couldn't believe my ears. "No – look," he continued as he pointed at the soaring cement overpasses ahead. "30a goes south, 30b goes north, but neither will let us just double back. Should I wait for the next exit?"

I just wanted to marry Annette. That's all. I could only shrug in response to Bob's inquiry.

He opted to take 30a. We found ourselves headed south on another superhighway with no exit in sight ahead. I shook my head dejectedly.

Suddenly the car lurched to the right and ground to a halt on the shoulder. I wordlessly searched for an explanation.

"Look!" He nodded hard to his right as he shifted into reverse and backed the big Hemi into a gravel farm access road we had just passed. In just a second, we were positioned perpendicular to the highway, staring beyond our lanes to a thin dirt break in the median that would allow us to join traffic returning north toward the Beltway.

If we could get through the traffic. It was after seven by then and rush hour was upon us. The highway was a roiling river of chrome in both directions.

"Maybe there will be a break from a stoplight we can't see," Ellen suggested hopefully. The cars passing were so closely spaced I couldn't have thrown a snowball across the first two lanes. Even if we got that far, the puny median offered no refuge: Our grille would be poking into the northbound high speed lane before our tail had cleared the roadway south. It looked hopeless.

"Poor Annette," I shook my head. "Let's keep an eye out for a phone."

"We can do this. Are you belted?" Bob asked quietly. The car rocked momentarily as he revved the engine ominously. "Just look south and tell me when there's any kind of break." He raced the mighty engine again, higher.

"OK, but I don't think. . ." The rest of my comment was lost in the thunderous roar of the huge Hemi. Ellen screamed as she was pushed back into her seat by the acceleration of four hundred horses clawing at asphalt and gravel. I panicked when I saw only a hint of access in the traffic coming north, so I spun my g-force constrained eyes about to look the other way. Horns were blaring and I watched in slow-motion fascination while two of Detroit's finest nearly drove in Bob's window. He shifted into second in a heartbeat as we fishtailed across the median, turning parallel to the traffic while we were still sliding sideways. The Hemi screamed like a rabid panther as he redlined it in second, the fat

111

tires spraying debris and smoke behind us. His shift to third was like Mohammed Ali's right jab – it was more of an instinctive flinch than a distinct movement. Then –

It was over. The raging red beast was headed due north, back to Beltway Exit 30. The engine purred as Bob synchronized his speed with the car in front of him. Ellen sat silently in the back seat. She seemed fine, but her eyes reminded me of Little Orphan Annie. Bob checked the rear view mirror, then looked over at me.

"This time we go west, right?" He smiled at me as he tipped his head toward the exit sign – but I saw glimmerings of primal fire in his deep brown eyes. "Don't you just love this car?" He peeled out of the traffic and on to the Beltway ramp. The speedometer registered eighty-five before we were out of the interchange.

The Washington Temple of the Church rises up like a virgin version of the Emerald City when you drive west on the Beltway. During its construction pranksters were fond of painting "Free Dorothy!" on the overpass just before the structure looms into sight. The morning sun was behind us as we approached the dazzling marble spires.

It looked like heaven to me.

She was outside, dressed in pristine white, sitting on the curb. She didn't recognize the snorting crimson Chrysler and registered dazed surprise when we stopped a few feet from her and I sprang out.

"Timber!" Annette arose with a smile as bright as the spires behind her. "I was so worried! I thought – I thought, maybe – " Her voice faltered as she reflected on her thoughts of the last few minutes. Suddenly she looked serious."Is everything OK?"

"Fine!" I said confidently. "We had a little car trouble. Are you OK?"

She looked up at me as she contemplated an answer. Then she reached up to touch my shoulder and I enfolded her into my arms. We kissed, deeply – far more passionately than was appropriate at the door of the Temple. Under the circumstances, though, I hope He understood.

"Come on in, folks," said a man dressed completely in white who was standing at the door. "It looks like you're a little late, but I think we can still take care of you." He smiled warmly.

I looked at my watch. Seven-twenty-one. The first day of spring.

Annette and I were married for time and all eternity later that morning. As we entered the room where we were to be sealed together, the gentleman officiating looked appreciatively at my beautiful bride.

"Your Father is so pleased with you today," he said to her, little knowing the trials she had faced to be there. But Annette told me she was overwhelmed with a conviction that the gentleman spoke the truth, and that the pleasure felt by her Heavenly Father that day would someday be experienced, in some measure, by her dad.

I clasped her hands as we knelt together across the altar. She was the very embodiment of beauty as I solemnly contemplated the privilege of being her husband. Then, as our vows were recited, I saw something I've never seen before or since: Annette was surrounded first by a gentle glow, and within moments by a vibrant rainbow of colors and hues, extending to the periphery of my sight. When she said, "I do," I witnessed as glorious a spectacle as ever I expect to see in this life.

The rest of the day was somewhat anticlimactic – but it was still interesting.

To our surprise and delight, several young couples from the congregation in New Haven made the long trip south to join us for our ceremony at the Temple. We emerged into the sunlight as husband and wife to hear Katrina's happy squeal. She and Mimo ran up to greet us. They had left Annette's father at a Congressional hearing on The Hill. Suzie explained that she had arranged for all of us to have lunch together at a charming nearby inn, so our modest wedding was garnished with a delightfully intimate reception. She had even provided a small, tiered cake which was served with the appropriate flourish.

The Yalies needed to get back to New Haven. Katrina and Mimo had to find Dr. Lantos before he was prompted to ask too many questions about the day's activities. While Annette and I were saying goodbye and expressing our thanks, Suzie faced a somewhat perplexing problem. Packed into the trunk of the Valiant were ribbons, pennants and signs celebrating our marriage. Suzie's original idea had been to decorate the Mercedes while we dined, but the white car was still immobilized by the roadside. After a quick consultation, Bob agreed that he would chauffeur us back to Annette's car, and we would have to make a new plan from that point. Suzie proceeded to transform the snarling bulldog of a Chrysler Hemi into a pom-pommed poodle of a carriage to transport us to our as-yet-undetermined honeymoon suite.

Only a few guests remained as Annette gathered up the abbreviated train of her veil and wedding dress and climbed with me into the back seat of the car. Bob dutifully assumed his post as driver, but as he coaxed the big engine to life Suzie rapped on the back window.

"Wait!" She ran around to the passenger's door, stopping briefly to remove a sign she had previously taped to the trunk of the car. "This belongs inside where you can see it." She quickly affixed the big poster to the back of the front seats:

TOGETHER FOREVER
– ANNETTE AND TIMBER –

Then she gave my new wife a hug and kiss and we drove away. The rest of the afternoon was a bit weird, but fun. We found the Mercedes as we left it, unmolested and inoperable. A half a dozen calls resulted in commitments for prompt repair service and a free tow to the dealer. As we waited for the car to be hauled away, I came to grips with the realization that there was little likelihood we would spend our honeymoon at Disney World. Annette commented that she found Olde Towne Alexandria charming when she had briefly visited earlier in the week with her sister. Katrina was living only a couple miles from the restored harbor village and she had given Annette and Mimo a quick tour on their way home from the airport as they arrived.

I found a hotel and made reservations as Annette stood out by the car. She still wore her wedding dress, the hood of the car was up, and our luggage was piled on the sidewalk. People smiled, honked and waved, and many offered to help. The tow truck had no trouble finding us in the midst of the commotion.

"Where to, Boss?" Bob inquired.

"The Olde Towne Inn, Robert."

"Would you prefer the scenic route, sir?"

"I think we'd just like to see the hotel."

Rush hour was again upon us. By the time we crossed downtown and headed over the Potomac, traffic was stop and go. My bride and I just snuggled down and chatted about the events of the preceding 24 hours . Another forty minutes passed before we unloaded our luggage and checked into our room. We both thanked Bob profusely, but nothing could fully express our appreciation for his steadfast service. He had been incredible.

My appreciation of his friendship was soon tested, however. At 7:40 AM the following morning, I was rousted from blissful exhaustion by the phone ringing.

"Hi, Timber." It was Bob. Good Ol' Bob.

"Hi, Bob," I responded groggily but politely. This was, after all, the guy who had tamed the savage Hemi to rescue me from an agonizing predicament.

"Uh, are you guys OK? I mean, was everything OK last night?"

I shook my head as I tried to process his query. Bob didn't date a lot. Maybe he just didn't understand about honeymoon nights. On the other hand, maybe he did.

"Fine, Bob, fine. Can I help you with anything?" I was really hoping to cut the call short. By this time, my new bride had opened one lovely eye and was using it to stare at me just a little skeptically.

"Nothing happened last night?"

I couldn't believe this. Bob generally had a great sense of humor, but the conversation was taking a turn toward the bizarre.

"Of course something happened last night. Bob, why are you calling me now?"

"Because when I got home, Katrina called me."

Annette's sister had phoned him last night. Of course. That's why my bliss was disrupted.

"OK, Timber. Look, I'm sorry. I'm a little confused and nervous. See, when I got home last night after I dropped you off, my mom said I had an urgent call from Katrina, but she couldn't talk."

That explained everything, I thought.

Annette was now fully awake and messing with my toes. She had decided this was all very amusing

"Bob, is this important?"

It was important – and admittedly rather hard to explain. After telling Bob that she had to call him back, Katrina had left her parents in her apartment to call him from a pay phone. She then breathlessly explained that as Dr. Lantos drove them home after his long day on the Hill, they were caught in terrible traffic out of DC.

Dr. Lantos is a very careful driver. As a matter of fact, he drives very much like Bob usually drives – almost identically. In this particular case, Dr. Lantos had inexplicably pulled into traffic directly behind Bob's car as we made our way across the bridge and along the Potomac. While neither driver had a clue about the occupants of the other car,

Katrina and Mimo instantly recognized the red Hemi rumbling in front of them, its trunk covered with "Just Married" signs and Yale blue pom-poms. Once they were on the bridge there was no alternate route, and nothing Mimo or Katrina contrived had prompted Dr. Lantos to slow down or speed up to distance their car from Bob's. Instead, Katrina's father calmly followed Bob's bumper for miles and obliviously discussed the proceedings of the hearings he'd attended all day. Katrina struggled to maintain her composure and avoid staring into the Chrysler in front of her. She could easily make out the tops of our heads as we reclined, along with just the first line of Suzie's poster:

TOGETHER FOREVER

Chapter 5

The Clerk with Gifted Hands

Friday Afternoon, 19 May 1995
Arvada, Colorado

The big windows of Safeline's 5th floor offices offered a sweeping view of Denver's western suburbs as they crept up the flanks of the Rockies. Each December my co-workers and I would watch the storms from Canada descend like a soft, shivering quilt to envelop first the peaks, then the foothills, then the shingled roofs below. Sometimes our view of the cars crawling along the street would vanish into the silent isolation created by the swirling, downy flakes. In May, the windows instead often opened into the belly of spring's savage storms. Lightning, thunder and grape-sized raindrops commanded the glass to succumb to the weather's wrath.

This particular afternoon, wind-whipped curtains of water rippled a few feet from my desk. As the windows trembled around us, Justin, Shelley and the others sat at their computers, productively engaged yet uneasily aware of our vulnerability. If they only knew, I thought. The flailing storm outside was the least of our worries.

The phone warbled. Shelly was busy on another line. I picked up the receiver to hear my wife sounding distant and tense. Her voice conveyed her obvious relief that I was the person who answered the direct line.

"Look – I'm standing in the rain, so I'll keep this short. Could you please call Tomicah? I called him this morning and told him about the twins, and I'm worried about him. I don't want him to feel that Didi and Mimo are the only ones he can talk to. "

"He'll be okay, Honey," I replied. "He can handle it."

117

My expression of confidence was both well-founded and selfish. Tomicah had grown to be a capable young man. As the oldest kid in the crew, he frequently assumed responsibilities that many adults found staggering. If Annette and I went on a date to a movie, he'd marshal the whole platoon of his siblings to get their dinner, do the dishes and brush their teeth. On family campouts, he was the quartermaster. He got his blond hair and flashing smile from Annette, and he ended up with my green eyes and broadcasting voice. A couple of years earlier he had successfully auditioned for a job as a teen movie reviewer for a local radio station, and subsequently parlayed his position into a job as a reporter for Reuters. Now, at sixteen, he was serving in Washington as the youngest-ever White House intern. Tomicah was blessed with a dependable sense of emotional equilibrium. I wasn't particularly concerned about Annette's call to him earlier.

From a more self-centered perspective, I was painfully burdened by events at Safeline. There was no time in my schedule to shmooze. In the days since Annette's ultrasound, my workload had been building like a pressure cooker left too long on the stove. I had to put out some of the fires on my desk, I told her, or the company could go up in smoke.

"Please. Do it for my sake," she pleaded. "He may not need it, but I need you to let me know he's doing okay. Just give him a quick call – will you, please?"

I suppose I could have refused. Instead I assured her that I'd be on the phone to DC as soon as I hung up with her. Tomicah and I talked for only a few minutes. He convinced me that he was doing fine and was primarily concerned about his mom and me. He had enough experience dealing with his grandparents that he'd be able to avoid discussing the subject with them, he said. I was glad I had called, but not sure it had been necessary.

The afternoon's buffeting winds and fusillade of rain seemed to leave everyone at Safeline drained. The clouds had since headed further east and the sun reappeared. We often worked late, but this Friday no one seemed disposed to stay. By 4:45 the desktops were cleared. I was the last one out at a few minutes after five.

The walkway to our back door was littered with green confetti blown down earlier from the canopy of trees above. The house bustled quietly as I climbed the stairs to the sunlit kitchen. Kimi smiled a quick hello and offered me a taste of the vegetable melange soup she'd concocted for dinner. It was excellent, as was often the case when she

118

took her turn at the stove. Her rich chestnut hair was pulled into a thick ponytail that caressed her neck and cascaded over her shoulder nearly to her waist. She stood barefoot in jeans as she gave her thirteen year old brother Levi a sample. He similarly pronounced it ready for the table and turned his attentions back to the long loaves of bread he was smearing with garlic butter. They resumed a discussion about his upcoming Eagle Scout project as I made my way past them into the dining room.

Chari was singing softly to herself as she set the table, but she stopped as soon as I entered.

"Daddy, smell these!" She commanded, and pulled me toward the profusion of lilacs that graced the center of the long table. "Corbi found them on some bushes that're kind of hidden back by the swing set. Aren't they heavenly?"

She was still wearing the magenta sweatshirt and dark slacks that constituted the uniform for her chorale group. I'd forgotten they'd had a performance earlier that afternoon. Like the majority of the kids in our crew, she was blonde. Her gentle curls had grown to reach the small of her back. Charity was going on twelve. She was endowed with her mom's perfect oval face and my high cheekbones. Daughter number two and child number four, Charity Sunshine had received her name well after a innocuous little puppy we called Goliath had matured into a feisty and fearsome furball. Perhaps that's why we were inspired to give her a name that we hoped would reflect her personality. The tactic proved strategically successful. She was usually determinedly optimistic and – at times – almost irritatingly good natured. I bridled momentarily as she shoved me into the white and purple blossoms, but their sensational perfume soon transported me to a more cooperative state of mind.

"Thanks, sweetheart," I replied just a little apologetically as she awaited my response. "These are really wonderful. And the table looks nice."

I headed down the long hall to our bedroom where I found Annette. She was propped up on five or six pillows in bed, reading. With my head still filled with the tranquilizing essence of lilac, I patiently stood waiting for her to finish her sentence – or paragraph – or page?

"Honey?" I finally interrupted her.

"Give me just a minute more – I've got to finish this, and then I need to tell you the most amazing story. Wait just a second...." Her eyes never left the paperback clenched before her. I shrugged off my jacket and sat down beside her.

119

"This book is incredible!" She finally tore her gaze from its pages. Even then it was clear to me that I hadn't won her full attention. I had at best achieved a momentary victory: She still held the book on the smooth mound of her midsection – open but face down – in both hands.

"I have to tell you what happened to me today!" She was excited and happy – two emotions that were usually her ready companions, but that had deserted her for most of the preceding week.

"OK, tell me," I instructed. If I didn't get the story right away it might remain untold until she finished her mysterious book. My invitation to have her recite her tale won a small triumph for me as she let go of its pages and folded her arms atop the volume. This signaled that I was about to get the full story and not the shorthand version.

"Well, I told you I called Tomicah this morning," Annette began. She had found him at the office of the Press Secretary, across the street from the White House. Most of the people he was working with were between their junior and senior years of college, or were graduate students. He was awarded the intensely competitive internship partly because his grandfather had used his influence to lobby on his behalf, and partly because he was a straight-A college sophomore with three years of professional broadcasting experience in Denver.

Tomicah had been in Washington for three weeks and didn't know anything might be amiss with the pregnancy. Annette hadn't really planned to call him. She and I had gathered all the other kids together earlier that morning and told them that she was pregnant with twins, but that they had very serious problems. It would be necessary to go to Salt Lake the following day, we told them, for tests to try to find out how bad the twins' condition was. We decided not to tell the kids the details until after Dr. DeVore gave us his prognosis.

It was my general practice to discuss almost everything with the kids. They were all thoughtful and capable, and I respected their judgment. I was also of the opinion that the process of analyzing the various situations the family faced was a vital part of the kids' education. Annette usually agreed with me, but only to a point. She opted to shield the kids from some things, and the twins' medical status was one such detail. That morning's family discussion was a compromise that we as parents had agreed to beforehand.

"I didn't mean to call him," my wife continued from her pillowed throne. "I didn't want to burden him, but I ended up just blurting out everything. Tomicah was really good – he just listened

120

calmly, and was really understanding and supportive. He asked if he should come home, but I told him that I didn't think he could do anything to help." Her eyes begged me for reassurance. "There isn't, is there?"

"No – I don't think so. We're doing fine." I squeezed her hand.

"He said that the internship wasn't that big a deal, but I didn't want him to feel like he has to come home – I just wanted him to know we were thinking about him." She sniffed, and I realized her eyes were brimming. As challenging as these days had been for me, I was only beginning to understand that I had no way to comprehend the burden Annette was bearing – both literally and figuratively. I nodded affirmatively.

She went on to say that at the time she felt almost compelled to discuss the twins with Tomicah. She craved any signs of support, and compassion, and a shared sense of appreciation for just how strange and hard it all was. Annette recognized afterward that one of the emotional challenges of the situation was she just wanted to talk about it. It was only later, when she had phoned me at the office, that she regretted it.

"Anyway, he said we should let him know what's happening, and he'll do whatever we want. Then I told him to try not to say anything yet to Mimo or Didi."

Annette's father, in particular, would almost certainly insist that he be involved in every facet of her treatment. His behavior was at times highly predictable. Annette and Tomicah both knew her father would be strongly inclined to join those who advocated an immediate abortion. Tomicah had agreed that for now he should say nothing.

She quickly collected her emotions and continued to tell me about the afternoon. It was only a short time later that she had left the house to take Corbi and Chari to their Chorale performance. After she dropped them at the auditorium, the big storm hit. She hated driving in the downpour.

"The rain was awful! It was so intense that I could only see flashes of the road, even with the wipers on high. It was so hard to see that I started to get this horrible headache. I finally just pulled over into the parking lot of a store on the corner."

She had felt almost ill, she said. The feeling was deep in her gut, and she momentarily toyed with the thought of eating a hot dog to make herself feel better. She quickly decided that wasn't the solution. She wasn't suffering from the pregnancy nausea to which she was so well accustomed. She was just sad and depressed – and afraid. A cold drip of fear was seeping into her soul. The comfort and peace that usually graced her life were gone. She wanted to go to sleep and forget the whole week.

She traced the thread of her dread back to her call with Tomicah. In addition to all the other emotions coursing through her life, now she felt guilty for her decision to be candid with him. He would be facing the same need to talk that she had felt, but he had no one to unburden himself on. A sixteen-year-old shouldn't have to face that kind of pressure, she had concluded. It was 2:30 PM in Denver – two hours later in Washington. It was then she decided to phone me to see if I would call Tomicah before he went home for the night. That way, she thought, at least he could talk to me for a while. There was a pay phone outside the store. Without making a conscious decision, she threw open the car door and vaulted out into the deluge. She was wet but not soaked as she reached the phone. To her dismay, she realized that the clamshell-type enclosure afforded her little protection from the driving rain. Only by wedging herself tightly next to the phone had she been able to avoid being drenched as she dialed my office.

As we sat together on our bed, she again apologized for pressuring me. She told me that she didn't want to beg on the phone, but if I had continued to resist her pleas she had been getting close to tears. She was swamped with waves of anxiety at the thought that Tomicah would soon head home from his work to face his grandfather by himself. She had felt a little better when I agreed to call him as soon as she got off the phone.

She had hung up the pay phone and was about to sprint back to the van when she realized that we were going to Salt Lake the following day and the kids needed milk and fresh veggies. She had frustratedly jammed her wet hands into her pockets in search of another quarter to call and let them know she was stopping by the grocery store. Finally, she found a coin wadded up with several bills in her hip pocket. As she shoved the money into the phone with her cold, wet fingers, it had slipped from her grasp. She once again felt a rising tide of desperation and depression as she watched the coin bounce off her shoe and roll into a filthy puddle.

"I couldn't understand it," she explained to me. "Everything was so hard. I was cold and wet and bummed and mad, and then I dropped my last quarter. It felt like God had just left me there alone, and I couldn't figure out why. I was <u>not</u> going to dive into that mud – and then I realized the solution was as close as the store a few feet away."

The convenience store was empty, and the clerk had been watching Annette's struggles with the phone from her position behind the register.

"She was so nice. I came barging through the door, sopping wet, and she said, 'You look like you're having a rough day. Why don't you wait a few minutes before you go back out there – Maybe the rain will let up.' I think she saw me drop the quarter, because she even offered to let me use her phone if I needed to make another call."

Annette said she realized the stress of the past days had clearly taken its toll when the clerk's compassionate greeting moved her to tears. Even with her face dripping from the torrent outside, she couldn't hide her emotions. The clerk had looked at her with obvious concern.

"It was just like when I was on the phone with Tomicah. I started to tell her not to worry about me, that it was OK, and that I'd just found out that I was pregnant with twins – and then I realized what I was saying didn't make any sense unless I told her what was really going on."

Once she had started, she couldn't stop – she told the stunned young woman the whole story. The clerk reached over and rested one hand on Annette's sodden forearm and simply listened. As the tale unfolded, Annette said she was surprised to see a look of astonishment and wonderment fill the clerk's face.

"When I was finally able to stop talking, do you know what she said?"Annette looked to me as if I might actually know the answer. I had no idea and shook my head accordingly.

"She said there was a doctor who spoke in her church last Sunday night who separated Siamese twins. He wrote a book about it, and they put him on the national news. I couldn't believe it! Right here, in Denver!"

"Why haven't we heard about him before?" I asked her incredulously. "Why didn't the Porters know about him?"

"No – they wouldn't know him – or maybe they would, but he's not from here – he was just speaking here," she replied enthusiastically. "I mean, he's from back East, but he was in Denver last week for some conference, and he took the time to go and speak in her church. The clerk was a Seventh Day Adventist, and so was he. He wrote this book, and she told me where I could buy it." Annette lofted the book from where it lay as I reached to examine it.

"Wait!" She pulled it away. "I'm not finished yet. I'll let you see it when you hear the rest."

Annette said she felt the tide of her depression receding with each of the clerk's words.

"The clerk said the doctor seemed really nice, and it was an incredible story how they separated the twins. They were joined at the head. That has to be one of the hardest operations, don't you think? Ours wouldn't be that hard to separate, would they?"

I told her I just didn't know.

The clerk had given her the name of the inspirational bookstore and the cross streets where it was located. The rain had subsided somewhat. It was a long drive across town to the address. Annette took a short cut to the highway, and as she pulled onto I-70 she happened to look up to see a large sign: Coming Home. It was the same name as the bookshop. Although she was miles from the intersection described by the clerk, Annette had decided to take the next exit and pull around into the lot. Minutes later, she stood dripping at the counter of the small bookstore. The proprietor had been helpful, but perplexed.

"And this is really weird. I told him that a friend told me I could get the book at this store, but at a different address. He said I was in the right place and they had a good supply of the book, but – this is the strange part – he's been at that same location since he opened. There's no other store by that name in the state. She must've been totally confused. So how in the world did I find it?" Annette triumphantly handed me the book. "Read the back cover."

Gifted Hands was the autobiography of Dr. Ben Carson, a young man who had come from the streets of Detroit to study at Yale shortly before Annette and I were there together. He earned his medical degree and went on to lead the neurosurgical department at Johns-Hopkins University Hospital. Much of the book was devoted to the events surrounding the successful separation of twin boys from Germany who were conjoined at the back of head.

Annette said she bought two copies of the paperback before she headed on to the grocery store.

"Honey, how many people have you talked to about the twins?" I asked as I leafed through Dr. Carson's book .

"Almost none – just Tomicah, Greg DeVore, and of course, that clerk at the store. I thought we needed to know more before I could tell Katrina, or Suzie – or anyone."

"Look at what's happening," I asked her as I put the book down on one of the pillows. "The doctors wanted to give us some useful information, and they found almost nothing. It took Dr. Porter two days to track down that article he faxed us. You and I worked through the largest library system in the state and we found very little that was meaningful. So using our own skills and resources, we learned literally nothing about separating twins, and not a whole lot about conjoined twins in general."

"And now we find the book." Annette almost whispered as she sensed my thoughts.

"We found the book, and also the Nova program last night. I guess my point is that actually we didn't find them. We tried, but we couldn't find them – Then they were just plopped in our laps." I continued. "The separation of Siamese twins isn't a real common topic for either TV or books. Now, when it's truly of life or death importance to us – boom! – there's the information we need."

I paused to collect my thoughts.

"In spite of what the doctors say, these twins are not a 'random occurrence'. I don't believe it was a random event that I turned on the stupid TV last night, I don't believe that it was a random occurrence that you dropped your last quarter into the mud, and I don't believe that the friend who helped us to deliver Tomicah has just randomly gone on to become the world's leading expert on prenatal heart problems. There's a reason that we're facing this, and I think it's pretty important that we keep an open mind about how we proceed.

"I don't know what we're going to find out tomorrow, but I do know that it would be wrong, given what's been happening, to just blindly do what the doctors say. These are our sons. When we make this decision, we'd better make sure we'll be at peace with our choice. Clearly, this is a choice with eternal implications for our family."

"If we're supposed to raise them, I'd be so happy," Annette said sincerely. "I don't care whether they can be separated or not. I would love to be their mother."

"And obviously, you can't carry them if its going to kill you," I added gently. "I wish the doctors would just give us the facts. I get the feeling that they're pushing us, like they're advocating a business, or even a political decision, instead of a choice about three lives – about our whole family. What's that scripture from the Old Testament?" I grabbed our thick, gilt-edged volume from my night stand, and began searching through it. "Something about, 'As for me and my family...'" The pages rustled under my fingers.

"House," she corrected. "'*As for me and my house, we will serve the Lord.*' Is that the one? Try the end of Joshua."

"I love you. I really wish I could do that."

She smiled at me playfully. "You'll just have to keep me around to answer all your scriptural questions. I love you, too. Let's get some dinner."

V. Goliath and the Intern

December 19, 1978
Bethany and New Haven, Connecticut

"UUhhhhnnh, I feel terrible..."

My mind snapped into razor sharp focus at the sound of her voice – but my body was not cooperating. I deliberately took a moment to analyze the situation and establish some important facts: We were in bed; my eyes were open, but not seeing much; it was therefore probably still dark outside. I was pretty sure it was Tuesday – or Saturday. I tried closing my right eye in a valiant attempt to force the other to focus on my new digital watch glowing inches from my nose. Success! Five thirty-five. And fourteen point three seconds. Cool.

"Are you having pains?" I inquired. I sounded a little groggy, but was reassured to note that my words were arranged in a reasonable order. They seemed to make sense. Scanning the small room tucked under the gabled roof of the ancient house, I noted that while frost coated the window, there was no sign of new snow. We were staying for a few months with the 90-year-old mother of a friend of my mom's. In return for reduced rent, we helped her keep the place clean and took care of her needs. Her home had been built in colonial times, as had our bathtub-sized bed. I looked at my watch again – mainly because it was pretty neat to be able to tell the time in a dark room.

Rats. Something was wrong. It seemed to be showing eight thirty-three – but why was the room so dark? I thrashed around until I found my glasses.

"No... No pains... But my stomach hurts. I think I have to go to the bathroom. Owwww. Oww... I feel gross..."

It was clear that Annette was not entirely coherent. Still, this stomach problem deserved further investigation. It would be wrong to just ignore her distress – wouldn't it? Especially since she was pregnant. Nine months. Well, pushing nine and a half. If my watch was working properly, I could check the exact date.

Now my right eye was refusing to open. However, I was pleased to note that the left one seemed to be working just fine. I groped for the lamp. After twisting the switch backwards three times I succeeded in turning it on. Searing white light blazed through the room. Both my eyes involuntarily clenched shut. My watchband evidently caught the lampshade, because the lamp then flew off the table onto one of the cats sleeping peacefully beside the bed. The accompanying clatter and yowl helped me to get a better handle on consciousness. Anyway, the light was easier on my eyes with the lamp on the floor.

Annette obviously disagreed. "Turn it off! Turn it off – Turn It Off!" she moaned. "Why did you turn that on??? Oh, I feel sooo gross."

"I'm sorry, Honey. I just have to make sure you're okay." I congratulated myself once again for sounding both coherent and compassionate. She had a swell husband.

My left eye was once again functioning. I looked at my beloved, if temporarily cranky, young wife. She was on her back next to me in the lofty but cramped bed, her hands cradling her huge tummy. This looked serious, I thought as I swung my legs around to sit up. I unfortunately misjudged how close I was to the edge of the tiny bed and started to tumble off. To compound my predicament, I realized with a start that I was about to land on top of the lamp. It took a heroic effort to grasp the rough-hewn wooden bedpost and twist around to land on my knees, straddling the still-burning lamp.

That could've been dangerous. I readjusted my glasses off my upper lip and back onto the bridge of my nose. I could feel the warmth of the lightbulb wafting up my drawers. If I'd smacked down on that light bulb in just my skivvies . . .

The thought of my close brush with disaster pulled me further into the realm of the conscious. It felt like my right knee was bruised, and I rubbed it with my left hand while I used my one good eye to look in my other hand for a suspected splinter from the bedpost.

"What are you doing?" my dear wife demanded, but then she promptly lost interest. "Oh, my stomach hurts. Is it morning? I feel like I'm gonna throw up. Can you please turn off that light?" She didn't offer me a moment's pause between her questions.

Normally, I might have growled back something about her total lack of compassion for the wounded, but this time I tried to ignore her comments.

"Honey, I need to know what's going on. Do you feel pains?" She was almost two weeks overdue, and the doctor said to head to the hospital when the pains lasted longer than thirty seconds and were less than five minutes apart.

"NO! Not pains, PAIN!" she snapped. "I've just got one big cramp! I feel horrible. Please leave me alone." Her eyes remained clenched shut, but her remarks were sufficiently stimulating that mine both opened wide.

"So you do feel pains? Are you sure?" This new revelation was not completely unexpected, but it was nonetheless alarming.

"Tell me when it starts and stops, and I'll time how long it lasts."

There. That should reassure her I've got everything under control. Now if I could just remember how to set the stopwatch function.

"OHhhhhHHHhhhh, it doesn't stop. It just hurts!"

Thank heavens she wasn't like this all the time! She was being such a whiner this morning. Did they tell us in class what to do if the pains didn't stop? Hmmm. I carefully scanned the room before determining that I had no idea what I was looking for.

"Leave me alone. Get me some ice. Ow-Ow-Owww! Hold my hand, please!" she pleaded.

I felt vaguely like a driver tooling down a dark street who suddenly discovers he's neglected to flip on his headlights. It was disturbing to realize I may not have yet regained the full use of my capacities. In my diminished condition, I wondered if she realized how hard this was on me. This was all getting pretty stressful, and she wasn't making it any easier. Momentarily, I considered asking her to let me just go back to sleep. She might even feel better if we just hit the snooze button for a few minutes.

128

No. Not yet, anyway. That would be irresponsible. My stupid stopwatch was hard to set to zero. Although I had pushed all the buttons at least once, the bold, glowing characters of the display on my watch said it was JUNE.

"Annette," I said firmly, mustering my most authoritative tone. She usually settled down when I talked like that. "We have to see if you're in labor. Tell me what you're feeling." Good job, I told myself. I was firm. Confident. Calm.

"I'M FEELING TERRIBLE!" she practically roared. "Just leave me alone if you're not going to help me. OHhhh, it HURTS!"

An almost imperceptible series of taps on the door caught my attention as Annette's clamoring paused. This is embarrassing, I thought, and I grabbed for my jeans.

"Is everything all right?" came a tremulous voice through the cracks in the ancient wooden door. Billie, a grad student staying across the hall while she worked on her Ph.D. thesis, peeked into the room. Neither Annette nor I knew her well. An acquaintance of the elderly lady who owned the house, she was considerate, meek, and quite bookish. She had planned to leave for her Christmas vacation the day before but was delayed for some reason.

"I think so – I don't know. Come on in," I said as I snapped the waist button of my jeans and zipped my fly. Annette moaned pitifully as Billie, dressed in a chin-to-ankle flannel nightgown, tentatively nosed open the door. She was a little taller than Annette, slender, with short brown hair and wire framed glasses. She spent long hours at the library researching archaic bibliographic systems, or something like that. She was nice, in her quiet way, but we'd scarcely seen her in the weeks since we'd moved into our bedroom in the creaking, clapboard farmhouse.

I was, for the moment, preoccupied. As I looked up to engage Billie in conversation, I found her staring at my crotch. In my haste to dress, I had jammed my zipper on a large, loose fold of my baggy underwear. She seemed mesmerized by my efforts to remedy the problem. With a start, she raised her eyes to mine and then started to back quickly out of the room.

"I'm sorry," she stammered – about what I wasn't sure. I finally unjammed the zipper and at least got <u>that</u> matter under control.

"No, no, come in! <u>I'm</u> sorry. Look, Annette may be in labor. If she is, we'll need to be heading off to New Haven."

129

Billie stood in the doorway, her hand on the old, wrought iron latch. Craning her neck to see past me, she stared in mute fascination at Annette's prone form.

"No, I'm _not_ in labor! I just don't feel good." She sounded grim, but she had regained some composure with Billie's arrival. I placed my hand knowledgeably on her tummy and Billie took a step closer to the bed. Within a matter of seconds, Annette's stomach went from firm to the tautness of a basketball.

"Billie, I think she's having a contraction." I was sounding very authoritative, almost like a doctor on a TV drama. I momentarily wondered whether I could make my own stomach muscles that tight. It certainly felt like the book's description of a contraction – but a little knowledge is a dangerous thing, I reminded myself. I had a fleeting, but almost uncontrollable, urge to thump her tummy: It was impressively hard. Somehow I sensed she wouldn't like me testing just how hard. Still, it was pretty easy to imagine what it would sound like – maybe kind of like a watermelon.

My adrenaline-enhanced vision was once again drawn to my new watch. The contraction had started perhaps ten seconds ago, I calculated. Boy, this digital readout is great, I thought, even if it is impossible to set it to zero. Annette groaned. The tenths of seconds flickered across the watch face as I did the mental math to time the duration of her pains. Thirty. Thirty-five. Forty.

"There," I announced with finality. "It's getting better, right?" I was truly trying to be helpful.

"NNnooooo! It's getting _worse_! Just leave me _alone_," she snapped.

A soldier under fire must not retreat. I bravely held my position. Fifty. Fifty-five.

Sixty. Her stomach was still as hard as the tire of an eighteen wheeler.

"Honey, is it stopping _now_?" I inquired cautiously.

"Just shut UP!" Seventy-five. Eighty. Eighty-five.

That really wasn't nice, I thought petulantly.

Ninety seconds. I thought I sensed a slight relaxation in the corrugated steel wall of her tummy, but not much.

"Is it any better?" I asked almost plaintively. Hummm... Ninety seconds. I looked at her and shook my head. There must be a mistake. Contractions only last for thirty seconds, or at most a minute. This,

130

however, was not a major problem. Another contraction should come along in five to ten minutes. I'd just have to figure out how to reset my watch, and then time <u>that</u> one accurately.

"OuchOuchOuchOUCH!"

My wife's caterwauling was getting out of hand, I concluded. I glanced over at Billie apologetically. Annette should at least wait for a contraction before she makes such a fuss. I patted her, perhaps a little condescendingly, on the tummy.

It thumped.

"Oh, shoot! Billie, we've gotta get her to Yale-New Haven <u>now</u>."

"Now? Right now?" I could see the whites all the way around Billie's eyes. She hesitantly moved back toward the door, but stopped halfway through. "Uh, what should I do?"

By this time, I was struggling to pull on a boot and slip into my shirt at the same time. Billie's question was a good one, I thought while heaving mightily on my bootstraps. The exertion successfully planted my heel firmly in the boot, but it also caused me to lose my equilibrium. I flailed wildly in an attempt to stand up and regained my balance only as I kicked the lamp from its resting place on the floor into the far wall. Darkness once again flooded the room. The cat growled menacingly.

"I guess you can start by turning on that wall switch," I replied sheepishly.

"OOHhhhhOohhhh, KEEP IT <u>OFF</u>!" Annette was not her usual polite self, I reflected.

Billie avoided the controversy by leaving. I found Annette's robe and loafers and slipped them on her, and threw on my split leather jacket. I was easing her down the stairs when Billie reappeared, dressed in street clothes.

"I can come with you," she suggested cautiously.

I got the feeling she did everything cautiously, but I genuinely appreciated the offer. The first problem was getting Annette into the car. It was parked down by the road about 50 yards from the door of the old New England homestead. I figured it was possible to drive across the frozen grass to the front door.

"Here are the keys," I replied gratefully. "Can you bring our car up to the front steps? The heater knob's in the center of the dash. Turn it all the way to the right." I paused for just a moment. "While you're at it, would you grab a few clean sheets from the closet on your way out?"

Why not? We couldn't boil water.

131

"I've gotta call Suzie! And take me to the bathroom –
OWWWW!!!"

Annette was really out of it, I noted. We had to get moving. I
had learned early in our relationship that it could be very exasperating to
try to force my petite but potent wife into a proverbial corner. I had to
choose my battles carefully. If she insisted that both her demands be
honored, then I figured this was neither the time nor the issue to debate
her. I dragged over the old dial phone so she could call her best friend
from her seat on the toilet. The conversation seemed to me to be more
moans and gibberish than anything else. After a minute or two, I cut it
short.

"Annette, if you don't start walking now, I'm going to pick you
up and carry you out."

Wow.

I was taking the reins of command. I was firm. I was calm. I was
confident. And in truth I was getting very queasy about the whole
situation.

A blast of frigid Connecticut winter hit us as we opened the
front door. Billie had succeeded in driving the aging Mercedes sedan
across the large yard of the 200 year old country house. The car was
waiting with the engine running at the base of the steps. I was practically
dragging Annette from the door out to the car when she stopped with a
shout.

"WAIT! Wait – Get the dogs!" she commanded.

"What???" I guess I'd heard her plainly enough, but I was
stupefied. "The dogs?!!?"

"I'm not going unless you bring the dogs!" She waved her arm
weakly back toward the front of the house, but her voice was remarkably
strong.

"Annette, that is ridiculous. Now let's move!" We had to get one
thing settled: As her husband – and the soon-to-be father of our
household – I was in control.

She promptly sat down in the middle of the stone porch.

A few stray snow flakes swirled around her in the dim morning
light. I quickly calculated whether I should haul her struggling the rest of
the way to the car or just bring the two little dogs. One was a tiny, pure
white Maltese in our custody while Annette's mother was traveling. She
was adorable, but I had determined that the only way you could make a
dog that small was to leave something out – and in Magic's case, it was

her brain that must have been left back in the assembly room. The second dog, a Lhasa, had been a charmingly inconvenient wedding gift. I had successfully lobbied Annette to name the adorable handful of brown fuzz "Goliath" and had lived to regret it as the growing young dog abandoned all feminine graces and assumed the character of her belligerent namesake. Both dogs were fully capable of staying alone for a day.

A man has to do what a man has to do. No one in his right mind would take two yapping fluffballs to the hospital to deliver a baby. Annette was obviously delirious. She may have been strong-willed, but I had strength of a different kind on my side. It didn't matter that she was a little heavier than when I'd carried her across the threshold. I could handle this situation.

Five minutes later, we were speeding along the country road toward Yale-New Haven Hospital at precisely five miles an hour under the speed limit. Billie was at the wheel, her knuckles white and jaw clenched as she valiantly fought the almost nonexistent traffic on her courageous mission of compassion. Her skill at hitting almost every red light exceeded even Bob's on the morning Annette and I got married. I thought I caught her slowing down several times for green lights, just in case they might soon turn red. Although it was normally a half-hour drive from the old country house to the hospital, I took comfort from the fact that first births were the result of an average of fourteen hours of labor. I had picked that little item up as one of the best students in our natural childbirth class.

Months previously, I'd informed Annette that I really was not up to the prospect of attending the delivery of our baby. On several occasions as I was growing up, the sight of blood (usually my own, let me say in my own defense) had caused me to faint dead away. I even got to take two days off from fifth grade when the fellow in front of me got a spontaneous bloody nose in the middle of our annual achievement tests. We were all standing in rows and doing breathing exercises between tests. Several scarlet drops appeared on the floor at the feet of the kid ahead. The last thing I remember is the panic in his eyes as he turned toward me clutching his chin and nose with a bloody hand. For some reason he was still holding his pencil and as my senses ebbed away I thought he had managed to impale it through his cheek. I chipped a front tooth and completely mashed my lips and nose by falling face down in the middle of the gym. Worse, the teacher apparently saw me (by then a placid, bloody mess on the floor) and concluded that poor Barbie McIntyre had somehow pushed me and knocked me out. As the girl of my dreams for that month, I had painstakingly arranged to sit right in front of her. The whole episode did nothing for our relationship.

I subsequently tried to avoid situations conducive to my loss of consciousness. I figured that whatever intangible bonding might occur between father and child would be negated if I collapsed in a heap in the delivery room. Like a good husband, I'd faithfully attended all the prenatal classes – but I forewarned Annette that when the going got gory, I'd get going. As we drove along, I took comfort from the prospect that it wouldn't be too long before I'd be sitting peacefully in the waiting room reading Popular Science.

It was somewhat awkward in the back seat with Annette. She continued to make a tremendous ruckus, groaning and moaning almost incessantly. I was, however, afforded one small measure of vindication when she was forced to interrupt her activities to remove Magic, the little white Maltese, from a perch atop the great mound of her tummy.

"Get off me, you stupid dog!" she had yelled.

I soothed my injured pride with the knowledge that I had been right all along. She grabbed Magic and shoved her onto the rear deck beside Goliath. At least the dogs were being nice to each other. Annette was not trying to be very nice to anyone. When we had clambered into the car, it was bitter cold, and she had been terse with Billie for not turning on the heater. Billie mutely responded by handing me the heater control knob with a couple of wires still attached. Then she explained how on her car you had to pull the knob to get heat. This made Annette even more upset. It was far from a pleasant trip. For a lot of reasons, it seemed interminable.

The car crawled to yet another stop, and I stared at the red light in front of us. I dispelled my rising anxiety with the notion that we had plenty of time. Her water hadn't broken. It might be evening before this was all over.

"I'VE GOT TO PUSH!" It certainly didn't sound like Annette's voice, but her desperate expression affirmed that it was indeed my increasingly uncooperative sweetheart who had spoken.

These were not the words I wanted to hear when we were still five miles from the hospital. The steady drip of adrenaline into my guts increased to a small torrent. Billie's knuckles got whiter as she looked nervously over her right shoulder. The light finally turned green, but the car didn't move.

"Do you want me to slow down?" Billie asked, her voice quivering. "I can stop the car."

The dogs were yapping incessantly.

"No! NO! Please, no! Just go, and be careful!" I instructed, and turned my attention to my dear wife.

Her jaw was set. I could see every muscle and tendon in her neck – it looked like an illustration from one of those biology textbooks. Her eyes were clenched shut, and her brow was completely furrowed and sweaty from the turmoil inside her.

"I GOTTA – I GOTTA PUSH!!!"

This was not according to plan. But – Wait! They taught us how to deal with this contingency in childbirth class, I realized with relief. Annette should be doing her exercises! And I should be her coach.

"NO, Annette! It's too early! Breathe! BREATHE!" Perhaps I sounded a little excited, but this was pretty much my first time coaching anyone doing anything. In any case – in my heart – I knew I was firm. Confident. Calm.

"YOU BREATHE!! — I GOTTA — OHHHHHH!!!!! HEAVENLY FATHER, HELP ME!!! TIMBER — THE BABY'S COMING!!!!

This was getting entirely out of hand. I moved into a position on the floor of the car at her knees. I grabbed one of the sheets and shoved it under her bottom as she yelled again.

"AAAHHHHHHHH!!!!! IT'S COMING!!!!"

In the gray light of the car, I could make out the top of the baby's head, just like in the movie in the prenatal class. The blood drained from my brain. My vision blurred and warped, and a huge, pounding noise filled my ears.

I blinked and shook my head – hard. That helped. With renewed acuity, I reached the irrefutable and terrifying conclusion that I was about to have a baby!

"OK, Honey, hang on! Don't push – You'll hurt yourself! Breathe, baby, Breathe!"

"AAAAHHHHHHHHHH!!!!" With a small explosion of fluid, her amniotic sac burst as the baby's head slipped into my waiting hands. My intense interest in technical matters was paying off as I remembered little

135

bits and procedures I'd seen in books and on TV over the past months and years.

"Hold on, Honey – Wait just a minute!" I succeeded in catching the baby at the shoulders and gently holding it in place while I checked to make sure the umbilical cord wasn't wrapped around its neck. Annette, however, had no idea what I was doing.

"What's happening???!!" She was anxious, confused, and exhausted.

I tried to remain calm. "Well, I have the baby's head here..." She jumped to the alarming conclusion that something had gone bizarrely wrong.

"Oh, Dear God!" she cried in fear and agony. "What <u>happened</u> to the rest of my baby???"

"No, no, Honey, it's <u>okay</u>. Everything's fine. I just had to check something. You can push again."

She looked at me with disbelief before deciding to follow my suggestion. With an outpouring of arms, legs, fluids, and relief, the astonishingly soft, warm little body slipped into my hands. Never had I felt anything so extraordinarily, wondrously alive. I quickly cradled the tiny form in one arm while I grabbed another clean sheet to swaddle the baby from the bitter cold. The baby's breathing passages were already clear, and within a second or two the uniquely miraculous sound of a newborn's cry quavered through the car.

"Oh, it's my beautiful little Kimber!" Annette proclaimed. "Let me hold her!" Annette was crying and laughing at the same time as we drove into the deserted emergency entrance of Yale-New Haven Hospital.

All things considered, she was now in an amazingly good mood, I concluded. She must be feeling better. I was still a little queasy.

We crawled to a stop. I opened the rear door and unfolded myself from the back seat to find some help. Dazed, sodden, and streaked with blood, I was promptly stopped by the hospital's security guard.

"Just what's thah prahblam, buddy?" he asked suspiciously.

I deserved a more ceremonious greeting. I raked the hair out of my eyes, pushed up my spattered glasses, and swiped at a drop of bloody amniotic fluid crawling down my cheek.

"We just had a baby! I mean, my wife did, in the car. I think I need some help, though."

The guard looked over my shoulder to Annette, who was beaming broadly from her den in the back seat of the car. The only sign of the baby was a little pink hand which grabbed at fold of the bundled-up sheet. Billie smiled weakly from her position at the wheel.

His concerns allayed, the guard brightened considerably. He patted me on the back and escorted me to the nearest doctor, who was in this case a young intern new to the E.R. The doctor listened with incredulity and growing anxiety as I blurted out the events of the last half hour.

So, I realized with a sense of triumph, they didn't teach this in his classes either. We trotted back to the car, and I proudly swung open the door so the intern could poke his head inside.

Anticipatory silence reigned for maybe a second. Then an explosive outburst of protective rage and snarling barks reverberated off the buildings surrounding us. Goliath lunged to defend the new mother and babe, launching on a trajectory straight toward the vital organs of the intruding doctor. Every fang was bared and no bark suppressed as the football of furry fury threw herself at the hapless young surgeon. The Lhasa's grim determination exceeded her competence as an attacker, however, and she tumbled harmlessly to the asphalt where she latched on to the doctor's pants cuff. Magic simultaneously jumped into the melee and viciously attacked his vulnerable dangling stethoscope. The intern smacked his head into the door jamb as he staggered backwards with the smaller pooch momentarily swinging from the rubber tubing like a frenetic, fuzzy pendulum. He surrendered the device to the tiny mutt, but she continued her assault and he chose to retreat in frantic panic and stunned confusion to the security of the guard's booth. I grabbed Goliath by the scruff of her neck as she skittered around the intern's heels. I then scooped up Magic (who was, being relieved of the 'scope, about as threatening as an enraged guinea pig) and plopped her back onto the rear deck. Annette collared both animals with her right hand, but they continued to yap enthusiastically. It was a testament to his professional dedication and humanitarian spirit that the intern was ultimately persuaded to return to the car and cut the baby's umbilical cord.

His trials, however, were not over. As he moved in to cut the umbilicus, I realized that Annette had simply assumed that she was the proud mother of a little girl. It was, for her, a natural conclusion. Except for her father, the relatives she had grown up with were all women. As

137

for me, I had been too concerned about protecting the baby from freezing to bother with checking its sex. A moment after the birth I had immediately wrapped up the baby in the sheets Billie put in the unheated car.

"Can you tell us, please," I asked apologetically, "if we have a boy or a girl?"

To me it seemed a completely reasonable question. The young doctor's face, however, registered only additional consternation and shock. His reaction was perplexing until I realized that, under more normal circumstances, the answer should have been apparent earlier – especially to a father who had just delivered his own baby. The intern somewhat squeamishly unwrapped the sheet, and with a look of obvious relief announced, "You have a perfectly normal little boy!"

Annette squealed with delight. She never thought that she, of all people, would make a boy! She beamed down at her handsome son, and then over to me.

I could see it in her eyes. It was all over her face. She thought I was <u>incredible</u>. Firm. Confident. Calm.

And as for me, I was very happy to see her happy again. She looked positively radiant.

Boy, I reflected. Women say labor's tough on <u>them</u>. The birth of a child could be kinda rough on the guy, too.

Billie carefully drove away to park the car in the lot. The still-shaken intern let me drive Annette in her wheelchair. As this triumphal new father wheeled his wife and son down the hall toward the delivery room to take care of the placenta, a familiar voice rang out.

"Timber! Is that you? Annette!" Dr. Greg DeVore, Chief Ob/Gyn Resident at Yale-New Haven Hospital, came running down the corridor.

"What's going on? Did you two have the baby already? How in the world did you manage that?"

Chapter 6

He Ain't Heavy... He's My Brother

Saturday Morning, 20 May 1995
Salt Lake City, Utah

Gray-blue rays flickered weakly from the sleek console's screen, creating an aura of light tinged with warmth and defining shapes that were becoming more and more familiar. The sterile examination room was illuminated not just by the beams and shadows reaching out from the convex pane on the face of the machine, but also by a trio of wall sconces which had been dimmed to sunset hues. I squinted to make sense of what I saw on the glass. The glimmering phosphors flashed and faded into images resembling those we had seen only a few long days before in Denver. But this time, the monitor was big – much larger than our TV at home – and mounted high on the wall of the darkened examination room. The pictures on the screen were still a jumble of strange shapes, but now some were in color: Oranges, reds, purples, and greens pulsed in front of us in addition to the bluish-white tones that we were growing accustomed to seeing. Annette was again straining to make sense of the dim forms dancing on the glowing tube, but this time she knew she was seeing her two sons on the big screen.

"This equipment allows us to see not just the babies' skeleton and tissue," explained Dr. DeVore. "We can see the vascular system and even indicators of the velocity and direction of flow of the blood. I can focus in and out to try to get a more detailed impression of the underlying structure. It's conceptually the same machine that you used in Denver, but the computer that processes the signals is much, much more powerful."

139

Annette and I had arrived a few minutes earlier. We had left a sleepy-eyed Kimi in charge of her siblings and caught the early flight into Salt Lake. Had we seen him on the street, either of us would have recognized Greg DeVore immediately – he really hadn't changed much since we last saw him. He had the same chestnut hair and crisp brown eyes, the same precise speech.

A few months after Tomicah was born, I graduated from school and our little family left Connecticut. Greg DeVore and his family had stayed at Yale-New Haven Hospital for several more years. It was a fruitful period. He was one of the first in his field to recognize that the use of ultrasonic waves had enormous diagnostic potential. Others had foreseen the technology's utility to monitor fetal development, but he envisioned the use of ultrasound to give neonatal pediatricians a window into a baby's heart even before the child was born. Yale-New Haven had plenty of high risk pregnancies, and the Med School was fertile with gifted researchers who were excited to work with a visionary Ob/Gyn. They structured a mutually beneficial relationship with the companies that were developing the new machines. These firms were delighted to find new capabilities for their equipment, and they cooperated in providing the Medical Center with their most advanced technology. Dr. DeVore soon became recognized as a brilliant pioneer in his field. He and his family moved from Yale to UCLA, and then finally to the Salt Lake Valley. He also worked with his wife, Dorothy, to build a family. They eventually had six kids – including identical twin boys.

Dr. DeVore smiled appreciatively at 20 month-old Glorianna's pink cheeks and halo of blond curls. The toddler had fallen asleep in her Sit'n'Stroll as we drove our rental car in from the airport. She remained blissfully oblivious as I converted the device into a stroller and wheeled her into the suite of medical offices. We greeted one another, exchanged the latest updates on kids and careers, then the doctor had looked to Annette.

"I think we should see how your little guys are getting along. I'm sure you know the drill. Let's have you get up on the table," he said as he seated himself at the console. He gestured toward the large screen on the wall.

"Actually, that monitor up there is just to help me explain to parents what's going on. The screen that I have here," he said, pointing to the glowing panel directly in front of him, "has a much higher resolution than the one you get to look at. A trained person can see things that we never dreamed existed until they developed this generation of machine. I've been working with the company that makes these things, and the technology is now driving the diagnosis. What I mean is that I get to try to figure out how to use the detailed information the machine makes available. For example, you probably know that amniocentesis poses some risk to both the mother and baby – "

"Yes," Annette interrupted soberly. "One of my best friends went into labor right after her amnio, and she lost her baby at five months."

"It's rare, but it does happen," Dr. DeVore continued. "We've developed a database and a procedure so we can now tell with more than 95% accuracy whether a baby has certain genetic defects, and we do it with this machine. It's a completely non-invasive procedure – we just use the sonograph."

I pondered the significance of this information.

"So what you're saying doesn't apply to us, because we've already had the genetic analysis done," I posited carefully. "But it would mean that a mother who had a hard time conceiving could get a pretty good idea if she had, say, a Down's baby without increasing the risk that she'd miscarry a perfectly healthy baby by having an amniocentesis."

"Exactly," said the doctor. By this time Annette was reclined on the upholstered table. Dr. DeVore arranged the apparatus. "This gel has only been in the warmer for a few minutes. I hope it's not too cold." He spun his chair back toward his equipment and sighed deeply as he studied the screen.

"Wow," he exclaimed with a voice devoid of enthusiasm. "Your Dr. Porter wasn't kidding. This pericardium is worse than the L.A. freeway system."

His comment was more a factual observation than an attempt at humor. The picture on the monitor was a maze of pulsing passages. In many respects, the pictures were even more confusing than those we had seen before. Dr. DeVore told us that just as an encyclopedia is harder to read than a road sign, the additional data generated by this apparatus took considerable training to master. He spent several minutes reviewing with us the basic information presented on the screen. He affirmed most of what we had learned in Denver, and answered all my questions about how he used the real-time movement in the pictures to trace the pressure pulses in the babies' arteries. The colors on the screen represented differing densities and velocities of the tissues and fluids in Annette's abdomen, he said. He could use the equipment to zoom in on specific areas, then he'd flash back to the big picture again.

"That's incredible." Annette almost whispered as she stared at the monitor. The room echoed with the subdued sounds of the babies' beating heart. With each beat, we could simultaneously see the contraction of the organ on the screen.

"Timber, look!" She gripped my hand so tightly it almost hurt.

I was at loss to understand her intensity and her accompanying tear-filled eyes. Then I saw it. The red and orange figure beating on the screen was undeniably in the silhouette of a classic heart. It moved and pulsed, each time returning to a shape that clearly resembled a little Valentine.

"Hmmm. Interesting. You two obviously know a normal heart doesn't look like that." Dr. DeVore shook his head. "There's no doubt in my mind that the biggest problem with these guys is their hearts," he continued. "The whole vascular system in the twins' pericardium – their chest – has severe malformations. It's not surprising, given their condition, but I really don't like the looks of this at all.

"Do me a favor, please. This equipment does a remarkable job, but when I come across a situation like this one – uh – well, the machine can't do my thinking for me. I need you to be very quiet." Dr. DeVore's focus was drawn to the screen in front of him, and his voice faded. "I've got to see if there's anything we can do."

His words drifted off and became inaudible, although I noticed that he kept talking to himself. He concentrated intently as he moved the probe. Without appearing too obvious, I tried to decipher the notes the doctor was making as he worked. They were diagrams and arrows, and cryptic coordinates that seemed to correspond to locations on Annette's stomach. At times, Dr. DeVore would bring his face within inches of the console. Twice, he pushed himself away, stood up and stretched, all without ever taking his sight off the images on the screen.

"I think I've got it," Dr. DeVore said.

I looked at my watch in the dim light. The first exam in Denver had taken about half an hour. Annette had been on the table in Dr. DeVore's office for almost 90 minutes.

"I'm going to turn up the lights, so you may want to shield your eyes. Timber, while you help Annette get cleaned up, I'd like to take a look at the amnio test results you brought from Denver. I'll be just a few

142

minutes, and then we'll go over things." I handed over the sheaf of fax papers sent by Regina in Dr. Porter's office. As the lights flickered on, Glori stirred. She had slept through the whole procedure, but now she turned her slightly dazed little face to watch the doctor open the door and head down the hallway.

"Why did he need the test results?" Annette was wiping off the accumulation of dried gelatinous goo while I sweet-talked Glorianna back to sleep. "I thought you told him they were all okay on the phone."

"As far as I can tell, they are," I replied, "but there's a lot of language in there that I could barely understand. It clearly stated that there were no genetic abnormalities, but there may well be some other information in the report that he can use either for the twins or for his research."

"I seems like a month since we were in Dr. Porter's office." Annette was staring at the blank screen looming above her. "I thought the most difficult thing we'd confront coming out of that room might be the possibility of a Down Syndrome baby. After living with Ben for the past fifteen years, that just wasn't a problem. I really think I was all prepared for that – but can't say I was prepared for all this." She looked from the big monitor to the bank of equipment and then to me.

"Ben's taught us a lot," I concurred as I reflected upon the countless hours we'd spent with our neighbor's son. With all his challenges and eccentricities, we loved him almost as we loved our own kids. He served as an almost daily reminder that every person – even those with fairly severe limitations – can make meaningful contributions to the lives of those around him.

"I remember thinking on the drive over to Dr. Porter's that we might have twin Down's babies," I continued, "and I was a little surprised to realize that it didn't faze me. It never occurred to me we'd be dealing with anything like these guys." We grabbed our belongings and headed down the hall after Dr. DeVore. He was standing at a filing cabinet, but he motioned us into seats across from his unassuming desk.

"I could show you all of this on the videotape," the doctor began, "but I've found that most people find these discussions easier to understand if I just make a simple sketch."

He began drawing on a large pad of graph paper.

"As I told you before, I agree with Dr. Porter's diagnosis in most respects. The key problem areas are the GI tract, the liver, and the hearts. The gastrointestinal commingling is the easiest of the three. Even if they

143

share one tract, rather than having two that are mixed up, we can fix that surgically. It's a serious problem, but not insurmountable.

"The liver is much more problematic. These twins share one big organ. I think I see two bile ducts, so its possible that it could be split, and conceivably each twin could end up with a functioning liver. However, that surgery would likely be a nightmare. We don't yet have very effective techniques for operating on the countless blood vessels in the liver. It's very difficult to control bleeding, and operating on a tiny baby's liver is just that much trickier.

"If those were the only problems we were facing, we'd be looking at some very sick babies who could possibly make it to term, but then might not survive the surgical efforts required to keep them alive.

"I'm sorry I kept you on the table so long, Annette. I had to make sure I understood their cardiovascular system, because when all's said and done, that's what is likely to determine whether these guys can live or die."

Annette and I were listening intently, and as we watched Dr. DeVore drew a detailed profile of the twins' stomach and liver. Now he moved his pencil up the page and began to draw the major arteries.

"I've never seen a more complex circulatory system than this. There are in fact two separate hearts. I know they're not just one big mass of tissue because one of the hearts – the little guy's – is barely functioning. What I saw, and what you heard, is the bigger twin's heart doing the work for both of them. If these were separate twins *in utero*, the little guy would have suffered a fetal demise long ago. As it is, because they are conjoined, the arteries and veins of the larger twin have grown over through the shared liver and interlinked with the circulatory system of the little guy.

"In essence, the big twin is giving full-time life support to the little one. The smaller baby is clearly alive and moving, but that's why he's smaller. His heart doesn't work, and his healthier brother's carrying him.

"And, quite frankly, it looks to me like it's killing the bigger twin. His heart is enlarged for his age because he's pumping blood for both of them. To make matters worse, the interlinking of the circulatory systems through the liver is both incomplete and inefficient, so he's forced to work way too hard to get only a small amount of blood through to his little brother. The fluid that they noticed in Denver – the stuff they thought was an indicator of a genetic defect? – is an indicator that the

144

big guy's heart is also beginning to fail. This liquid is like lymph fluid, and it starts to accumulate when there's cardiac stress."

Annette sat silently, one hand cradling her tummy, the other holding my hand tightly as she leaned into the desk. She was pouring over the drawing. I could see in Greg DeVore's eyes that thousands of rough pregnancies and thousands of talks with devoted parents still weren't adequate preparation for a discussion like this.

The doctor spoke again, gently and with great conviction.

"I really tried to find out exactly what was going on, because I knew you'd want to make this work if you possibly could. About all I have is bad news. First, the hearts are inseparable. There's no way I can see to untangle these two. Second, the job of keeping both of them alive is wearing out the big twin. I doubt he'll make it to term. And it's not like he'd be out of the woods even then. I suppose you could then try to save him by sacrificing the little guy, but you'd almost certainly end up losing them both. Forget the liver and GI tract – we just don't have the surgical techniques to fix these hearts."

Annette quietly broke down. As she saw her tears falling onto the desk – onto the corner of the drawing of her little boys – she turned to bury her face in my shoulder.

"I know you'd tell us," I managed to say haltingly, "but I've gotta ask anyway. Given what you're saying, do you think there's any way we could operate on them before the babies progressed much further?"

Annette seized the shred of hope my question offered. "Could we do something now that might save one of them?" she asked. "I've heard they sometimes can operate while the baby's still in the womb. There's a doctor we read about at Johns-Hopkins who has separated twins. Couldn't we do something now – before they're born – and maybe save the bigger twin?"

Dr. DeVore shook his head slowly, pensively. "If there was a way that I could in good conscience give you even a little hope, I would, Annette. If you assume that we could somehow operate on the hearts and save the larger twin, you'd still have to deal with the liver and GI problems at the same time. Three of the most critical organs of the body would need massive surgery, all at the same time, and all on a tiny baby who's not ready yet to live outside the womb. It would require a whole series of operations that would all need to take place very soon – within the next month – because these babies are already weak and getting weaker. Then, if we assume a miracle and the big guy survives, he's still

145

going to be a very sick boy. His heart would need additional reconstructive surgery to allow him to grow. I've been sitting here wracking my brain for a strategy, but I don't see any chance of a surgical solution. They just have too many strikes against them."

I closed my eyes and took a deep breath as I tried to organize my thoughts.

"Dr. DeVore – Greg – what if this were Dorothy? I mean, what would you do if you two were facing this situation?"

Dr. DeVore sat up straight and rocked his head back and then to each side to get out the kinks and relieve some of the tension. Then he swung forward, leaned over the desk, and looked directly at us.

"I know why you two are here. I've dealt with enough parents over the last two decades to know which parents are really seeking a solution and which ones aren't ready to face the reality of a child with a birth defect. I know that you want these babies – whatever their condition. You want them so bad that you told me you'd pay for these tests yourselves. You jumped on the plane, in spite of what the doctors in Denver said, because if there was any chance these little guys could make it, you wanted to know. I respect that, and I'm pretty sure I would have done the same thing.

"Let me digress a minute. A lot of people don't know that more than 60% of conceptions end in early, spontaneous miscarriages. It seems to me, as a doctor who's seen it all, that a lot of us take it for granted that it's easy for God to make a baby. But it's evidently not. The way I look at it, every time a healthy baby is born, it is a bona fide miracle. Truly. After all these years, I'm still in awe as I try to comprehend all the things that have to go right to allow a healthy, thinking baby to be delivered.

"A few years ago – no, it was longer than that – anyway, I got a call from a committee of the top leaders of the Church. They were taking a hard look at the Church's position on abortion, and they wanted my perspective. I ended up suggesting some wording that's pretty much what was adopted as the official policy of the Church. In fact, the legislature here also consulted me before drafting the new state law.

"As a person who cherishes every life born into this world, and as a man who truly believes that our future as a planet and a race depends on bearing and nurturing children, the thought of destroying healthy babies tears at my heart. If our Heavenly Father brings less than

146

forty percent of conceptions to delivery, it seems the height of arrogance and disrespect to abort so many of the best of those.

"The language I suggested to both the Church and the legislature said basically that if the life of the mother is at risk, or the baby has a fatal abnormality, then after prayerful deliberation the pregnancy may be terminated. In regards to the first part of the wording, I've known children who lost their mother as they were born. If a healthy baby is carried at the acknowledged, substantial threat to its mother's life, we are risking that it will be born forever crippled spiritually and emotionally – perhaps in the worst possible way. I really don't think we're doing that baby any favor. To deliver the baby but lose the mom leaves the world less well off than the alternatives. It's hard to contemplate losing a baby, but I also know it does the world no good at all to lose a loving mother," he said, looking at Annette. "You're too important – to your other children, now or in the future, and to your husband. So if we risk the mother's life, we are jeopardizing an essential part of our Heavenly Father's plan.

"Similarly, childbearing always poses risks for mothers, even under the best of circumstances. If we can tell using the diagnostic tools God has given us that a fetus has no realistic chance for survival, is it wise stewardship to force that mother to bear the physical and emotional burdens of the pregnancy to term? I didn't think so back then, and I feel the same now.

"In a more straightforward case, these aren't easy issues to contend with. In your situation, both factors weigh against you: The twins have almost no chance of survival, and they actually pose a threat to your life.

"Let me tell you about two cases. I had the daughter of a senior leader of the Church come in, and we found her baby had a fatal heart defect. The baby was alive in the womb, but barely. The condition was clearly inoperable and terminal. Perhaps the baby could have made it to delivery, but it wasn't very likely. In my opinion, the baby would have been stillborn, but I'll leave open the possibility it might have survived until birth. They left here to pray about what to do. She subsequently chose to terminate the pregnancy.

"Several months ago, another couple was referred to me with a baby thought to have severe physical defects. The ultrasound showed this baby was profoundly malformed and its heart and other organs offered no hope. The mother chose to carry the baby to term. She and

147

her husband came back in here a few weeks ago and told me the pregnancy had turned into the most powerfully positive experience of their marriage. The whole family had bonded through prayer and trial, and as the delivery date approached they were completely at peace. The little guy only lived about ten minutes, but that was long enough for his dad to give him his name and a father's blessing.

"It's a fundamental article of faith that, as we pray in faith, we are entitled to personal revelation from the Holy Ghost, and that our inspiration will be in harmony with God's established principles. The doctrine of the Church, as well as my experience as a doctor, both say in this circumstance you are free to choose in accordance with the dictates of the divine inspiration that you personally receive.

"Timber, I wanted to give you a full and respectful answer to your question, and I hope you can forgive me for being so long-winded. In short, if I were sitting next to Dorothy, the way you're sitting with Annette, I'd have to tell her that the twins aren't likely to live much longer. It'd be one for the medical journals if they made it through the trauma of a C-section, and then there's simply no way I can see the big guy," and he pointed to the larger twin in the drawing, "supporting his twin for long outside the environment of the womb. And we can't separate them: When the little guy goes, he'll end up taking his brother with him."

He looked across the desk to Annette. "If they live and grow over the next months, we can't foresee all the complications. You could go toxic, or they could grow enough to rupture your uterus or cervix and make you hemorrhage. Even just a few decades ago – say, at the time when I was born – you almost certainly wouldn't have survived this pregnancy.

"In this case, you're blessed to be able to know what's happening and make an informed choice. If you," he said, nodding toward Annette, "were Dorothy, I'd have to tell you we should prayerfully consider terminating the pregnancy."

VI. The Zenobian Queen

1980-1992
Denver, Colorado

Please let me offer a little advice to all of you newlywed guys:
Think twice – or even three times – before you buy a house your spouse
hasn't seen. This little rule should be obvious to any savvy guy. Take
someone like me, for example. In this enlightened age, a guy like me
shouldn't even think of buying a house before his wife has had a chance
to look it over, check out the neighborhood and offer her opinion.
Ideally, that opinion should be favorable. A guy would have to be crazy
to sign the papers and commit to a thirty-year mortgage without his wife
having first seen the place.

Then again, there are situations in life when acting crazy may be
the best you can do. In the fall of 1980, I took a deep breath and told
Annette on the phone long distance that I'd found a house that looked
ideal for our purposes. Let me note without further comment on my
judgment that she must have loved me a lot when she said, "If you think
it's the right thing . . . Buy it." And she didn't make me sleep on the
couch even one night of the twelve years we lived in our snug home on
Zenobia Street in Denver.

It was only in retrospect that I realized how reckless I was to buy
our first house before Annette inspected it. She was back in California
with our 22 month old Tomicah and our new baby girl, Kimber. She
knew little about Denver and almost nothing of the area where the house
was located. It wasn't near any friends or acquaintances.

She opted to trust me. Then she stood by her word and made the
best of it. The time in Suzie's Valiant before we married had been well
spent. As we drove about focusing our energies on other people's needs,
Annette and I had talked for hour upon hour. Together, we forged the
goals and understandings that would serve as the tools and rules of our
future lives. As much as we were attracted to one another, and as much
as we liked to be together in the moment, we both wanted to craft a
relationship that would last forever. We explored areas of agreement and
dispute and after a few months both of us could accurately cite the

other's opinions on politics and poverty, religion and race, morality and money.

We knew before we married that we wanted kids – lots of kids. As our wedding date approached, someone asked the inevitable, "Do you think you'll be starting a family soon?" Annette had replied without hesitating that she was planning to have twenty-two children. Where she got the number I'll never know, but I shared with her a deep desire to nurture any and all the little people who came into our lives.

After we married I had a full semester to complete before my accelerated graduation. We faced a choice: We could return to New Haven for the fall semester or we could take a break from school. If we took the latter option I would then graduate with the rest of my class in the spring. The choice was made easier when my mother asked that we come to Denver to work on her political campaign. A spirited statewide primary campaign in the summer became a hard-fought battle in the fall. As November arrived my increasingly pregnant Annette and I helped to elect Mom as Colorado's first woman Lieutenant Governor. We then returned to Connecticut for Tomicah's birth and my final classes.

The months after our wedding found us waging another kind of campaign. Annette had reconciled with her dad, but only to a limited extent. Public displays – including an impressive celebration of our marriage – indicated that he had made his peace with us, but privately her father was still furious.

When Dr. Lantos decided to run for a Congressional seat in California soon after my graduation, we saw an opportunity to rebuild the relationship that had been fractured with our matrimony. We worked feverishly on his campaign. Six months after Kimber was born, Annette's father was sworn in as the first Holocaust survivor to serve in the US Congress. In two short years we had been blessed with two lovely kids, my mom had become Colorado's Lieutenant Governor and Annette's dad was elected a Congressman.

We – or perhaps more accurately, I – bought the house on Zenobia Street at the conclusion of the campaign of 1980. Annette was still in San Francisco helping to mop up after the election, but it was clear to us both that our relationship with her father was still making life difficult for us all. There were forces at work that were more powerful than our heartfelt attempts to coexist harmoniously. As a result, I came to Denver to find a job and a place for our little family to live. The realtor eventually suggested a compact, century-old red brick Victorian with two bedrooms and an attached garage which had long ago been converted into a den. The living and dining rooms were generously trimmed with original wood molding and antique lighting fixtures. Surrounded by big trees and low fences, the houses of the neighborhood felt like a small town. Within minutes of walking through the door for the first time Annette ripped down the mustard colored curtains, but she agreed that – given the circumstances – I had made a good choice.

It was a chance only an inexperienced husband would dare to take. Nonetheless, she was right. The house served us well. Levi was born at Thanksgiving a year after we moved in. Annette insisted on leaving the hospital immediately to cook dinner for visitors from out of town. Charity arrived all blonde and pretty in 1983. Soon I converted the den into a playroom and then into a multi-kid dorm. There was a good-sized walk-in closet under the eaves upstairs, and as Corban arrived in '85 and Liberty in '87, I got creative and slipped a few bunks up there, too – along with a slide to make it easier to get down in the morning.

One reason I chose that particular property was that it included a tiny, two room frame house in the back we could rent for extra income. For the first few years we had a variety of tenants, but eventually we used it as a school room by day and dorm by night.

In the early 80's home schooling was considered a radical approach to education. Some folks did it for political or religious reasons. When we started to teach Tomicah at home at age four our motives weren't so ideologically pure. He was too young for the public schools and he was determined to learn. We continued to teach our kids ourselves because we enjoyed spending time with them and the appreciation was clearly mutual. While I was confident that they were unlikely to find a better teacher than their mother, I also pursued another agenda: Much of the nasty trouble I got into as a kid – whether disciplinary, or suffering abuse at the hands of my peers, or doing stupid things as I sought social acceptance – started at school. (Annette never got into trouble, so she had to take my word for it.) I figured that we could avoid the bullies, the temptations and the cliques – and have a much clearer idea why a kid had a problem with their teacher – if we taught all of them ourselves.

Our general curriculum included the basics of reading, writing and arithmetic taught in the context of our daily lives. Annette transformed a morning of baking into lessons on fractions, chemistry and culture. The kids were soon steeped in the history of the world and

151

immersed in science and art. The kids studied Christianity, of course, but also Judaism, Islam, and the other established religions. Our educational process was at times intense, but the kids seemed to learn at a stunning clip. So over the years I installed chalkboards and bookshelves in the little house out back: Our home had became a school as well.

Annette's commitment to our family was total. Her energy was astonishing, her vision of our collective potential inspiring. In ways far exceeding my hopes or imagination, she served as an amazing mother and wife. She didn't limit her involvement to the walls of our home. We encouraged the kids to get involved with whatever worthwhile activities they found to be of interest. They had ample social interaction. In fact, unconstrained by the scheduling limitations imposed by conventional school, they found opportunities abounding. To our surprise, people began to take notice of the kids' success.

Tomicah played soccer and was a Scout, but he also started the family tradition of singing with the Colorado Children's Chorale. He loved to talk with people and he read voraciously. He soon struck up a friendship with the local librarian which in turn led to a stint – at age eight – as a reviewer of children 's books for the Rocky Mountain News and the local public television station.

The kids were blessed in many of their undertakings. At eight Kimber was one of thirty chosen from among thousands of elementary-aged students nationally to write an episode concept for a new television show. Kimber's abilities as a singer were such that she was named Grand Champion at the State Fair and she was subsequently invited to perform with Levi at that year's national convention of state fair organizers.

One result of their high profile successes was that parents began to seek us out for advice on how to teach kids. By the mid-80's newspaper and television reporters – even magazines like <u>Forbes</u> and <u>Newsday</u> – were featuring Annette in stories about cutting-edge educational trends. With no intent or conscious design she became a local leader – of sorts – in the field of education. She was asked to testify before the state legislature and was sought out by educators and policy makers. In many respects it was a natural development. She had been awarded her teaching certificate as an undergraduate, she had earned a couple of Masters degrees, and her father was a tenured professor.

In truth, it was an uphill fight. Among those closest to us were a multitude of skeptics. Some of the opposition we faced was political in origin. There were those who thought either my wife or I would make an attractive candidate, but we had our hands full with the kids and other responsibilities. I managed the opening months of my mom's tumultuous and ultimately futile campaign for the U.S. Senate in 1984 and later led successful efforts to re-elect Annette's father. In each case, many people involved in public education were very helpful. Annette's dad, in particular, had strong support from the teachers' unions. They didn't yet understand that home schooling offered innovative, collaborative opportunities for teachers, schools, and – especially – kids. Perhaps that contributed to his discomfort with our children's education. It also may have been an unconscious response to our choice to wed in the face of his objections. Whatever the cause, for years he voiced a conviction that we were jeopardizing our children's chances for happiness and success. While he had graciously ignored his pledge to ostracize us after our wedding, in his subsequent relations with us he didn't hesitate to be critical of how we were raising our family.

In 1990, I poured my heart out to him in a long letter:

> You don't seem to feel any joy in the fact that Annette has repeatedly been singled out as an example of the very best in teaching. How often do you reflect with satisfaction that she has several times been the focus of statewide television features as a result of her excellence as a teacher? Annette has been accorded more recognition and has more accomplishments to her credit as a <u>teacher</u> than do most <u>schools</u>. And never have I seen a school where the students had similar access to technology or, through field trips, to facilities.
>
> In this context I find your attitude toward our schooling unproductive. You keep making comments critical of this or that detail of the kids' education, and casting aspersions about Annette's capabilities. How can you reconcile the acclaim she continues to receive with your criticism?

As happens in many families, our relationship with Annette's father was paradoxical. He was the second most important and influential person in my wife's life. He was offended by her faith and was openly frustrated with the unconventional practice of her chosen professions as an educator and a mother. It remained unclear whether the rocky relationship I had with her dad was a cause or a symptom. Our personal rapport improved at a glacial pace. Yet he obviously loved his daughter and grandchildren and craved our family's company. Twice we moved at his request from Denver to San Francisco to be near him. When his seat in Congress was seriously threatened, he trusted me to manage two of his most brutal campaigns. We won handsomely each time, yet we remained unable to sit comfortably in the same room together. He doted upon our children, and bought them thoughtful gifts and endearing trinkets. They loved him in return. Every few years he would purchase our family a new car or a major appliance. It was a complex and intense relationship marked by painful contradictions.

My career didn't offer Annette a whole lot of emotional cover. It might have been easier had I been wonderfully successful in the business world. Then Annette could have said she was living in the lap of luxury and driving the kids to soccer lessons in a Lexus. While we were blessed with a bounty of joy and plenty of life's necessities, our circumstances were relatively modest. After a couple of stints as an executive within multinational corporations and then as a consultant, I grew weary of the incessant demands that I give my job a higher priority than my family. The best way to balance home, career and church seemed to be that I focus on one of my inventions and start my own company. The results were predictably slow in coming. It was all too easy for Annette's dad to maintain that another man could have provided more for her.

What our young family lacked in substance we balanced with spirit. Annette had inscribed a quotation from the scriptures on the inside cover of the Bible she gave me when we married. It read:

> Organize yourselves; prepare every needful thing; and establish a house, even a house of prayer, a house of fasting, a house of faith, a house of learning, a house of Glory, a house of order, a house of God. [D&C 88:119]

The house on Zenobia Street was such a house – at least some of the time. I suppose it's more accurate to say we were truly a house of order only on special occasions, and it's also important to note that this particular scripture mentions nothing about pets. It would have been helpful if I had been offered at least some counsel on pets.

We certainly had a house of pets.

Early on, I established a rule that a child could not acquire a pet until that child had written an extensive report on the care and history of that specific type of critter. It was a useful if temporary technique for slowing the transformation of our living quarters into a landlocked Noah's ark. At age six, Tomicah wrote a report on guinea pigs that was 12 pages long – with perhaps 12 words per page. To his disappointment the guinea pig wasn't a long-term resident of our ark. She made her way to that big pigpen in the sky after just a couple of years. We gave Tomicah the consolation prize of ownership of a svelte white cat. He plumbed the depths of his creativity to name her "Miss Meow." Kimi's treatise on rabbits was more substantial. It had a bright blue cover and pictures she'd cut from magazines. She named her pure white Mini-Lop "Loverly" and fed him prodigious amounts of leftover guinea pig food.

Loverly liked Kimber and hesitantly tolerated the rest of the family. He soon grew to be a mild-mannered but substantial and remarkably vigorous armful. I never understood what distinguished him as a "Mini-Lop" – a Maxi- sized version of this beast could have been gainfully employed in building demolition. He'd regularly rip out the wire mesh of his cage and tour the house. He'd go in and out the dog door I contrived to accommodate Levi's new pet, an irrepressible golden/lab pup. The hare and hound had a somewhat confused idea of which one of them was the predator. Initially Loverly was larger than Francis, the dog. If the puppy got too aggressive, with one good kick the lop would send him flying across the kitchen. We'd hear a pained yap momentarily followed by a soft thud as the dog slammed into the baseboards. Within seconds Francis would have scampered back for more. The relationship changed as Francis grew larger. One day we were surprised to hear the customary pained yap only to see the rabbit slide on its back across the kitchen floor. As Loverly smacked into the baseboards with the accustomed thud, I used the episode to illustrate Newtonian physics to the kids: Francis had grown so he was now substantially bigger than the rabbit. The same force that previously sent the little puppy across the room now propelled him nowhere, and instead sent the bunny gliding. They were obviously having a little difficulty adjusting to the new dynamics.

155

The neighbors soon became accustomed to the hum of activity at the house. We entertained a steady stream of six-, four- and two-legged visitors. Levi enlisted his little brother Corban in the task of filling aquariums with frogs and salamanders, stocking mayonnaise jars with beetles and snakes, and furnishing boxes as nests for baby birds and mice. Most of our animal visitors were reasonably well behaved. Quite a few stayed with us for years. Levi tenderly raised a starling from the time it fell from its nest in our yard. For months after he released it, the little bird would return from the treetops to sit on his shoulder. If you were a critter, life was good on Zenobia Street.

Most of the time, anyway.

Drusilla and Fay Ferree were living legends in our corner of town. They came to Denver during World War II and stayed. They taught square dancing, organized a citizens band radio community response network to take care of the elderly and reduce crime, and advocated the latest in reflexology and home herbal remedies. Fay was wiry, spry and in his eighties when a thug held up the local community center. The young man brandished a pistol at Fay and demanded the evening's charity receipts. When Fay refused, the guy shot him, grabbed the money and boldly walked off. Fay got up and decked the man with the empty cash box. He shot Fay again before running into a nearby alley. Fay was seriously – although not mortally – wounded, but so was the thief. He was arrested a short while later as he sought treatment for the nasty gash Fay inflicted on his head.

Although the Ferrees attended our ward, they liked to join in our celebration of the Jewish holy days. We'd perform the Seder, and several times a year we'd get together for a festive feast to honor Chanukah, Sukkoth or Purim. On less formal occasions Fay delighted the kids with tales of old Denver while Drusilla played our vintage upright piano. We were just gathering to eat on one such a night when Annette sent Kimber out to the little house in back to get her brother. Most of the family was seated around our big dining room table when we heard a scream seemingly ripped straight from Kimber's heart. I bolted from my chair at the table to see her stagger in the back door.

"Francis killed Loverly!!!" she wailed.

Total pandemonium swept the household. Where peaceful anticipation reigned moments before there was now a chorus of pitiful, highly demonstrative mourning. Annette rose from the table clutching our new baby, Liberty, and led the children in a cacophonous dirge of

156

horror and grief. Fay and Drusilla were stunned and dazed by the maelstrom of emotion pummeling the family. They had no idea who had killed whom, but they looked close to having heart attacks of their own.

Francis had enthusiastically bounded in the door with Kimi, excited at all the commotion. His curiosity was met with a raging torrent of recrimination. He cowered against the wall as his name was shouted punitively at him by five furious little people and several big ones.

The scene was completely chaotic. In an effort to wrestle control from the spirit of wrath that had seized our home, I bellowed for everyone to be still. To my surprise, they complied.

Francis had been reduced to a quivering mass in the corner of the room by the door. He held his forepaw over his nose as he attempted to shrink himself into invisibility. There was no questioning his abject misery. I stepped past him out on to the back stoop. It was dusk, but almost immediately I saw the dirty white pile of fur out on the lawn.

"Someone get me a box big enough to hold him," I ordered dejectedly over my shoulder. An array of anguished faces peered past me toward Loverly. "I'll take care of things."

It was in my job description somewhere. Dads are the ones in a family who do this type of work. I took a deep breath and walked over to the filthy, almost shapeless critter before me. As I took the first step, someone started crying again behind me. By the time I knelt in the grass next to the hapless bunny the sobs of my children echoed through our peaceful neighborhood.

There was no blood, I observed gratefully. That would make it easier on the little guys. What a shame, I thought. I gingerly slid my fingers under the still-warm body to lift him carefully into the cardboard box Tomicah had obediently fetched. The bunny had not been an easy pet – his propensity to escape from his cage was matched by his willingness to urinate behind the piano and in other almost inaccessible spots of the house – but we loved him. Loverly was incredibly soft, as white as our snowfalls and lots of fun to have around. I found myself scripting a brief eulogy in my mind. I had to keep my balance as I transferred his plump remains to the box.

In an acrobatic squirm, he flipped from my hands to the grass below.

One of the kids gave a startled yip. The others fell silent with confusion and wonder. Startled and deprived of the counterbalancing weight of the big white bunny, I fell over.

"Did you drop him?" Kimi inquired tentatively, not daring to hope. I wasn't quite sure what had happened. I scrambled onto my knees near the rabbit.

Loverly cocked his head to examine me with one wild pink eye.

"Come here, bunny," I cooed as I offered my open hands.

Hop.

Hop-hop. The rabbit gingerly moved toward me.

"He's alive!!!" Tomicah crowed. The neighborhood resounded with more screams, more sobs. The racket sounded similar to the previous cacophony, but the emotions conveyed were entirely different.

Loverly was fine. No broken bones, no abrasions. He was filthy, but apparently no harm was done. Whether he'd been sleeping, playin' possum, or unconscious, I'll never know. Charity was sure the bunny had been raised from the dead – and who am I to argue with the faith of a child? Francis also recovered almost immediately from the assault on his character and was welcomed back into the bosom of the family. The Ferrees were a little shaken, but very good sports under the circumstances. As they departed for the evening Fay said they had enjoyed dinner immensely.

Another couple of years passed in our red brick Victorian on Zenobia Street. The city was struggling economically, and we along with it. I was called to serve as the bishop of Denver's Second Ward, and with my brother and a partner I started Safeline Children's Products.

We also had a couple more kids.

The children grew in capability and sought increased independence. Annette and I held the kids accountable to most of the standards we kept ourselves. Kids who argued found the consequence was an hour spent in exile in the empty bathtub. If they had a complaint, they were called upon to express themselves in a manner that would help to solve the problem. Disrespect to either parents or siblings meant the perpetrator received an immediate assignment of extra chores, as well as an interminable, although perhaps ineffective, lecture. Our home was rarely quiet. Although the kids regularly quarreled and found fault with one another, they were all best friends. They each had companions outside the family, but when the time came to join a team, or participate in clubs, or try out for a play, they were happiest when a sibling joined in.

In March of 1989 we were blessed with a perfectly beautiful baby boy. Lincoln Justice was lively, happy, and crowned with a fuzzy mane of reddish hair – just like my father. He died in bed without warning one evening three months later. The doctors initially attributed his death to Sudden Infant Death Syndrome, but an autopsy revealed some unexplained inflamation of the lining around his heart. Perhaps a virus, they said. It really didn't matter to us.

Losing Lincoln was the most painful experience of my life. I still feel the repercussions. I find myself awake in the middle of the night and compelled to walk quietly to my youngest children's rooms. At each door, I pause to hold my own breath silent. Only after I'm able to hear each child's slumbering sighs can I again breathe easily. I know my fears are irrational, but they're not unprovoked. Kids are remarkably tough – yet their lives can be so fragile.

After Lincoln died, the level of appreciation that the kids held for one another grew even more. Shiloh, our next baby, required constant medical attention for the first two years of his life. He suffered from a rare condition called laryngomalacia which was so severe that his breathing passage would often collapse without warning. Moments later, his heart would also stop. The doctors bluntly told the family that Shiloh would die unless steps were taken each time to immediately revive him. Our HMO had oxygen bottles regularly delivered and Shiloh learned to crawl trailing his clear tubular lifeline. We kept him wired to an apnea monitor to alert us to his breathing cessations and a cardiac monitor for his bradycardia. Several times each day and night, the alarms would shriek, and Annette, I, or one of the kids would vault to his side to begin resuscitation efforts and get him started up again. It may sound odd, but we were happy to do it.

Thirty pounds of oxygen bottles and electronic monitors didn't phase the kids. Levi might grab the baby, Tomicah the oxygen cylinder, and perhaps Charity the monitors, and they'd head out through the grocery store or the mall tethered as a tight little group. Shiloh loved the attention and he started to talk a blue streak at an early age. Gradually the heart stoppages and breathing difficulties abated, and by his second birthday he was weaned from all the equipment. The only lasting effect was that, after being carried everywhere for his early years, he acquired the heft, if not the strength, of a miniature football linebacker.

Annette took care of the food, medicine and schooling. I tried to keep the bills paid. As one of our friends quipped, we seemed surrounded by insurmountable opportunities. Our challenges very nearly overwhelmed our capabilities, but somehow we managed to thrive.

159

Chapter 7

The Blessing .

Saturday Afternoon, 20 May 1995
Salt Lake City and Bountiful, Utah

Babies were everywhere. It was springtime, the sun was shining brightly, and downtown Salt Lake City must have had more strollers per capita that day than any city in North America. Most of the mothers looked as if they'd been lifted straight from a 1972 Sears catalog. Smiling, with permed hair and crisp, print dresses that just covered their knees, these women had huge, frilly strollers. The babies riding within stared with wide eyes as their mothers talked and walked together. Occasionally they would pass other mothers who seemed to have come from a parallel universe. They wore tight, black jeans and had straight, tar-and-copper-colored hair and purplish-black lipstick. These women – or to my aging eye, these girls – often smoked cigarettes and wheeled their babies about in flimsy, imported umbrella strollers.

The strollers generally captured a disproportionate amount of my attention. I rarely got out of the office, and when I did, part of my mind kept working in the baby products business. Annette seemed bemused and gratified to catch me ogling carseats and carriages when many other husbands were gawking at convertibles and cleavage. As we walked down the street or sometimes even when we were driving, I'd have the urge to glance in passing minivans and look in the back seat to identify who made the baby carrier. Every once in a while, I was gratified to see a Sit'n'Stroll.

When Annette would glance in the same direction, she focused first on the baby. She scarcely saw the plastic and cloth and metal. Today she saw lots more babies than she usually did in Denver. She absently stroked her pregnant belly as we drove slowly along the city's

160

wide streets. Normally, she loved to see all the round cheeks, tiny little hands, and sparkling eyes. I'm sure the same was true that afternoon, but her expression belied more complex emotions. She said she felt a little uneasy.

Glorianna was hungry. She'd made it clear as Annette and I departed Dr. DeVore's office that her cooperation was going to cease unless food was forthcoming immediately. We drove the rental car a few blocks west to the heart of the city. As we passed the entrance to the big downtown mall, a car pulled away and left both a prime parking spot and a fully stoked meter.

"I think they have a food court," Annette recalled. "I don't feel much like eating, but you and Glori should be able to find something."

I pulled into the space. Within moments we'd unloaded and were on our way inside. The restaurants were adjacent to the door we entered, and we found a table near one of the tall windows looking out on Temple Square. Glori was comfortable and there were no booster seats around, so I converted the Sit'n'Stroll back from a stroller to a carseat and placed her on top of the tabletop next to us. Her bright blue eyes followed the trays of food passing by with great interest. It was warm inside.

"Sweetheart," I said in a low voice as I helped Annette remove her jacket, "you may want to leave that on. You must've put your dress on backwards after the exam."

I motioned to the two front pockets now positioned behind her hips.

She shrugged her shoulders, then mustered an impish grin.

"It's been that way since we left Denver – I never took it all the way off at the doctor's office," she explained. "I love this dress, and you always say it looks nice on me. But I'm so big now, it doesn't fit frontwards. So I tried it backwards. What do ya' think?" She performed a model's pirouette, subdued but nonetheless endearing with her pockets in back and volleyball-sized dome in front.

I smiled back at her. I found Glori some cheese soup and got a veggie sub for me. I picked at the sandwich while Annette shoveled bread and soup into the baby.

"Excuse me," said one of the women from the '72 Sears catalog. She had quietly walked up without attracting our attention. "I hope I'm not bothering you, but I saw you when you came in. Is that stroller also a carseat?"

161

It happened all the time, and it could be a little humiliating: The carseat/stroller attracted more attention than the cute, curl-bedecked blonde in it. I didn't have the energy to graciously answer her, but Annette was drawn into five minutes of conversation about where to get it, how much it cost, and how I had worked together with my brother to develop it. I had to admire her stamina. Finally, the mother wheeled her own carriage away and left us, for all intents and purposes, alone.

"It doesn't sound good, does it?" I asked rhetorically. "The logical thing to do is to abort the babies. It's safer for you, and if they aren't going to make it anyway . . . "

"But we don't <u>know</u> that!" Annette interrupted emphatically. "I can feel them moving, and I want these babies so much. <u>If</u> they could make it, we'd find a way to take care of them. I'll be OK. I can't imagine doing anything to them." Her eyes shone with tears. "The little guy may already be dying, and the big one is giving his life to keep him alive. Oh, I know they aren't thinking it all out like that, but what <u>is</u> going on, Timber?" Her deep blue eyes sparkled in the sunlight streaming down through the adjacent windows, demanding an answer – but not necessarily from me. "Do we really have the right to decide that <u>we</u> should end their chance at life? They're trying so hard."

"Baby, it's apparently more complicated than that," I said quietly. "The article Dr. Porter faxed said twins conjoined like this just don't live longer than three months, even under the best circumstances. They'd be struggling that whole time. And it's not just their lives that are at stake. You're an incredible mother and teacher and wife." I was having a hard time articulating my fears.

"I don't know if I buy that stuff about my life being at risk," she said forcefully but somehow without conviction. She paused.

Outside on the broad sidewalk mothers and babies continued about their affairs. Across the street a profusion of bright flowers surrounded the soaring spires of the Salt Lake Temple. Just to the north was the complex of office buildings housing the main headquarters of the Church.

We'd spoken with Dr. DeVore for a long time before leaving his office. He was a person of great spirituality and understanding and he had urged us to seek out the counsel of those who would see the twins' problems through eyes of faith. As we sat together in the mall, Annette wanted to get the perspective of the person who had taught her the first

162

principles of the Gospel, and of his wife who'd faced similar pain when they first met.

"Do you think we can call Jeff? I'd really like to just talk with him and Pat."

Annette was an undergraduate when she first met Jeffrey and Pat Holland. He was pursuing a Ph.D. in American Studies from the grad school at Yale. Jeff taught an evening religion class sponsored by the Church. As a new convert Annette was deeply impressed with his ebullient wisdom, remarkable knowledge and profound faith. Pat was likewise brilliant and sweetly spiritual, and the young couple established a fast bond of loving friendship with the effervescent Annette. It was through Pat's miscarriage at five months – her third – that Annette learned something of the agony and bewilderment that can accompany the miracle of conception.

Once Jeff finished his Ph.D., he left New Haven and a job offer from Yale to return to Utah with Pat and their kids. He took a relatively unremarkable administrative job with the Church Education System. Annette went on to Stanford, and then returned in 1976 to Yale's Divinity School. Although she saw the Hollands infrequently, the foundation to her friendship was sure.

I was first introduced to Jeff, Pat, and two of their three kids the summer after we got married. As we drove up to their home in suburban Bountiful, I found him on his knees in the front yard. He may have been praying for help, but the gray pipes and yard tools helped convince me he was also installing a sprinkler system. I'm afraid I wasn't much of an answer to his problems. He had taught Annette the Gospel, and that afternoon he had to teach me the proper technique for solvent welding PVC tubing. It wasn't until later that evening that I began to better appreciate Jeff Holland's keen spirituality and warm humanity.

The occasion was an after-dinner fireside talk he was giving in a nearby chapel. Annette and I had been invited to join him.

"I come from St. George," he began.

Jeff was a tall man, solidly built, simultaneously handsome and slightly cherubic. He really didn't need the microphone on the podium in front of him. Most in attendance were faithful church members. Quite a few knew him well.

"St. George has earned the uncomfortable the distinction of being the hottest town in the state. Most of you know it's way down in the corner of Utah, only a couple of hours from Las Vegas. I like to think St. George is so warm because it's so far south, and it's at the lowest elevation of anyplace around here," he continued, and then he assumed a comically pained expression. "But it always kind of worried me that there are some folks who say it's so blasted hot there because it's the town in Utah that's closest to Hell."

The crowd gasped, then erupted into good-natured laughter.

That evening and many times thereafter I was deeply impressed with this man who would endear us with his self-deprecating humor and unhesitatingly bear as powerful a testimony of the divinity and mission of Christ as anyone I'd ever known. I found it quietly reassuring that in an institution as conservative and staid as the Church, Jeff experienced a meteoric rise in his assigned responsibilities. Within a few years, he was the Director of the Church Education System, and then he was appointed President of Brigham Young University. The school, which was the nation's largest private university, flourished under his stewardship. In 1994, Elder Jeffrey Holland was called as the youngest member of The Council of The Twelve Apostles, the highest governing body of the Church.

"We can try to reach them, Honey," I offered to Annette as Glori finished off her soup, "But I'd be real surprised if their number was listed. Let me call Kimi and get their number from the Rolodex."

I found a pay phone, and Kimber was able to locate the Hollands' home phone number. She wanted to know the results of the tests with Dr. DeVore, but I appeased her with the assurance that she'd get the full lowdown later that night.

Annette placed the call, and twenty minutes later we were headed north on I-15. Jeff had answered the phone. When he'd heard why we were in town, he insisted upon meeting with us immediately. He said he was happy to meet us downtown, or if we wanted to see Pat, he'd welcome us to his house. We pulled up in front of their well-tended home in a neighborhood that was probably populated by accountants, dentists, and perhaps some small businessmen. I unbuckled the baby as Annette started up the front walk ahead of us.

"Annette! Timber! And who's that beautiful little charmer? Come on in and take the load off your feet!" I looked over my shoulder to see a large figure in a crisp white shirt and dark slacks striding toward us, arms outstretched.

Although Annette had years previously coached me on the etiquette of referring to him as "Elder Holland" now that he was serving as an Apostle, the bonds of friendship and the outpouring of warmth from the Hollands were stronger than her resolve to keep her own counsel.

"Jeff – Pat!" was all she could say as she broke away and ran up the pathway to be welcomed into a loving three-way embrace. Glori snuggled her forehead into my cheek as I stood a few steps down the walk, just a little self-consciously, while Annette was bathed in the warmth of reunion and the Hollands' compassion.

Elder Jeff Holland looked over Annette's head and his eyes locked into mine. He nodded almost imperceptibly in greeting, but to me it was clearly more – it was a gesture conveying both respect and communion. If his words had been spoken, rather than expressed through that indefinable touching of souls, he would have said simply, "I'm glad you're here. I know this is hard, and I'm glad to be here with you." He held out a big, welcoming hand to me without ever quite depriving Annette of the supportive hug that meant so much to her at that moment.

"Elder Holland, thank you so – " I mustered.

"Now, quit that!" He responded with a warm smile. "I hope I'll always be 'Jeff' to you two, so just cut it out with the formal stuff. I'm just happy to see you."

I had met him personally on perhaps half a dozen different occasions, and each time I was a little stunned at how he made me feel like a long lost younger brother returning from some valiant endeavor. Jeff Holland was a man of great personal power, untainted by artifice or insecurity. His wife similarly manifest a profound appreciation of how any particular moment offered an opportunity to choose the better path. Not quite as tall as her husband, she had moved to stand in the doorway, slender and elegant. Every time I saw Pat, she seemed to be dressed for church. Her appearance and demeanor fit precisely with the image that I used to envision in my childhood mind when in a conversation someone would ask me to "remember that lovely woman who . . ."

"Please come on in," Sister Holland said graciously. "You've had a trying day, I'm sure."

We were ushered into their comfortable living room. On the wall was a large painting of irises and the calming tones of lavender, purple, green and white were subtly echoed throughout the wallpaper and upholstery. The carpet was thick and plush and Annette and I luxuriated in the serene ambiance of the home.

165

After a few digressions into our kids' activities and the whereabouts of mutual acquaintances, Elder Holland steered the discussion to the point of our visit. The Hollands listened intently as Annette told them of the events of the past few days. I did my best to fill in the technical details. It only took a few minutes to summarize what we knew.

"If we're to try to study this out, and learn all we can from this situation, then it seems there are a couple of key issues," Elder Holland analyzed. "First, are the twins alive now, spiritually united with their bodies, and struggling to make it into this world? Second, what is the proper path for you to take when it seems that continuing the pregnancy poses at least some kind of threat to you, Annette? In response to the first question, we don't have a precise answer to the question of when a spirit takes permanent possession of its body," he reflected. "The Scriptures only hint at what happens."

He grabbed a large, leather-bound volume from the credenza. "Some of what we know is just logical, and the Scriptures tell us more. Science still doesn't have a very good handle on the onset of life, but Pat tells me that when she feels the baby move in her womb, it's a profound event." The two women looked to one another with shared understanding and nodded in agreement.

"With every pregnancy, Annette's somehow been able to tell me the sex, and even the disposition, of the baby well before birth," I concurred. "There's no doubt in my mind that the spirit of an unborn child at least visits its body. Annette says she just feels it."

"Well, I was almost sure Glorianna was a boy," Annette corrected me as she gave the tousled cherub in her lap an emphatic kiss.

"OK. I forgot."

"As far as what Pat's told me, when the baby moves, it's a testimony of sorts to her that the being in her womb is alive as a person," Elder Holland continued as he leafed rapidly through the big book. "It's clearly not all that simple a medical issue, but see – In John 6, verse 63, the Savior said, 'It is the spirit that quickeneth; . . .the words that I speak unto you, they are spirit, and they are life.'

"And in Romans 8, verse 11," he continued as the pages fluttered under his practiced fingers, "We read, 'He that raised up Christ from the dead shall also quicken your mortal bodies by his Spirit that dwelleth in you.'

"And in <u>James</u>, we're told again very simply that 'the body without the spirit is dead.'

"From the way you've been talking, Annette, you clearly feel that the twins are alive. As a mother, you have a sense of their vitality. Scripturally, there's plenty to support that conclusion. I don't know that we can conclude that the spirits for the twins have taken up permanent residence in their bodies, but from what you've said, and from what we find in the scriptures, I believe there are indeed spirits associated with those bodies."

Sister Holland nodded again in agreement. She had at some point opened her own Bible. "Just look at the beginning of Jeremiah: 'Then the word of the Lord came unto me, saying, Before I formed thee in the belly I knew thee; and before thou camest out of the womb I sanctified thee, and I ordained thee a prophet unto the nations.'"

"I know," Annette said emphatically. "I don't know whether the Lord wants these children to be born alive, but I can tell you that they feel alive in me now." Her breath caught as she inhaled sharply and stared down at the pattern of the carpet. "And when the doctors tell me to terminate the pregnancy, they are asking me to kill my twins." Her eyes glistened, and the only sound in the room for a time was the firm, steady tick of their grandfather clock and the faint chirping of birds outside.

Elder Holland broke the silence. "The position of the Church on elective abortion is clear. Except in cases of rape or incest, or when the fetus isn't viable or the mother's health is in serious jeopardy, abortion is a grievous sin. Every baby is a precious, priceless creation, and we are called to be their stewards for our time as parents. A healthy mother should never choose to end the life of a healthy child.

"The concepts of stewardship and responsibility are of paramount importance in understanding the Lord's general position on parenthood," he continued, "but that's not what's in question here. In any case, I don't know of two more faithful, dedicated parents than you.

"That's the issue that we haven't talked about here: the larger issue of stewardship over your whole family. Your responsibilities extend well beyond the obligation to nurture the babies in your womb." He was focusing on Annette. "You're a wife, and the mother of a houseful of kids, Annette. You've been told by Dr. DeVore and the folks back in Denver that it's highly unlikely the twins will live to breathe even one breath. As I understand it, the medical position is that, if by some miracle they make it through delivery, they can't survive for long after that. And the doctors have told you that you are putting your welfare increasingly at risk the longer you carry them.

"This is clearly a case where, if you decide after prayerful consideration that you should terminate the pregnancy, you would have nothing but loving support from faithful members of the Church. And from me." He looked over to his wife.

"And obviously from me, too," Pat added almost without a pause. "We've spent a lot of time thinking and praying about these issues. During my last miscarriage I had massive hemorrhaging, so we've had to grapple with at least a few of the same fears and possibilities that you two are facing. In your case, the only wrong choice you could make would be if you chose not to follow the promptings of the Holy Ghost. You need the Lord's direction, and that's _all_ you really need." Her voice was tempered by experience.

Elder Holland picked up her train of thought.

"Some brilliant theologians, like Bruce McConkie, believe that we will count among the members of our eternal families every conception – miscarriages, stillborn babies, every little body that is the fruit of our union will join us in the eternities," he explained. "It's an enormously comforting doctrine to those of us who have faced this loss – as some of us have, over and over again." I saw power and intensity in his eyes as he momentarily focused on his wife, and I realized he was speaking to her as much as to us. A long, still moment passed before he resumed.

"Other people, of course, claim that a baby must take a breath of its own accord to lay claim to life, but I'm not sure that feels right to me. There's no official policy of the Church on what happens eternally to babies who never make it into this world – but that's why we're entitled to individual, personal inspiration from the Holy Ghost.

"Annette," Elder Holland's intonation shifted from instructive to solicitous. "Would you like a blessing? I'd be honored to administer to you, if you feel it would help."

A blessing received through the priesthood was distinct from personal revelation. Every worthy person was entitled to the inspiration of the Holy Ghost in times of trial. Priesthood blessings afforded additional strength and insight to those who asked, and listened, in faith. By placing his hands on her head and calling upon the power of the priesthood, the man performing the ordinance became a simple mouthpiece for the Lord. Annette knew that all blessings administered by any worthy priesthood bearer were the same in the eyes of God. Theologically, it made no difference who served as the voice for the blessing. I could administer to her with the same consequence as an Apostle. Nonetheless, emotionally, both Annette and I were enormously relieved by the prospect of hearing Jeff offer the Lord's words of comfort and direction to us in the midst of our conflicting concerns.

Elder Holland stood behind Annette and invited me to join him in laying his hands upon her head as she sat, eyes closed, in a straight-backed chair. He spoke clearly, solemnly, and without pause or apparent forethought.

Calling upon the power of the priesthood, he blessed Annette to know that her Heavenly Father cherished her and that these and the other trials she faced had a powerful eternal purpose. He blessed her to be at peace and to know that the Holy Ghost would surely speak to her and give her the assurance and direction she required as she proceeded in faith. And he blessed her to know with certainty that these twins were hers to raise up in the Millennium as members of her eternal family, from that moment onward.

" . . . and I proclaim these things," Elder Holland concluded, "with the full power and authority afforded by the Melchizedek Priesthood to me in my Apostolic calling, in the name of Our Savior, The Almighty Jesus Christ. Amen."

Annette's cheeks were streaked with tears. As she looked around, she was not alone.

"Honey, we're going to miss the plane," I prodded gently, but firmly. We were once again in the clear sunshine, now tinged with yellow as the shadows reached across the neatly mown lawn. I had buckled Glori into the back seat and was folding myself into the driver's seat of the little rental car. Annette was enthusiastically engaged in animated conversation with the Hollands as the three of them stood on the sidewalk next to the car.

"I would have thought that Greg DeVore would have ended up in New York or Chicago," Sister Holland was remarking. "He was always so good at everything he did. This has been a little Yale reunion for you today, hasn't it? And in Salt Lake, of all places!" She laughed self-effacingly.

"I'm so grateful you could see us," Annette said sincerely.

169

"I'm just amazed you caught us," Sister Holland exclaimed. "We were both gone this morning and had only been home a few minutes when you called. Now we've got to leave to attend a funeral."

"You know, the remarkable thing is that we were in town at all," Elder Holland reflected as he helped Annette into her seat and latched the car door securely. "We're traveling continually these days – especially on weekends. Pat, when was the last time we were even here on a Saturday?"

"Oh, my – It must have been six months." she calculated. "Well, anyway, we're so glad we were here today. Please keep in touch – Let us know how things go. Now, scoot! Timber's right – You'll miss your flight."

VII.   Gentle Ben

Wednesday Evening, 14 October 1989
Denver, Colorado

The office was modestly appointed. The only substantial furniture was a large, old wooden desk set diagonally into one corner. A half dozen ladder-back oak chairs were arrayed in a semi-circle around the room's periphery. The beige walls were plain, painted cinder block. There were no windows. It did have a skylight, however. Ben Sandoval was sitting directly beneath it in one of the wooden chairs. He sat with his shoulders hunched over, his hands knit together in his lap and his knees splayed apart. Ben was twelve. He was stockily built, with brown hair cut short and a lower lip that seemed to always have a crack that wouldn't heal. He sat quietly behind a shy smile that would wax and wane as he looked at me across the big desk.

"This is a big day, huh, Ben?" It was more of a comment than a question. I didn't really expect an answer. That was part of the dilemma facing both of us.

Ben grinned broadly.

"How in the world am I going to do this?" I pondered under my breath. I had known the young man across my desk since he was a toddler. Tomicah and Ben were close in age, and when Annette and I had moved to our Northwest Denver neighborhood in 1980, the two boys got to know one another as they attended the same classes in church.

"Daddy, what's the matter with Ben?" Tomicah had asked me one Sunday afternoon when he was about three years old.

The question had prompted an extended, albeit simplistic, lesson on genetics, birth defects and personality. Ben was the first Down Syndrome child that our family had an opportunity to know well. Annette had been immediately drawn to the boisterous little boy and she formed a fast bond of love and respect with his mother. I admit that I was at the outset much less comfortable with this child who was so hard to talk with, and whose reasoning processes were so different from those of the other children in my life. Still, Ben was unusually good-natured and generally a fun companion – first for Tomicah, and then for Levi, and Corban. As each of our sons grew older and made new friends, Ben would shift his attention to the next younger child down the line in the Tillemann-Dick household. When he was eight or nine, he announced that he was going to marry Kimi. She was flattered, and even though she never accepted his proposal she remained his heart's desire. For reasons that defy simple explanation, Ben became virtually a member of the family.

Enmeshed therein lay the bittersweet choice confronting me. Six months earlier, I had been called to serve as the unpaid lay minister of our congregation. As bishop of the Denver Second Ward I was the formal, local authority for roughly eight hundred members of the Church of Jesus Christ of Latter Day Saints in our corner of the city. If my buddies from high school could see me now, I had mused. In high school I certainly would not have been voted "The Most Likely to be Made a Bishop."

After failing at New College and in the months prior to leaving for New Haven I spent a lot of time pondering the elements of success. It was to me a paradox that my worldly accomplishments were unrelated to any enduring sense of well-being. A new sales record at the radio station afforded no companionship. A patent on my invention was just an abstraction represented by a piece of paper. Yet these were celebrated, while the human interactions that gave me honest pleasure went unheralded. I craved meaning in my life but I had no idea where a commitment to build a positive, constructive life would lead. I decided I really didn't care. My guts told me the path ahead was the right one.

Nonetheless, at the conclusion of my first year at Yale I would never have believed a crystal ball showing me a dozen years hence seated in a windowless office, not just as a Mormon, but as a bishop.

Annette and I often reflected wryly upon the fact that while I served as the local church leader, she was the one who had earned a Master of Arts in Religion from Divinity School. Annette had joined the Church while she was a new student at Yale – three years before we met – and she long ago reached an inner assurance that the Church functioned with an appropriate division of responsibility. The Church's doctrine precluding women from holding offices in the priesthood was consistent with her understanding of how the Lord's organization was first established. If Sarah, Esther and Mary were content to have their men bear the burden of the priesthood's responsibilities, then it was acceptable to her.

Perhaps her transition from non-practicing Jew to an active member of the Church was made easier by the many commonalities she saw in the two faiths. Even though her father wasn't particularly observant, the traditional, patriarchal structure of the Torah was echoed in her home as a child. The powerful role her father played in her life was typical of many Eastern European families. As she grew into young adulthood her search for faith led her to investigate the Church. She found there a set of beliefs that were essentially consistent with the Jewish heritage she knew and loved – plus a recognition that Jesus Christ was the promised Messiah. When she accepted the challenge to pray to receive a confirmation of this Restored Gospel, she obtained a personal conviction that it was true.

After she graduated from Yale College she had applied to and was accepted by the graduate schools of Divinity at Yale and Harvard. Once back at Yale, she found her new faith offered her unique insights into her studies. Nonetheless, she couldn't share the professional aspirations of her classmates. She was a gifted scriptorian, but in the Church of Jesus Christ leaders are called to positions not by a weighing of their credentials but through a process of prayerful deliberation. The Church functions with a lay ministry. There was no professional path leading from the Div School to a position in the ministry of the Church. As the only Mormon in the school, she was there primarily to grow in faith and knowledge. Her Div School peers had the added goal of advancing their careers.

So here I was a decade later, serving as the bishop, qualified not by my education but by a commitment to do the will of the Lord. Annette, who was my superior in formal theological training and at least my equal in her desire and ability to serve, held no priesthood calling. Instead, she served capably and faithfully as a teacher of gospel doctrine to the adults, as an administrator in the children's organization and – especially – as a mother.

Although there were those both within and outside the Church who hotly debated issues such as the efficacy of a lay clergy and the granting of priesthood callings to women, that quiet October night I faced a new twist on the question of who should hold ecclesiastical office in the Church. Ben Sandoval's smiling willingness to serve presented me with a dilemma that I found particularly perplexing.

Upon reaching the age of twelve, young men in the Church are offered the opportunity to be ordained to a position in a preparatory priesthood. If the young man is found in an interview with his bishop to be morally worthy and appropriately knowledgeable, he assumes the responsibilities of a deacon. Ben was probably as ready that night as he would ever be for his ordination interview.

"OK, buddy, do you know why you're here?" I inquired gently.

"Yesss," Ben responded. Twisting and wringing his hands, he smiled even more broadly. He squirmed in the slick wooden chair, slouching down as he beamed across the desk at me.

"Do you want to be a deacon?"

He grinned so broadly that his cheeks rose to meet his eyebrows and the bright buttons of his eyes almost disappeared into joyful squints.

"Yessss!"

I had little doubt about Ben's sincerity. He loved the Church. He begged his family to take him to every meeting and activity. He didn't like school and he drove his Mom crazy at home, but he was wildly enthusiastic about almost everything connected with church.

"What does a deacon do?"

"Passa sacrament!" came the immediate reply.

"Good!"

Pretty good, anyway, I thought. I reflected on the events of the Sunday three weeks before. It had been a lovely, sunny day. Sacrament service was just beginning to get underway. As I stood at the podium, the Sandoval kids were sitting together with Annette and our family near the front of the room. I cleared my throat.

"Welcome, everyone. It's good to have you with us. There will be a baptism tonight at the Green Mountain building . . ."

A muffled scream interrupted my opening announcements. I had quickly glanced around the room, searching the faces of the startled Saints for the source of the confusion and alarm. Ben's eight-year-old sister, Mara, could be a chatterbox, but usually she was well behaved. Now, however, she gave a small, strangling noise. She staggered out of her place in the pews and bolted sobbing from the chapel.

The customary background drone of chitchat in the chapel uneasily subsided. Ben, who was very protective of Mara (at least when she wasn't begging him to leave her alone), promptly heightened the sense of impending chaos by abruptly standing up and running out in hot pursuit while yelling something unintelligible. The Denver Second Ward wasn't well known for its reverence, but this kind of disturbance was highly unusual. A few kids snickered, and the adults in the congregation looked up to the podium for guidance. Within seconds, even as I motioned to one of the youth leaders in the front row to follow the two kids and find out what was happening, Ben reappeared in the front aisle between me and the congregation. He stood wringing his hands as he looked pleadingly, first at the wide-eyed church-goers seated before him and then, as he turned, he focused up at me.

"Oh, man, thisziz terrible!" Ben had bawled, and then he stormed out the door on the opposite side of the room, slamming it behind him with a thunderous, wall-rattling wham. Bits of dust filtered down on the congregation from the lighting fixtures overhead.

For once, the crowded chapel was silent. I shoved the announcements into my counselor's flustered hands and headed out the door after Mara. It took perhaps five minutes to piece together the events of those few moments, and then I spent a similar period presenting the somewhat embarrassing explanation to the mystified congregation. The sacrament service never did revert to a sense of normalcy that day.

In some respects, it had been all my fault. I like gadgets. I love my wife. I was a little worried that, with all the time I was spending at work and fulfilling my church responsibilities, I wasn't taking care of Annette as I should have been. She needed something to protect her when I was working late, something that would afford her reliable security when I was not at her side. And, really, the little gadget I purchased for her was a great solution. Even Mara thought so – at least at first. In an effort to quiet the kids in the minutes before services

174

began, Annette had asked Mara to find and distribute some mints that were in her purse. Mara had been bored by my announcements, but was fascinated by the intriguing gift she found in my wife's handbag: a self-defense tear gas key ring. It took her only a moment to twist the nifty little safety release open, and only a moment more to experience firsthand just how effective the stinging aerosol was.

I had found her unhurt but whimpering at the drinking fountain as her mother helped to splash cold water on her face. I joined her mother's efforts to comfort her and then realized that Ben was upset and still unattended. The faces of the congregation turned in unison when I transited the aisle across the front of the chapel. With an apologetic shrug I proffered a few reassuring words to them and trotted down the hall in search of Ben. I finally spotted him in an alcove with his head buried in the corner. He was dazed, confused, and completely at a loss as to what had happened to Mara.

"It's OK, Ben," I had said soothingly, but no explanation seemed to help him to understand what had hurt his sister so deeply.

The events of that recent Sacrament service flashed through my thoughts as I looked at Ben in the rapidly fading glow of the skylight. He was sitting alertly, excited and full of all the power and enthusiasm of a twelve-year-old. He knew why he was there to meet with me and he was eager to get on with the evening's business.

But there were many aspects of his life that Ben would perhaps never understand. At age twelve, his speech was often incomprehensible. He couldn't read at all. There were times when he would sit next to Tomicah, enthusiastically singing nonsense words as he held the hymnal upside-down. Second only to whichever of my children that was his current intellectual peer, his favorite playmates were the Barbie dolls that gave him unending delight.

In many regards, Ben was a twelve-year-old toddler. I had grown to love him, and as my initial uneasiness abated I would take quiet pride in his mischievous explanation to friend and stranger alike that "Thisiz my Daaad!" Annette was happy to have him over to play with our kids, in part because he never drew them into activities that were sordid. His enduring romantic devotion toward Kimi was completely chaste. He'd do things that were perhaps silly and occasionally stupid, but he steadfastly avoided the moral pitfalls that trapped many of his more capable peers. He was a sweet, good kid.

In spite of the chasm separating us – a gap of perception and conception, of age and intellect – Ben challenged me to acknowledge and accept our spiritual kinship. It was a challenge both Annette and I embraced, and when Ben impishly demanded, "Call me <u>son</u>!" we felt his little game had profound meaning. As I sat with Ben that Wednesday evening and contemplated his conspicuous limitations, I realized that I had developed a deep respect for both his spirit and his capabilities. But that night, Ben and I shared a profound responsibility to discern whether he could realistically bear the burdens of the preparatory priesthood he sought.

"Ben, what's this?" I held up a copy of the scriptures.

"S'a Bible."

"And what's in The Bible?"

"S'about Jesus! N'all He did, n'what <u>you</u> gotta do, if yer g'na be good. 'Sgot lotsa stories!" His words came fast and sure, and Ben straightened his posture to assume an air of authority that left no doubt that he knew <u>exactly</u> what he was talking about.

Later that night, Annette's impossibly blue eyes followed my every move as I wearily untangled my tie from the button-down collar of my shirt. She was already in our bed, reading. I sat down heavily next to her and struggled to pull off my boots.

"How'd it go with Ben?" she inquired.

"After all these years, I keep learning more about him," I replied. "It seems like, when he gets mad or irrational, a lot of it comes from being incredibly frustrated by facing, day after day, some insurmountable barrier to communication. I'm convinced he's able to listen and comprehend things a whole lot better than he can express himself to us." I paused to collect my impressions. "At times, I get this sense that parts of his spirit are every bit as competent as mine. There's just something in him that makes it <u>so hard</u> for him to get through to others. But I'm still not sure whether it's appropriate to ordain him to the priesthood."

It goes with saying that in most religions Ben's priesthood ordination would never have been considered. It was immediately apparent to even a casual observer that he was severely limited in his mental faculties. Intellect, however, was not a major criterion for the decision I had to make. Just as I needed no academic degree to serve as a bishop, Ben's ability to advance in the priesthood required more in the way of courage and commitment than it did any minimum score on an IQ test. Jesus chose fishermen and laborers as His disciples. The training of the Pharisees and scribes afforded them no special capabilities in the Lord's eyes. In the Bible, the priesthood was open to all worthy males. The doctrine of the Church of Jesus Christ stipulates that of paramount importance is a simple willingness to obey the commandments and serve diligently. Ben wanted to travel the path that countless other young men had followed in their attempt to live their faith. I deeply respected his resolve.

"Wait a second," she urged gently. "How much do you trust Ben – on spiritual matters, I mean?"

"Actually, in a lot of ways, I trust him <u>more</u> than some of the guys who are now deacons," I reflected, and stood to hang up my shirt and trousers. "He knows right and wrong, and when he's bad he's really sorry. He's less calculating than some other kids."

I couldn't help staring at the soft contours of her shoulder and the exquisite sculpting of her neck where her long blonde curls flowed down her cheek. As she reclined on the pillows before me, her slender curves offered just a hint that she was carrying our seventh child. She was, I thought for the ten- thousandth time, remarkably beautiful. A dozen years of loving service as co-worker, wife, and mother to six lively kids had not diminished her appeal. I suddenly found it hard to conduct a coherent conversation. After a moment's indulgence in just contemplating the woman in my bed, however, I forced my thoughts back to the matter at hand. The wisdom behind Annette's inquiry was dawning upon me.

"Ben <u>wants</u> to be a deacon. He's committed to keeping the Commandments and he seems capable of doing the work. I guess he deserves to be a deacon as much as a lot of kids," I concluded.

"I agree."

"He can do it, don't you think?"

"Mmmm – humm," she nodded affirmatively. "He's a good boy – better than most out there. Pray about it," she instructed, and then she smiled in a way that unambiguously expressed her desire to move on to a new subject.

Chapter 8

Shadow and Light

Saturday Evening, 20 May 1995
Denver, Colorado

At the subdued sound of tires crunching on gravel, Annette's eyes fluttered open. She hadn't really been sleeping. The drive back from Denver's flashy new international airport was a lot longer than the fifteen minute jaunt to Stapleton Field that she was accustomed to. The rhythmic thump of the wheels on the concrete panels of the highway seemed to act upon her like a mild sedative. It had been dark when we'd left that morning for Salt Lake. Now it was nearing midnight as we nosed into the alley to park the car behind the house. She was clearly exhausted. As I pulled the minivan into its place next to the apple tree and turned off the engine, she blinked and surveyed the area in an attempt to orient herself.

I peeled off my glasses and tried to relieve some of the day's strain by massaging my eyes. When my vision refocused, I found Annette staring at our big white house. The dogs were inside, so the only perceptible sounds were some indefinable metallic tinking noises from the motor as it cooled and Glori's measured breathing as she slept in her Sit'n'Stroll.

"Let's not go in yet," Annette entreated. "I want to talk with you just a little more before we discuss all this with the kids."

"They've probably gone to sleep," I calculated. "We've got church tomorrow, and they didn't know how late we'd get home."

I rested my hand on my wife's smooth forearm and studied her face. The automatic outdoor light I had installed above the parking area had been triggered by the arrival of the minivan. Its harsh glare cut

178

through the windshield but left her half obscured. Her cheeks and chin were pale in the light's beam, her eyes colorless in shadow. Annette's gaze was focused not on me, but inward.

"Why is this happening, Timber? I still don't know if I fully understand."

As a young man in college I had been captivated by the same question in a wholly different context.

Why?

My children asked me incessantly about almost everything: Why? I struggled to find the right responses. But for every answer I offered to satisfy them, they could always look past my wisdom to ask yet again: Yes – but why, Daddy? It was the ultimate recursive query.

Why?

Because the cells didn't divide properly.

Because one twin is keeping his brother alive, and they can't be separated.

Because they probably can't live outside the protection of the womb.

Because carrying them could even kill their mother.

Because – when you understand it – they were conceived with one heart.

"Timber, did we do something?" Annette's plaintive inquiry drew me once again to my place in the car. "Why is this happening? Why is it happening to us?"

I had no answer. I had to answer her.

"Maybe – but I don't think so. If life were so simple – " I stalled out.

"I know – at least I hope you're right." She was more pensive than self-critical. "But I don't want to be so arrogant that I just assume I'm blameless, or that there's nothing I'm supposed to learn here." Her emotional stability helped me to focus on the spirit of her question. Then she began to glance nervously about like a cornered colt. "I'm finding it incomprehensible that we have to consider – – consider ending their lives before they've even begun." Her eyes shone.

"Well, let's talk about it." Her nearly instantaneous transition from reflection to tears scared me. I knew I was too tired to gracefully handle this kind of talk if it wandered too far unbridled. We were both traversing an emotional knife-edge ridge, with fear threatening us on the

179

one side and self-pity looming on the other. If the discussion could be steered rationally, we might avoid the beckoning abyss of fatigue, guilt and stress. Caution was in order.

"First, we can feel a little better in that there doesn't seem to be anything either of us did medically or biologically to cause this. I mean, the doctors insist this is a completely random occurrence."

"That's not what I meant."

"I know," I continued. "I'm just trying to get my thoughts organized. My point is just that we didn't provoke this by eating the wrong thing or not taking the right vitamin, or whatever – So if there's a cause and effect, or a lesson here, it's gotta be deeper. Let me get back to your question: Did we do something?" I was straining my battle-fatigued brain to analyze our situation.

"It's hard to even say it, but I think you're really asking whether we're being punished – whether one or both of us has caused this because we've offended the Lord, or something like that." As I spoke, the car was plunged into darkness. It took me a moment to realize the automatic timer on the light outside had run out. Paradoxically, as my eyes adjusted I realized I could see better in the natural light of the night. Enough moonlight reflected off the broad expanse of the white walls in front of us that Annette's eyes were lit by just a hint of amethyst. She looked to me expectantly.

"Neither one of us has been behaving perfectly lately," I confessed. "You've been better than I have – the stress of everything going on at Safeline's killing me, and I know I've been a grouch at home. I'm sorry about being a jerk, too – But I can't believe that's why this is all happening. Think about it: We've been bad in the past – fighting, or whatever – but that's part of most marriages, at least to some extent. Lots of people have been worse. A lot worse, and nothing like this happens to them. This is a pretty scary situation and if it was a punishment – well, it just doesn't seem to fit our crimes, if you know what I mean." I hoped what I lacked in eloquence I made up with some measured common sense. "And look: Should we consider Ben's life a punishment, or a blessing?"

"That's a ridiculous question, Timber," she replied firmly.

"To us it is, but not to some people. And I guess that's my point. If we truly believe that all things can work together for good, then I think we're wrong to fear that this is some kind of punishment for us. The Lord just doesn't seem to work that way."

180

"So I still have to ask why this is happening – What are we supposed to learn?" She was firmly persistent. "There has to be some good that comes out of this. There has to be a reason, doesn't there?"

"Maybe we need to start by taking a big step back," I suggested. "Look at us: We've been incredibly blessed. I love you so much, and we love the kids – and they love us. We're kind of stressed out sometimes, but basically we're happy and healthy. Honey, do you realize that by the time I was Levi's age, I'd cracked my head open seven times and broken at least a dozen bones? I'd fallen out of a moving car and nearly been electrocuted a couple of times. I think about what I put my poor mom through, and then I look at our kids. They've hardly had anything like that happen to them."

"That's not entirely true," Annette responded carefully. "Glori could have died from that virus she got right after she was born – that RSV thing."

"I know. I've thought about that over the past few days. And Mercina got that horrible infection, too." When she had been barely a toddler, an opportunistic bacteria had covered Mercina with oozing sores. She had lain bandaged and intubated as the doctors administered massive doses of antibiotics in an attempt to control the infection ravaging her little body. Annette stayed with her in the hospital for the better part a week. It was terrifying, but Mia suffered no lasting effects – not even a scar.

"Annette, I'm covered with scars. If you X-ray me, it looks like I got hit by a truck. You have to wear your contact lenses and I'm so blind I couldn't see a car that was about to run me over – and yet not one of the kids needs glasses. Our kids barely have cavities. I'm exaggerating, but only a little. Even Shiloh. We came so close to losing him, but you'd never know it to see him today."

When Shiloh was a couple of weeks old, Annette had traveled with him to Canada to visit her aging grandmother. She'd been there only a day when the little guy began to gag and choke without provocation. Initially the doctors at Vancouver's Children's Hospital thought he had contracted a virus. His breathing difficulties were attributed to the associated diminished pulmonary function. He was admitted to the hospital for several days, but Shiloh seemed to respond well to treatment and he was sent home. Annette immediately hopped on a Denver-bound plane with him. She arrived terribly tired and still recovering from labor and delivery, so the night they came home I sat in

181

a big chair in the living room with my blond baby boy in my lap. It was late, and I was similarly exhausted from the workload at Safeline plus caring for the whole household while Annette was gone.

Late in the night as I had dozed in the overstuffed chair I realized something was terribly wrong. I'd convinced myself Shiloh was fine, that the doctors had released him and he was just fine. But it seemed like he wasn't breathing. I squeezed his pallid cheeks and shook him gently as I examined him more closely. He again seemed fine. Unnerved, I watched him closely until exhaustion again seduced me. A strange snorkling sound jolted me awake. He struggled to inhale until I lifted him to my shoulder – and then he sweetly drifted back to sleep.

The cycle repeated. I refused to believe what was happening. Five – fifteen – forty times I had to lift him, squeeze him, and put him up on my shoulder where he'd gasp and gag and cough – and then his breathing would again seem completely normal. I spent the night in a wretched fog of fear and fatigue, living an unrelenting nightmare of bad judgment and desperate rationalization.

Shiloh couldn't be so sick. Not like Lincoln. Not two in a row. That never happened. And then I'd look at him laying peacefully in my lap. So still.

Completely still.

"So where does Lincoln fit in?" She sat calmly next to me in the darkened car.

I was grateful for Annette's interruption. They never tell you in church or childbirth class that every parent lives with a secret dread they'll somehow hurt their child. Shortly after my brother had his first son he phoned me, fearful and tentative. He'd just heard a report on the radio that a man in our corner of town had backed a minivan over their toddler, killing him. He had to be sure it wasn't us. For the first time in his life he was feeling the hidden, hard edge of the burden of parenting, the sharp part that unexpectedly cuts into your sense of well-being, the part that hurts. What makes the fear real is its immediacy. In a moment we can do the unthinkable. Our enemies are many: Distraction. Rage. Neglect. Misjudgment. As their primary guardians, we're uniquely situated to be our kids' worst threat. Most parents are wise enough to avoid dwelling on the thought that we might fail utterly to do our job – but the possibility's always there, menacing but concealed, gleaming like an unexpected glimpse of a polished blade at the carnival.

I only thought about that night with Shiloh when I felt forced to. It had been one of the most horrifying of my life – especially in hindsight. My determination to nurse him through those long hours myself instead of calling 9-1-1 was inexcusable. It was a miracle he survived. When I finally phoned at 8 AM the doctor told us to bring Shiloh in immediately. It took a team of specialists two weeks shuttling in and out of the Intensive Care Unit to diagnose the problems with his larynx and heart. It took the little guy almost two years to grow out of his affliction. Now he was fine. Smart. Fun. Healthy. I wished we could say the same for Lincoln.

"Lincoln's a lot like the twins," I reflected. "Nobody hurt him. He was wanted and loved and cared for every minute of his life. And I don't really understand why he's gone."

"But we do, Timber." Annette was gentle in her contradiction. "We've grown to understand at least some of the purpose behind his life. And think: how many times have we been able to comfort other parents who've lost babies of their own? How many times has our understanding of Lincoln's death enabled us to help others – and ourselves – to better understand the importance of viewing this life from an eternal perspective? And really," she paused as the faint amethyst of her eyes shone into the darker corners of my soul, "Haven't we both been more committed, and more obedient, since he died? We both want to be together with him eternally – and so his death has made us better people. I don't think that's why he died, but I can see a lot of blessings that happened only because we lost him. That makes sense, doesn't it?"

"Uh-huh," I agreed. "And maybe you've just made my point. Every life seems to have its share of pain – even the Savior's. He suffered to save us from our suffering, and we need to feel at least some of life's pain to appreciate and understand what He did for us. Each of the children we've been given is extraordinary. Any suffering we've experienced has been far outweighed by the good in our lives.

"Honey, we need to search for the reason – for the benefit – of the twins' lives. It's there. There's no question in either of our minds that the Lord has a purpose here, and I'm quite sure he fully intends for something good to be the result of what we're going through."

My remarks prompted her eyes to narrow slightly in the dim light. She tilted her head thoughtfully.

"Sometimes I forget that we already have answers to some of these questions. Are my scriptures in the diaper bag?" Annette twisted

183

around in her seat to dig in the canvas sack next to Glori's carseat. In a moment she had the Bible open on her lap. I flicked on the overhead light. Its even glow was comforting, illuminating.

"Here. Read this." She handed me the thick gilt-edged volume. It was opened to St. John, Chapter 9:

> And as Jesus passed by, he saw a man who
> was blind from his birth. And his disciples asked him,
> saying, Master, who did sin, this man or his parents, that
> he was born blind? Jesus answered, Neither hath this
> man sinned, nor his parents: but that the works of God
> should be made manifest in him.

"That answers my question, at least for now," she continued softly, respectfully. Then her voice became more affirmative. "I want to name them. I want to name the bigger one Christian Gabriel, because he's giving his life for his brother, and the little one Jefferson Thomas, after Jeff Holland, and my dad, and Thomas Jefferson," she said definitively, with her own peculiar logic.

"I like those names," I replied sincerely, but without clearly focusing on what she meant. "We need to pray about this. I mean, before we talk to the kids, we owe it to them to try to get some resolution on what we're going to do. We've done just about everything we can do to study it all out. Now we just need to make sure we're doing what the Lord wants us to do."

"So what do you think we should pray about? What do you think we should do?"

"Oh, Honey," I replied, pleading for understanding. "I asked Dr. DeVore, and he said nowadays a lot of one-pound babies survive. That's so tiny! Four quarter-pounder hamburger patties stacked up." I cupped my hands together to approximately the size I envisioned.

"Don't be gross." Annette scowled.

"I didn't mean to be gross. I just mean that – well, a generation ago, a baby that weighed two pounds and pulled through was pretty much a miracle. Now babies half that size live and are healthy. Twenty-six weeks old and they can live outside the womb. These guys are already bigger than that, and they're almost that old. As I sat on the plane tonight, I replayed over and over what the doctors have said about aborting them. The logical side of me says this is a no-brainer. Even if they make it through birth, it doesn't sound like they'd have a decent life. I don't think we want to see them suffer. But I can't even think about it. Honey, the bottom line is I can't bring myself to even suggest to you that we ask the Lord to bless a decision to end the pregnancy now. I mean, if you feel we should terminate, then I totally respect your decision. Obviously that's the smart thing to do, and this is ultimately your decision." I was rambling.

"Thank you so much," she tenderly interrupted.

"Hunh?"

"Thank you. Thank you so much, Timber. It seems like almost everyone we've talked to wants to devalue their lives – just because they'll have problems. I'm so grateful that you care for them as much as I do. I can't pray and ask God to let us kill them. Maybe we'll have to get an abortion, but I think we should first choose to <u>try</u> to let them live. I can't have our first choice be to condemn them to die."

"We don't have to act immediately," I said cautiously. "Dr. Porter said we have about a week more before they'd grow so big that we'd need to terminate by some kind of procedure that's a lot harder on you – I forget what it's called – but in any case, we don't have to do anything for a few days."

"Can we pray about that plan?" she asked. "I'd really rather tell the kids we're going to try to make this work."

She didn't wait for an answer from me. Instead she leaned across the seat to tenderly seal our pact with a kiss.

VIII. Theopolis

1987-1994
Denver, Colorado

The first time either of us remembers seeing the big, white house we were out jogging. Annette and I had developed an exercise regimen that involved jogging about as frequently as a lot of folks attend church: Around the major holidays we'd get very energetic, but during the rest of the year we'd put on our running shoes only when we felt particularly moved to repent. As was the case in several areas of our life together,

185

Annette was more committed and I was more in need. Although we both got plenty of activity chasing after the kids and taking care of our home, occasionally we'd each find a bulge or wrinkle that we were sure would be banished by a series of good workouts. Out from the closet would come the tennis shoes and sweatpants and we'd try to pound along for a mile or two together before breakfast. After a couple of weeks the bulges would temporarily retreat and the demands on our respective schedules would advance to the point that the jogging shoes could retire for another season.

"Look at that place!" I panted to Annette as we jogged through the early morning sunlight along the tree-lined street. We slowed and then stopped to peek through a gap in the profusion of lilac bushes shielding the front of the property from traffic.

"I must have driven along here a hundred times going to and from the Sandoval's," Annette said quizzically, "And I don't remember noticing this place. It's beautiful."

The stately but aging house was located on a pleasant, residential avenue less than a mile from our first home in Northwest Denver. It was set well back from the street atop a low rise. The property occupied much of the block, and was bordered by a bank of dense lilacs punctuated by flowering crab apple trees along the sidewalk. Deeper in, a dozen oak, elm and maple trees towered over the broad expanse of lawn. Half hidden by the profusion of greenery, a series of stone steps climbed toward the yard from the sidewalk where we stood sweating. We cautiously climbed up to the point where they met a brick walkway that curved away toward the front door.

The structure was pleasantly symmetrical. The central mass was two very tall stories high and topped by a Mediterranean-style red tile roof. Three large arches across the main facade were supported by massive white columns, and the entrance consisted of a single door in the center. In front was an expansive raised porch reached by either of two curved staircases that cradled a brick-paved courtyard.

Angling back from this center block of the house were two wings on the main level, each apparently one story tall with harmonious tile roofs. Upon closer examination, however, we saw that the whole building was recessed into the crest of the hill which fell away to the rear of the house. While the wings were on the same level as the main entry, they were themselves two stories tall, with the second story descending toward the rear, rather than reaching the same level as the

186

center of the structure. While obviously classic in design, the house was unusual in that it was provided with an abundance of windows, from narrow slits reminiscent of a European castle to broad expanses of glass that dominated whole walls.

It was distinctive yet timeless, massive but graceful, detailed but not ornate, impressive but reserved.

"Ya'know, I really hate the thought of moving – but if we were ever going to move, it'd be a lot easier to face if we were moving in here," I told Annette. She nodded agreeably.

The property's appeal was captivating. Once we knew it was there, we found ourselves noticing it every time we drove by. A few months later Annette saw a white-haired woman clearing weeds from the front steps. She pulled to a stop, jumped out of the car and struck up a conversation.

Her name was Jessie and yes, the house was hers. She invited Annette to stroll around the grounds as they talked for perhaps twenty minutes, first about the house and gardening and then about Jessie's family – or lack thereof. She was divorced from her late husband, a dentist who used to have his office in the lower level of the big house. They were childless. She lived with a couple of boarders. Jessie evidently took a liking to Annette – she invited her back anytime.

Annette's schedule was full enough that she returned only infrequently. Since we'd made our decision to teach the kids at home she was pretty well booked with their classes, activities and field trips. Still, anytime she was taking Ben home and saw Jessie outside, if she had a few minutes to spare she would pull over and chat. They developed a pleasant, if not deep, friendship over the next couple of years.

By 1991 we had seven of our own kids living at home, plus Dulcia, an orphan we'd taken in from Honduras and another brother and sister whose parents were getting divorced. We had kids tucked in every corner of the house. We were cramped but surprisingly content.

The venture to manufacture and market the Sit'n'Stroll carseat/stroller was lurching off the ground. We had passed all the safety tests and were finally in production. Sales were hesitant but growing and the press reviews were exceptionally positive. Finances were tight but my partners were confident that the company would soon fly.

"There's an estate sale this weekend at Jessie's house – the big white one," Annette announced one evening as I arrived home for dinner. "Jessie isn't living there anymore."

187

"Wow – Is she OK?"

"Well, kind of. It's a wild story." She answered my questions as we set the table.

On the last several trips over to Ben's, Annette had noticed a sheet of paper taped to the front door of the house. Annette got curious enough to run up the front walkway and see what it said. It had a phone number and a brief explanation that deliveries should be directed to the neighbor across the street. Since she had a few minutes and was concerned about Jessie's welfare, she knocked on the neighbor's door. The woman who answered – Katie – was gracious and forthcoming. As Annette inquired about Jessie, Katie nodded knowingly.

Katie had grown increasingly worried about Jessie with each visit to her house. Katie was soon convinced that one of her boarders was trying to wrest legal control of the property from the elderly woman. One day while she was visiting, Katie noticed an official-looking paper on the floor. It was a copy of a formal power of attorney which gave the boarder and his girlfriend full authority over Jessie's assets. Katie asked Jessie why she had signed it.

"I didn't," Jessie replied blankly. "I would never do that." Yet her signature was on the paper.

Katie and Dorothy – another neighbor – went with Jessie to her attorney. Jessie's mental state was still lucid but deteriorating. At Jessie's request they established a trust and she was named the beneficiary. When the boarder and his girlfriend tried to challenge them in court, the judge sided with Jessie's lawyer and Katie. It took another two months to evict the guy and then to get a restraining order against him as he continued to hang around the house. Shortly thereafter Katie had come to the front door to check on Jessie and had heard what sounded like cascading water inside. Jessie was baffled when asked about the noise. Katie explored and soon found a small torrent overflowing from an upstairs bathtub. It had caused the plaster ceiling to collapse on the main floor. The water drained to a small lake at the foot of the ground floor stairs before streaming out the back door. The bathtub must have been running for days to have done so much damage. Jessie had either ignored it or hadn't noticed.

Clearly Jessie could no longer safely live alone. The confusion and bewilderment that Annette had noticed years before had given way to full-blown Alzheimer's. She had been moved to a comfortable nursing home nearby.

The house was soon to be listed for sale but wasn't yet on the market. Jessie's lawyer had already been approached by a firm that wanted to convert the home into a halfway house for drug offenders and another potential buyer who wanted to use it as a "Wedding Palace." Katie was hoping for a buyer who wanted it as a home, but it would be a tough sell. The house had been neglected for years. It was in need of extensive repairs and the local real estate market was in the doldrums.

A few days later Annette and I visited Katie. We eagerly accepted to her offer to walk us through Jessie's home. The big, white house was an amazing place. Just inside the front door was a broad, sunny room with vaulted ceilings like those in a church. The living room could have been designed for waltzes, with several alcoves and a massive brick fireplace. Twin polished walnut columns eleven feet high guarded the entrance to the dining room. Crystal chandeliers hung everywhere – except in the three kitchens. The west wing had been used as the dentist's office. It had a darkroom for developing X-rays and a derelict laboratory with real teeth scattered about the counter. The exterior walls consisted of two solid feet of masonry and concrete. We immediately dubbed one basement room "the Bomb Shelter" because there was little doubt in my mind that it would survive anything short of a nuclear blast.

There was no denying that inside and out the house was in rough shape. The gutters were hanging loose, several windows were shattered, and the hardwood floors were pitted and stained. There were large areas where the ceiling's plaster crunched beneath our feet. Jessie had obviously loved to hang pictures. The spalled nail holes and pockmarks on almost every vertical surface reminded me of a building I'd seen that was used for live-ammunition SWAT team exercises. The place had last been decorated in the dark browns, reds and pinks of the stylish, slightly psychedelic Sixties. The halls and anterooms were muddy blue or dirty aquamarine. Just looking at the paint was enough to induce a bad hangover.

After twenty minutes poking around, I pulled Annette aside.

"I love this place!"

Katie said the architect was one of the most distinguished in early Denver's history. Originally built in 1908 as a elegant country home near the city, it was used for many years as a retreat for nuns in need of a respite. Then Jessie and her husband had lived there for almost forty years. With the help of a full-time gardener, Dr. Schloss had meticulously kept the acre of grounds pruned and planted, but the property was now underwatered and overrun with weeds. The doors were ready to fall off the big garage in back. I kicked at the grass sprouting through the brick walkway and squeezed Annette's hand tightly as we walked back to the car.

It took almost a year to work out the details with Jessie's lawyer. It was his job to protect the interests of Jessie's trust, but I began to wonder if some of the delays in our negotiations were due to the fact that he was getting paid by the hour. We were blessed to have Katie and Dorothy involved as trustees. Once they were convinced that our kids wouldn't be swinging from heights of the big oak in front or shooting all the birds with BB guns, they became enthusiastic supporters of our attempt to buy the house.

A consulting engineer that examined the structure said the flaws were almost all cosmetic. It wasn't just the bomb shelter that was well built, he said. The whole building was constructed to withstand centuries of use.

Annette's dad had a hard time seeing any appeal behind the defects. He arranged for us to meet with a noted local architect to evaluate the property. As we sat together on the front steps of the gracious front entrance and surveyed the huge elms of the grounds, I asked the architect's opinion.

"Well, the best use of the property would be to subdivide it into six or eight parcels. Then you could knock down the existing buildings and take out most of these trees. It'd be a great site for some nice mid-sized homes," he speculated as he framed the new houses between his outstretched hands.

Annette and I respectfully declined the use of his services.

We were still shoehorned into our home on Zenobia Street. Shiloh's health had stabilized and the kids were all growing to fill their allotted nooks and crannies more snugly with each passing day. Occasionally familial tensions would get near the bursting point, but we were coping remarkably well.

In the midst of Safeline's turbulent ascent I finally worked out a plan that was acceptable to the lawyer. We would lease the white house for a year and secure our purchase option with a sizable, non-refundable earnest payment. We would share the expenses of repairing and upgrading the house, and I could use the time to persuade a lender to provide a mortgage. At the end of the year we would close on the purchase or be forced to walk away from it all.

The deal would risk essentially everything we owned. The only way I could swing the initial funding for the earnest payment and repairs would be by taking advantage of a stack of credit cards I'd been collecting as a curious hobby over the previous several years. Then we'd have to sell our home on Zenobia Street and hope to get some equity payment in the face of a recessionary real estate market. We'd get some cash out of the mortgage on Jessie's house to pay off the credit card debt, and Voila! – We'd be living in a home that could accommodate us all for years to come.

The lawyer may have liked my plan because the chance of our success was limited. He thus faced a high probability that he'd be called upon to rack up some more hours negotiating another deal with a subsequent buyer. The trustees were thoroughly fatigued with the process, and at their urging he tentatively approved the plan.

It was pretty crazy. I had successfully – and very conservatively – managed our family finances since our marriage. We had paid off all our student loans and we carried no debt other than our modest mortgage. If the scheme succeeded, we'd have a mortgage almost three times larger than the purchase price of our first house. If my plan failed, we'd be out on the street. This decision would affect the whole family.

The older kids had reached their teens. Big families were increasingly unusual, and we had long ago expanded way beyond what most folks considered to be big. The Tillemann-Dick family was now large enough that we amounted to a social curiosity. It was fascinating to watch the faces of people as they learned that the child in front of them came from a family with eight or nine kids at home. It was like telling them you kept llamas in your back yard, or you had built a cyclotron in your kitchen. Almost everyone thought it was interesting. Remarkably few voiced disapproval. Most couldn't understand why anyone would undertake such an ambitious project. A few commented how wonderful it was that anyone could still afford such a large family – and then they'd walk off shaking their heads. For whatever reasons, however, the customary adolescent rebellion within the ranks of our teens never materialized.

One reason may have been that Annette and I insisted upon mutual respect within the family. We listened to and valued the opinions of our kids, and asked for the same in return from them. In my mind, the decision to commit to this deal was one that should be made not by me alone, but by everyone affected. We could ask the Lord's blessing on our action, but not His guarantee. If things didn't work out, I wanted all of us to have the assurance that we had followed the Lord's will to arrive at the challenges that would then be before us.

As the day to sign the deal approached, Annette and I gathered everyone in the snug living room of our house on Zenobia Street. We carefully explained what we proposed to do and detailed both the risks and the benefits. In the months since Annette and I had first toured the big, white house everyone had spent time with Katie cleaning up, moving boxes and mowing the lawn. If we succeeded we all knew we faced a mountain of work. Although I had invested hundreds of hours structuring proposals and negotiating the deal, I wanted two things even more than I wanted to proceed. First, I wanted us to act with a prayerful affirmation that we were doing the right thing for our family. Second, I hoped – against any reasonable expectation – that we would be unified in our decision. I didn't want a vote. I wanted us to act in harmony – whether we stayed in our old house for a while longer, or whether we moved to the white house.

We were in the habit of praying as a family. Every night and morning and at every meal we would ask the Lord's blessings upon us. Only infrequently, however, did we kneel as a family to make a major decision through our collective inspiration. This time, we formed a circle and joined hands. I asked Annette to lead and invited anyone to contribute as they were so moved. At the conclusion I closed our appeal in the name of the Savior.

The mood after our prayer was excited, expectant and more than a little anxious. Starting with the youngest, I asked each child to report their feelings about whether the Lord would bless a decision to risk our home and savings in the effort to buy Jessie's house.

Since five month old Mercina's contribution to the prayer had been to quietly gnaw on the latest Newsweek, Shiloh led with his comments. Nobody expected much from him, but his mop of blond hair and piercing blue eyes interfaced with a brain that frequently processed events his siblings missed.

"Yeth." He nodded solemnly.

Liberty had grown to be a skinny, vivacious four-year-old with long, wavy blonde hair and blue eyes. She liked to play games, but she looked seriously at her siblings in the circle. "We should do it," she affirmed.

I figured Corban would be inclined to buy the house. He loved poking around the garage and the laboratory, and he told me he planned to raise frogs in the pond out back if we went ahead. He was still old enough to voice doubts, though, and this process gave him every opportunity to take a position of caution. "Even if we only stayed there for a year, I feel it would be a good thing," he concluded.

Charity was grinning with her customary enthusiasm. Her eyes sparkled and flashed as she slapped her palms to her thighs in speaking. She tossed her hair and cares aside.

"I love that house! I just feel really good about going ahead. To me, the wrong thing would be to turn away from this gift."

Levi's brow was furrowed, his tone measured. He was ten, and he felt the burden of his years. He was taking this responsibility very seriously. I was pleased to see his thoughtfulness. "Well, it will be a lot of work. Everybody's going to have to help if we go ahead. And maybe the whole deal will all fall apart, and that would be very, very bad." He looked soberly at his siblings. "But the answer I got was yes." He nodded with finality.

"This opportunity is a gift – like Charity said," Kimber began. "We'll have a lot more room, and we can use the house to do good things. My prayer said we should go ahead."

"My answer was yes," Tomicah said confidently.

Back in 1982 we were temporarily living in California when we received a call from our former bishop in Denver. A family we knew was facing a terrible situation. The single mother had died of uterine cancer and now her three teenaged kids were being evicted. The kids had only recently arrived from Honduras to live with their mom. The bishop was looking for families with some Spanish language ability and a willingness to help. He asked if we would take in the fourteen-year-old for a few months until he could find a better situation for her. We prayerfully agreed, and he never did find her a better place. Dulcia had joined our family for good. As we knelt together in the living room, she had grown into a young woman who had recently returned from serving a mission in California. While she wasn't likely to be at home much longer, we wanted to know her feelings.

"Uh, I felt good," she offered cautiously. "My answer was yes, too."

193

"Annette?" I asked.

"Yes. Definitely yes. I got a very clear answer." She looked from face to face around the circle, smiling and nodding. Her gaze settled on me. Not so many years before, she and I had prayed about accepting a very attractive position with IBM in California. Denver was deep in the bust phase of its boom-and-bust cycle. It was too good an offer to pass up. But when we prayed, the Lord indicated to me we should stay in the little brown house on Zenobia Street.

Not this time.

"OK, folks – I guess we're gonna be packing up here soon."

We could have been exultant. We probably should have been soberly concerned with the risk we were willing to accept. Instead, we shared a sense of awe that each of us had received the same, unambiguous answer to our prayers. Where ever this path would lead us, we were starting out with a common commitment and a mutual sense of direction.

Two weeks later, I signed the papers.

We'd thought we were busy before as we tried to manage our crew in the house on Zenobia Street. Now we learned more about the true limits of our capabilities. The intensity of the commotion and construction of the following months left us reeling. We had incredible help. People from church joined the Scout troop and neighbors in cleaning trash and undergrowth from the grounds. Not counting construction debris, we hauled off almost thirty tons of junk and branches.

Through a friend, we found a do-it-all handyman/contractor who was as welcome as any angel. Zane could pour concrete to fix the sidewalk and patch flashing to stop a leak in the roof. Never had I met such a talented and ingenious co-worker. He was imaginative – he liked to invent things, too – and he loved to speculate on the history of the structure he was revitalizing. We would find old papers or some strange piece of equipment and Zane would soon have an exotic account that he had pieced together from a few tantalizing clues.

While there was no telling how accurate Zane's historical recreations might have been, the house undeniably had its intrigues. A few months after we moved in Annette was standing while talking on the phone and Corbi was rolling around on the floor at her feet like a seven year old puppy. She saw his eyes go wide and he pointed up at her.

194

"Jewz!" he exclaimed through a mouthful of peanut butter sandwich. It wasn't his habit to launch into a theological discussion in the midst of lunch.

"Don't talk with your mouth full," she replied. "What are you trying to say?"

"Chules!" he coughed as he tried to scramble up without releasing his sandwich from his clenched little hand. "Look!"

Annette had been standing with her hip against a counter built into the pantry. Corbi reached beneath the countertop and extracted a handful of dusty, but still sparkling jewels. There were half a dozen rings and a bracelet hidden on a series of hooks that were invisible to anyone except a little boy.

When we brought the booty over to Katie, she reflected that Jessie had always elegantly received visitors even when she was working in the kitchen. With this secret stash, in a moment she could whip off her apron and grab her jewelry. It seemed a more plausible explanation for what we'd found than some of the tales Zane concocted.

Annette realized that we could take in foreign students from the nearby college as boarders. I still don't understand why they were willing to put up with the dust and chaos, but we were soon making friends with gracious visitors from all over the world – and making some extra money simultaneously. They walked wide-eyed through the white columns of the front entrance into a maelstrom of kids, commotion and critters. We rapidly learned details of distant cultures. To an Arab, for example, an affectionate puppy was about as welcome as an amorous python. Koreans loved fermented cabbage. And the Japanese seemed to think in linked idioms.

"Hey, Akihiro – Have you had lunch yet?"

"So kind of you to ask," the student would smilingly reply. "Your beautiful wife ran like the wind out of the blue and made me a first class meal fit for a king."

Annette somehow managed the various contractors, the students and our own family. Dinner table discussions were spiced with views from Indonesia and Yemen, Brazil and Switzerland. On occasion the rhetoric grew heated, but almost without exception we saw our students return home with a sincere invitation to come back to visit anytime.

I added only a little to the progress on the house – I was frankly overwhelmed with the task of managing Safeline. There were times, though, when I made my contribution.

195

I found Zane's note in a sealed envelope taped to the door of the bomb shelter. He knew that I almost always stopped by my rudimentary office in there before I went up to bed. A note on the door was the most reliable way to get a message to me.

"Timber – I quit early today," the note began. I had noticed the little Bobcat excavator parked askew where we were trying to level out a parking area. Zane was a hard worker – Had he hurt himself? I read on.

> "I had to stop. I uncovered a body when I was
> digging the drive. I didn't know what to do. Call me
> when you get home. I'll be awake.
>
> ---- Zane"

I swallowed, hard. It couldn't be. A body?

It was almost eleven PM, but he picked up the phone halfway through the first ring. He explained that while using the backhoe to loosen a pile of rocks buried near the house he'd uncovered a small, carefully wrapped bundle. The size, shape and heft left little doubt in his mind as to what was inside. He'd carefully re-covered his discovery and been disinclined to continue for the day.

"It was probably one of the nuns, Timber. She must've gotten pregnant. Poor thing. I've been thinking about it all evening. We'll never be able to find out what really happened. I thought about calling the police, but what could they do? They'd just get the whole family – the whole neighborhood – all upset. I think you and I should just have a quiet little ceremony and re-bury it. Poor thing." He wasn't completely coherent, but I could understand why.

Zane felt the most respectful thing we could do would be to take care of the situation ourselves.

"You're a bishop – Can't you do this?"He knew I was regularly called upon to officiate at funerals. "Poor thing," he said for the sixth or eighth time. We hung up with no clear resolution.

If he was right, the body had been there for half a century or longer. It was highly unlikely the police would be able to trace it to any previous occupant of the house. On the other hand, Zane said it was wrapped in some kind of plastic. They didn't have much plastic when the nuns lived in the house in the 1940's. What if it had been there only a short time? What if there had been a crime? And didn't this little body deserve a real, marked grave? It just didn't feel right.

Neither did I. The slice of pizza I grabbed for dinner wasn't accepting Zane's news gracefully. Annette had gone to sleep with Mercina before I opened Zane's envelope. I walked around inside the house for a while. In the cavernous living room, the couch was covered with plastic sheeting to protect it from the construction dust. I sat on it and stared out the big window toward the Bobcat. My fingers toyed with the filmy covering beneath me. I realized what I had to do.

I said a quick prayer and grabbed a flashlight I kept near the bed. Annette mumbled something sweet but unintelligible, then lapsed back to sleep. I picked up a big mixing spoon and some scissors from the kitchen and found a shovel standing guard by the Bobcat. I propped the light on the crooked arm of the backhoe and began to probe carefully into the fresh dirt next to the bucket. It took me only a few moments to find a soft, resilient shape in the pile. The back of my throat tasted like green peppers and bile. I straightened up to clear my head.

I should just call the police, I thought. They should be doing this, not me. I looked at my watch.

Midnight. Great. Just great. It was dead quiet outside. They'd have six cars there in a few minutes.

The problem with calling the police was that Zane was right. They would cordon off the area and perform an autopsy and interview the neighbors. Any of the nuns that they could track down would come under suspicion. Did they deserve to be treated that way after their years of service? The alley was only a few feet away and shrubs and brush had overtaken the area. Anyone could have driven through in the dead of night, any time during the last 50 years. They could have buried the body in twenty minutes and no one would have been the wiser.

I decided if there was evidence of foul play, then I'd have to call the police immediately. But before I could dial the phone, I had to make sure that some good would come from doing so. I gulped some air and started clearing away the dirt with the spoon I had brought along from the kitchen.

It was a little smaller that I expected, I reflected as the shape came into view. I glanced around nervously. What if the neighbors were watching? Zane could help me explain if we had to. I sincerely hoped it would not be necessary.

The body was carefully wrapped in many layers of what appeared to be Saran Wrap. This was not a good sign. Saran Wrap was from the Sixties era or later – after the nuns had sold the house to Jessie and her husband. We had a problem.

Maybe. As I examined the bundle before me more carefully, new questions arose. The shape was irregular. Within the plastic wrap, the body appeared to be wrapped in several pieces of bedsheet. That still didn't fully explain the form illuminated by the flashlight's yellow beam.

It took me another ten miserable minutes to gingerly snip and cut at the wrapping and find the answer I needed. If I had not been so susceptible to the suggestions of Zane's overactive imagination, I might have come to a less morbid explanation even before I started poking around the pile. I recognized her immediately when I had uncovered just a portion of her body. I had seen her picture many times on the wall of Jessie's dressing room. She looked to be a foreigner. Possibly a French – – poodle.

In retrospect, I was glad I hadn't called 911.

Zane and I had a little burial ceremony the next morning. Just the two of us.

By the year's end we had managed to fix the ceilings and walls and refinish the floors. We'd patched most of the plumbing and installed new wiring. The lawn was green and the roof didn't leak. I found a buyer for our house on Zenobia Street. After paying on that mortgage for twelve years and investing twenty grand in improvements, we sold our old house for a few thousand more than I originally paid for it. Even so, we financed the purchase of Jessie's house at the last possible moment and still were able to pay off the credit cards.

"We did it, Honey," I said to Annette as I poured some cranberry juice into stemware. We toasted our achievement with celebration and appreciation. "Congratulations!"

"I want to name it. Now that we own it, I think we should give it a name like they do some of those great old estates back east," she mused. "I've been thinking about it. How about 'Theopolis?' It means 'City of God', or maybe 'God's Place'. What do you think?"

"Theopolis, huh? Sounds good to me."

Truly, it was His house more than ours. We could claim ownership of the property not as the result of a single miracle, but only through many, many almost impossible occurrences which each redounded to our benefit. If the house belonged to anyone, it belonged to Him. I told Annette what I was thinking, and she was pleased.

In the morning she broached her idea to the kids. They really liked the idea but found the name Theopolis cumbersome to say and unintelligible to non-family members.

They had an alternative.

"How about we just call it our Big, White House?" Liberty suggested.

In this case, the majority ruled.

Chapter 9

The Council Meeting

Sunday Afternoon, 21 May 1995
Denver, Colorado

Denver was beautiful in the spring. The streets were lined with huge trees, and each presented an aerial explosion of intense, vibrant green. The bright, mile-high sunlight filtering through the clouds of translucent new leaves reached the ground with a faint emerald tint that made everything look fresh and alive.

As we drove home from church in the big van, I asked the kids to assemble for a family meeting to talk about the twins. They were subdued as they filed up the back stairs and through the dining room. The large window on the west side of our living room was flooding the piano and couch with shimmering sunbeams sheathed in shades from lemon to lime. The kids sensed the seriousness of the occasion and were unusually quiet and considerate as they gathered in the comfortable, high-ceilinged room. They sat – some on the couch, some on the floor – and talked in hushed tones.

They had made it clear over the previous days that they were delighted at the prospect of twins. Though sobered by the possibility of major medical problems, they without exception eagerly anticipated the new additions to the family. One might expect after the trauma of Lincoln and the stress of Shiloh that the kids would be hesitant to welcome yet another baby into their lives. Yet it's fair to say that few children enjoyed as much love and nurturing as did Mercina when she was born in January of '92 and, a year and a half later, Glorianna. They were cuddled and cherished, and pampered and preened, at the hands of their siblings.

The eight kids who were at home looked at each other and squirmed a little nervously. A couple of them stroked the closest available pet. I wasn't sure how to proceed.

"First off," I requested, "Since we missed having a prayer before we left for church this morning, Libi, would you ask the Lord's blessing upon us?" It was a safe, constructive first step.

Liberty was sprouting like the greenery outside. She was seven. Oval faced like her mother, willowy and trim, she was gregarious and a touch mischievous. She stood with folded arms to offer a sweet, careful invocation. The amens were said, and every face turned to look expectantly at Annette and me as we sat together on the couch.

"Well, guys, we've got both good and bad news," Annette began carefully. "We've got two little identical twin boys. Genetically, they're fine – I mean they don't have Down Syndrome, or anything like that, but they have a bad problem." She paused and glanced at the smooth mound of her waist. "When they were separating into twins, they didn't split all the way." She took a deep breath to regain control of her quavering voice. "They're still joined at the chest. They have two little bodies that seem to be in pretty good shape. Dr. DeVore says they have two hearts, but only one is really working, and its pumping the blood for both of them. One of them is bigger and stronger, and he's keeping his littler brother alive."

The children looked incredulously at their mother.

For all the chaos and turmoil of our home, each member of the family had a general, but unarticulated conviction that they were brought together for a purpose. No one was blind to the many shortcomings of their housemates, but under it all was a profound sense that each of them was, in their own way, a very important person.

By logical extension, the twins were very important people, too.

"So they're, like, *Siamese* twins?" Levi asked. Now thirteen, he was the self-taught family biologist. "Like on <u>Nova</u> the other night?"

"Yes," I replied. "The technical term is 'conjoined', and it hardly ever happens. Apparently in the first few days when the baby is forming, the cells resulting from the fertilized egg divide – just like they would for identical twins. In this case, however, the little bundle of cells didn't split all the way. So we have twins, but they're conjoined." I thought about Dr. DeVore's comments. "It really makes you stop and marvel at the human body, and how blessed we all are to be heathy."

"It also puts a lot of other birth defects into perspective," Annette interjected. "A withered arm or a cleft palate doesn't seem like that big a deal when you see how just a few cells improperly dividing can make the difference between a healthy baby, or healthy twins, or conjoined twins. One little step went wrong, I guess, and this is the result." Her voice drifted off, and the children sat in stunned silence contemplating the life within her.

I resumed. "The doctors are telling us that only a few conjoined twins are born each year. Our doctors in Denver have never even seen conjoined twins. It's one of the rarest forms of birth defects. Nobody is real sure how to handle our case. As you saw on TV, sometimes it's possible to surgically separate conjoined twins. Mommy and I were hoping that would work with these guys, but Dr. DeVore said their hearts are so commingled it would be impossible to sort them out." I lowered my voice in an attempt to soften the impact of my words. "Especially since the little guy's heart is barely functioning – It just wouldn't work to split them."

"That's OK," Corban said. His dark blond hair was perpetually in need of a cut, but you could still see his bright golden eyes as he focused in on the issue confronting him. The nine-year-old was determined to find a solution to this problem he barely understood.

"We can take care of'em. They'll be kinda hard to carry, but if we could carry Shiloh and all his stuff, we can handle these two guys. It'll be kinda like holding Mercina and Glori at the same time, and I can do that, easy. Hey, how will we do their clothes? Will regular diapers fit?" He looked expectantly to me and his mother.

"Corbi, I think you're right that we can handle them, if we get a chance," I said carefully. "But what we found out yesterday was not good news. Twins can be joined in lots of different ways, and unfortunately, these two are joined in about the worst possible way. The prognosis for them is lousy."

"What do you mean?" Charity demanded in a sober tone that was very much out of character. At eleven, she was between Corbi and Levi. In spite of her predisposition to look on the bright side her voice had suddenly become deadly serious.

Annette had maintained her composure remarkably well for the last three days and she was striving valiantly to present the facts without upsetting the kids more than necessary. But as she sat surrounded by the hopeful, expectant faces of those she'd labored to bring into our lives she lost her restraint.

"Oh, Chari – The doctors say they probably won't make it." Annette turned quickly from child to child, wordlessly trying to convey her burden of knowledge, but with awful anticipation of the pain it would cause.

"At all?" Charity rose up from her chair, her eyes flooding with tears.

"Oh, they'll make it, Mommy," Corban also stood up, bewildered but resolute, and he started to walk across the room to his mother. He waved his pudgy hands as he spoke, almost visibly pushing away the feeling of cold dread that was rapidly overwhelming the sunlight pouring into the room.

"We can take care of 'em. I'll put 'em in my wagon with lotsa soft blankets, and take 'em with us everywhere. I can just pull 'em around." He looked first to his mother, then to me, for any sort of affirmation. "I can help out a lot. They're gonna be just fine," he said reassuringly, as if by the power of his own will he could make it happen. But the corners of his mouth were being pulled down further and further with each word.

"It's gonna be okay – " he proclaimed. Then, as he looked into his mother's brimming eyes, his little face collapsed as tears streamed down his cheeks. It was all he could do to raise his arms to embrace his mom. He wept with the deep, heart-wrenching sobs of a child who's lost in a dreadful dream, or who has suffered a hurt far more cruel than any physical pain.

Charity fell to her knees beside him, and she buried her face in her mother's lap. All of the children were drawn by some natural force or instinct to the couch where Annette and I were sitting. We huddled together, crying and quaking as we struggled to breathe. The children hugged and stroked one another, seeking to both receive and provide comfort and protection. The sense of loss and grief we shared was beyond any rational explanation. It just hurt. It ached to the depths of our souls.

When I was finally confident that I could once again talk, I looked from child to child.

"You guys know how much we love and cherish each one of you," I said as we sat together. Their faces were gaunt and drawn. The

203

sunshine still streamed in the window, but no one noticed. The ache in our hearts hadn't really subsided – we were simply drained of emotion.

"We are incredibly blessed to have you. We appreciate your wisdom, your good natures, and your commitment to do what's right. Mommy and I need your help. As I said before, there's not much chance that these guys – " I laid my hand gently on Annette's stomach as I explained – "are going to make it. The doctors – all of them – have said that it would be safer for Mommy if we'd terminate the pregnancy immediately."

Charity gasped quietly. She looked with alarm to Kimber.

"Your mom and I have listened very carefully to what the doctors have said. You should also know that when we were with Elder Holland yesterday, Mommy was told in a blessing that whatever happens to these little twins, we will have them to raise in the Millennium."

"With Lincoln?" Corban sniffed guardedly, hopefully.

"Yes," I continued, "Even if they never make it to live with us in this lifetime. So here's the problem: The medically recommended thing to do is to terminate, and with the doctors all saying they can't live, there are no compelling spiritual reasons not to – except that your mom and I don't feel right about it. If the doctors say there's very little chance they'll make it, then there's still some chance that they <u>could</u> make it. We've prayed about it, and for the time being we feel it would be wrong to take action to end the pregnancy.

"If we wait, there's some risk that complications could develop that would put your mother's health at risk. But for now, that's balanced by the fact that we'd also know that we were giving these little guys every chance we could to live.

"We want you to know what we're doing, and why. Mommy and the twins – "

"I think we should name them Christian and Jefferson," Annette interjected, and she briefly explained briefly her rationale. The children nodded their assent.

"As I was saying, Mommy and Christian and Jefferson," I resumed, "need your prayers. If any of you start to feel we're pushing this unwisely – that the risk to Mommy outweighs any potential benefit to the twins – then I want you to tell me, pronto. I want this to be a family project, OK?"

Everyone nodded in unison. It was a solemn commitment.

We got on our knees and prayed together one more time, and then the family council was officially closed. Levi and Corbi hung around for a while and asked a lot of additional medical questions, but when Annette left to go into the bedroom with little Glori, the other kids drifted off.

All, that is, except Kimber. She sat alone on the couch. Her expression was a portrait of grief, along with something else.

"Sweetheart, are you all right?" I asked gently. Kimber wasn't prone to over-reaction and I was a little surprised to see the strain on her face. Her red-rimmed eyes were kaleidoscopic jewels of hazel and green. They probed my soul, searching for answers like her mother had done so many times before.

"Daddy, I knew."

"What do you mean, Kimi?"

"I've known from the start," she said with awed conviction.

"I'm still not sure I know what you mean, Honey. What are you saying?"

I could see her collecting her thoughts. She was blessed with a powerful intellect and I usually found it easy and invigorating to talk with her. This type of cryptic dialogue was not her style.

"Daddy, on the way home from the clinic on Tuesday you drove by Libi's performance, and I was outside working," she recounted accurately.

"I remember," I affirmed. Liberty had been singing with the Chorale, and as an alum Kimber occasionally helped out with the staging. I had stopped by to see if the two girls needed a ride home, but the performance was running very late. Kimber had asked about the ultrasound results. I simply told her to wait until everyone was together.

"You didn't tell me anything, but I knew right then." Her voice was soft – but absolutely sure. "I knew we had twins – and Daddy, I knew they were *joined*. I had a clear understanding of exactly what was going on, maybe even before you and mommy did." Her big eyes searched my own. "That's never happened to me before, and it scares me a little."

"Did you feel anything else?" I inquired, not at all sure that I wanted to hear what else she might have perceived.

"No," she replied after a moment's search of her memories. "And I really didn't feel it," she corrected. "I just knew." She paused reflectively. "What does it mean? How can that happen?"

205

"I don't know, Kimi. I'm doing my best to make sense of all of this, and I really don't know. I do know I love you very much." I bent over and kissed her on the cheek. She looked more comfortable than she had at the outset of our conversation, before the weight of her unseen burden had been shared. "You gonna be okay?"

"Yeah." Her voice trailed off as she pondered the unexplainable in the fading green sunlight filtering onto her lap.

"Thanks." She looked up at me with a tight-lipped smile. "I love you, too."

IX.   On the Road and on the Air

1994
Dirt roads and Interstates

There are times when you get a great idea, but you're pretty sure your spouse won't understand its merit. This seems to hold true for both sexes. Sometimes the idea relates to a project: She wants to put up wallpaper. He's convinced that the same paint has worked just fine for the last dozen years, so why change? Or maybe the guy wants to buy a new piece of equipment. To a man, it's a tool. But the woman sees it as just a toy. She doesn't realize that with the right attachment – like a paint stirrer – you can also use a power drill to make a real, fine milkshake. Or even pancake batter. But have you ever tried to drill through a two-by-four with a blender? Some things just seem to be hard for a woman to understand.

To compound my particular problems, when the Good Lord made my wife, he put in an extra large measure of the stuff that makes her a woman. She's 100% pure female, and that doesn't leave a lot of room for the guy part of her personality. I'm different. With a little concentration, I can get in touch with my feminine side. I've been known to shed a tear at a good movie – like when Rocky knocks the stuffing out of that huge foreign guy – and if Annette wants to be taken somewhere really elegant and stylish, then sometimes I'll wear lace-ups instead my boots. But I'm not sure the converse is true for her. Asking Annette to find her masculine side is like trying to find the inner side of a golf ball: If it's in there, it's mighty hard to get to.

The key to peaceful coexistence in the face of these incongruities can be found in proper strategic planning by the male. A dozen daisies hand-delivered the day before you buy the drill can make all the difference. Or packaging. A little thought about how and when things are presented is important.

I learned this fairly early in our marriage. It was Christmas. After weeks of research, I had splurged and bought her a really expensive gift. I was so proud of myself I dropped a few juicy hints: She was sure going to be happy with Santa that year! Being a sensitive and caring guy, I wrapped the big box in some of the nicest paper I could find. I took some ribbon off one of the boys' packages – he wouldn't have appreciated it anyway – and made a nice card from some notebook paper I found in the playroom. When she came down that morning and saw the beautiful package waiting for her, she was really excited! And as she unwrapped it, her eyes got bigger and bigger. I actually thought she was going to cry over my thoughtfulness. And when I explained that her new heavy-duty vacuum had a special bypass design and a twelve amp motor, she actually did cry. That was a Christmas to remember! Even though she eventually came to a sincere appreciation of the machine's capabilities, I've felt inclined to do the vacuuming ever since.

When the time came to purchase one of our family's most important tools, I kept these lessons in mind. First, I was even more careful about dropping hints. We had a big trip planned to Connecticut for our class reunions. She had a list of friends she wanted to visit on the way. And Disney World was almost on the way, she insisted. I mapped out the locations of the places Annette wanted to visit and played Connect The Dots. We were looking at a six thousand mile trip – in a van with nine kids. Given Annette's propensity to chat with old friends until approximately four hours past our scheduled departure time and our statistically predictable frequency of bathroom stops once we got on the road, the trip would take about three months and end up with me in an institution – a nice institution, I'm sure – somewhere near Mobile, Alabama. As delightful as this prospect may have been for the rest of the family, I had some concerns. It was time for a bold plan. And the bold plan began with a few gentle hints.

Phase One: I loaded the kids into the van at 5:45 for a planned 6 PM departure to the Natural History Museum. As Annette climbed in the car at 6:20, I started the engine and then asked, "Does anyone need to go?" Three hands shot skyward and those people disembarked to attend to their personal needs. As we departed ten minutes later, I commented, "Boy, it sure would be nice to have a vehicle with a toilet."

Nonchalantly. Just like that. A hint. This process was repeated several times over the course of the next few weeks.

Phase Two: I went downstairs to the laundry room while Annette was doing the wash with the kids. Looking around at the piles of clothes heaped on the floor and counters, I commented, "Gee, this is only three days' worth of clothes? What's it going to be like on our trip?" Then I just walked off, nonchalantly. This was also to be repeated several times, but I had to stop because I ended up folding too much laundry.

Phase Three: This was the sneaky part. "I have an appointment across town," I'd say nonchalantly. Then I'd take my lunch hour and the classified ads and drive like a bandit through all the industrial areas and truck stops around town. I was looking for a sleek, fiberglass body Annette would find appealing (See? Packaging!) and which would really impress our former classmates. Like Phase Two, this step was curtailed when I realized those sexy bodies cost a small fortune. Nonetheless, I soon found almost what I was seeking.

Phase Four: I loaded Annette and the kids into the van and headed across town, past the truck stop and through the gate of a big, fenced in parking lot.

"OK, everyone – Open your eyes! What do you think?"

"A bus!" chorused the boys.

"What's it for?" asked the girls.

"It's so ugly!" pronounced Annette.

This time I was ready.

"It's an orphan," I told her as we all tumbled out of the van. "Nobody wants it. It was made to carry little handicapped children, but now it's just sitting here. And it's not ugly. It's kinda cute – like a calico brown bulldog."

"Cool!" shouted the boys. "A bulldog!"

"What's it for?" the girls asked again.

"Timber, it's so ugly," Annette reiterated.

I could sense that she was softening.

"Look at all the luggage space!" I walked around it like one of those pretty women who show off the prizes on a TV game show. "It has a door in front, one in the back, and – Look! – a handicapped lift so we can take little old ladies to church!" I opened the door to demonstrate how the hydraulic wheelchair platform effortlessly raised up and down.

"Cool!" shouted the boys. "Can we ride on it?"

"Are you seriously thinking of buying this?" asked Kimi and Chari in disbelief.

"Oh, Timber. I can't stand the color!" Annette shook her head in disgust.

"It has a bathroom!" I played my strongest hand.

"Dad – Mom's right," Kimi opined. "The guy who came up with this color scheme should be shot. What's it supposed to be? 'Peanut Butter on Poop'?"

"Cool!" shouted the boys. "Peanut butter on poop!"

"Kimber! Now look what you've done!" Annette glared at the boys. "I'll have no more of that!"

Levi elbowed Corbi as they tried in vain to stifle their snickers. "We could call it the Poopmobile!" he whispered, and the two of them nearly collapsed with glee.

"It's an orphan," I tried again. "It was made to carry handicapped children."

"I'm not setting foot in there unless you get it painted another color."

"Me neither," said the girls.

"That means we get to buy it!" shouted the boys. "Cool!"

It was all a matter of careful strategic planning.

And packaging. Once it was painted Colorado Sky Blue, I bought the bus with the proceeds from the sale of one of our two fifteen-passenger vans. It looked a lot like a medium sized, bulldog-nosed school bus, but it had been outfitted with high-backed coach seats and a good air conditioner. It had originally been purchased by an area recreation center as part of a federal funding package. In order to get the money, they had to agree to provide handicapped-accessible transport. It was only after they bought the nicely equipped vehicle that they concluded that there was no one who wanted to be transported in the bus. They'd take it out to a community picnic or use it to haul equipment a few times a year, but the fourteen year old vehicle had just twelve thousand miles on it when we bought it.

It wasn't possible to fit a bench seat for the driver and navigator, but I was able to position two captain's chairs nearly side-by-side. I turned every second row of seats to be rear-facing and installed stowable, cushioned platforms in between the pairs so we could have five comfortable double beds. The luggage rack on the roof also served as a secure place to pitch a tent, and thus in a pinch we could sleep the whole family.

While it was neither fast nor glamorous, there was plenty of room to stretch out, and almost everyone could have a window seat. Best of all, as far as I was concerned, was the rudimentary bathroom in the back. Without it, our family had found it difficult to travel for more than half an hour before someone requested a stop.

Our first trip was very nearly a disaster. I spent almost every night of the two weeks prior to our departure modifying the bus. During the days, I had to get Safeline prepared for my absence. By the time we packed and left – sixteen hours behind schedule – I was exhausted. Annette wasn't trained on a manual transmission and I've traditionally done most of the long distance driving for the family, so I was the sole occupant of the driver's seat. The first day was blisteringly hot. I found that my seat was inconveniently located farthest from the air conditioner and nearly on top of the engine compartment. The metal floor beneath me got so warm I had to drive with one foot on the gas pedal and the other lofted a few inches high. We had driven perhaps six hours when, outside a small town in Nebraska, the engine bucked and coughed a few times. I pulled off at the next exit and as we neared the stop sign at the ramp's end the motor died completely.

It was four in the afternoon and over 100 degrees outside. The good news was that the air conditioner was driven by its own small gasoline engine, so the kids didn't roast. The bad news was that the air conditioner didn't cool at all under the hood where I was working with my tool kit. The kids ended up spending the rest of the afternoon reading inside and sunbathing on the roof, but so far the trip wasn't much fun. I made the long, sweltering hike into the little town's Ford dealership for advice and a new fuel filter. Then I put in a few more hours work on the engine. After inspecting the fuel and electrical systems, I still wasn't sure what had caused the problem. As I patched everything back together, I looked up to see ten faces staring down at me. I climbed back in my seat, uttered a quick prayer under my breath as I turned the key – and we were on our way once again.

The engine seemed happier as we drove into the night. Heat seemed to be part of the problem. In an effort to give Annette and the kids as much time as possible with those we were meeting along the way and minimize driving in the heat of the day, I settled on the practice of driving until three or four in the morning, or until we neared an attraction or rendevous point. The family would be conked out in their beds in back. I'd then sleep fitfully for a few hours, drive on to the destination, and they'd talk and play while I tried to grab a few more winks. As the days wore on, my temper grew along with my sleep deficit.

Annette and I are usually pretty well synchronized when it comes to disciplining the kids. We may bicker between ourselves, but we generally support each other and agree on the frequency and severity of the kids' punishments. Whether due to my fatigue or some other cause, as the trip progressed we soon couldn't seem to agree on anything. It would have been almost comical if it hadn't been so painful. I'd suggest we stop, but she'd want to drive closer. Then I'd say fine, I'll drive on, and she'd insist that we stop. The same pattern held with discipline. No item was too small for us to argue about. We were acting more childish than the kids.

We managed to hit the reunions, meet most of Annette's friends and see Niagra Falls. In Washington D.C. Annette's dad got us great rooms at the Hyatt. As we left the Capitol he said he had reserved a suite for us at Disney World. We splashed in the Atlantic surf and ate boiled peanuts and moon pies. I was bleary, cantankerous and scorched, but we made it safely home in three weeks. The bus sputtered a few times along the way but didn't quite stall. After living with my unceasing bad temper and the ominous unreliability of the bus, I was almost convinced that no one in the family would ever want to set foot in it again. I seriously contemplated selling it.

Then, just a couple of days after our return, Corbi asked that I take him in the bus on a church camp-out. It was another blazingly hot day. We were climbing up the mountains on a busy, narrow two-lane road when the engine coughed, bucked a few times, and died. The bus was wider than the road's shoulder and drivers glared at me as they squeezed past. It took three hours and the State Patrol to locate a monster tow truck. Just as it was scheduled to arrive, the patrolman said I should give it one more try. The big V8 roared to life.

"Get on out of here!," he yelled as he blocked traffic for us. "I'll take care of the tow truck!"

I very, very seriously contemplated selling it.

When the big blue bus did the 'roll over and play dead' trick for the third time with a group of fourteen Scouts aboard, I told Levi we had to acknowledge it was simply not a reliable means of transportation. We either had to sell it or plan to use it solely when we could afford to have it break down. His response was emphatic.

"Dad, we love the bus – really we do. I know you didn't have such a great time on our trip back east, but it was a blast for us. We could all see out the windows. I could brush my teeth after lunch. We played Monopoly in back. We got the big rigs to honk their air horns when they passed us, and I could grab a snack anytime I got hungry. Tomicah and I loved sleeping on top. We can't sell it."

I was a bit taken aback by his sincerity and depth of feeling. As he had so frequently done in the past, Levi had completely disarmed me with his comments. It was a trait he'd shown at an early age. In the grocery store as a toddler, he had a habit of accosting strangers.

"Hey, Lady – D'you wanna strawberry?" From his perch in the shopping cart, he'd managed to reach into the produce display – not for his own appetite, but to share with the woman nearby pinching peaches. She smiled as he tried to pass her the berry in his pudgy hand. I smiled in turn and tried to decide whether I had to make good on the little guy's offer or instead should just walk on down the aisle. A few moments would pass and he'd grab the sleeve of another passing shopper.

"Say, Mister – That's a nice jacket!"

As he ascended through puberty, Levi continued to cultivate his mother's gifts of communication while he acquired my voice. It was a persuasive package.

"I know what to do!" He suggested enthusiastically. "Let's call the Car Guys!"

He had a good idea. Tom and Ray Magliozzi co-hosted National Public Radio's "Car Talk," a syndicated radio call-in show that we frequently listened to on Saturday mornings while we did chores. Both brothers had earned engineering degrees from the Massachusetts Institute of Technology, but they sounded for all the world like your corner garage mechanics – albeit with a better sense of humor. They offered remarkably astute advice on their callers' problems – automotive or otherwise – and they were lots of fun to listen to as well. The next opportunity, I called the toll-free number and was both pleased and surprised to soon be on the show talking to the Car Guys. Our conversation was relatively brief, but their advice to install a booster pump to minimize the apparent vapor lock in the fuel system made sense.

A couple of months later I was surprised to get a call from someone working with the show's producer. When he asked if I'd be willing to participate in a new part of the show where they did follow-up calls, I was happy to comply.

"With great trepidation, we are inaugurating a new segment of our show. We call this the 'Listener Retaliation Portion' of our show, and – and, this is risky!" The voice, thick with Boston brogue, belonged to Tom Magliozzi.

"This is risky," Ray chimed in, "but I'm ready for it. I'm up for it!" His voice was deeper, coarser.

"Here it is – here's the essence of it: Every so often, we're gonna call back somebody who was already on our show, and find out whether we gave that person good advice."

"Ohhh," Ray groaned somberly.

"Now we've asked – and we have no participation in this, whatsoever, except to converse, or re-converse, with the caller – so we've asked our crack staff to pick somebody at random from the people we've talked to recently, and get that person on the phone. And we have no idea what's going to happen."

"We don't know who it is," said Ray with vaudevillian showmanship.

"All we have is a little description of who they are, and a summary, for the record, of what we told'em."

"Yeah."

"So, are you prepared to embarrass yourself on national radio by being publicly humiliated by our former callers?" Tom asked Ray.

"I can't wait," he replied, with a transparent, but bemused, lack of sincerity.

"OK. We're gonna talk to somebody named Timber, who we talked to, I guess, a month or two ago. And he had a 1980 Bluebird school bus . I remember that now!" Tom was warming to the challenge.

"Vaguely. The problem was it was running out of gas – " Ray's voice trailed off as he desperately tried to reconstruct the call from memory, but Tom jumped in and continued to read the notes they'd been given.

"...at the carburetor, causing the engine to cut out on hills," he recounted.

"And what did we say to him? I don't remember." Ray's comfort level with this new portion of the show was vaporizing.

"Here! We have notes. We said to test for a hole in the fuel line, and if that wasn't it, then to put in an electric fuel pump." In contrast, Tom's confidence seemed to be rising.

"I do vaguely remember that. Also, he had a bunch of kids, this guy did. That's why he had the bus, right?"

"Right!" Tom affirmed.

"Yeah. He used to take everyone on vacation by piling a thousand kids in the schoolbus. Alright." He paused to gather his courage. "So, do we got this guy on the line? Timber?" Ray's enthusiasm for the new feature seemed a little shaken by his difficulty in remembering the details of the earlier call, but he was still committed to making it a success.

"You've got me on the line," I replied warmly. It was one of the few times I'd heard myself over the air since I left the radio station two decades before. My voice was slightly muffled by long-distance static.

"Hey!!! Heh-heee – " Ray's utterances were reminiscent of those made by young kids as they pull away for their first ride on a big roller coaster. He was trying to say something coherent, but momentarily dissolved into friendly, if slightly anxious, laughter. "All right, now, this is the truth, this is absolute truth: We have no idea what you're gonna tell us. You're either gonna tell us, 'Boy you guys were right on the money', or you're going to stump the chumps."

"Right," I affirmed.

Earlier in the week, when the staffer for NPR had called to make sure I would be available for an on air follow-up call from Tom and Ray, that was all they had asked. Neither the radio hosts nor their producer knew anything about what I planned to say.

"I'm really glad you called," I launched in. "Your diagnosis turned out to be right on. The fuel line integrity was fine."

"Uh-huh. Good." Tom and Ray seemed to be feeling better.

"So I went ahead and installed an electric fuel pump. The first one we found was, uh, a little bit puny, so we got a high performance unit from a racing shop." I halted to make sure they were following me.

"Good!" Ray said encouragingly.

"Because the gas tank's way in the back. It's a long way. We hitched it up with an auxiliary switch on the dash, and everything looked fine," I recounted, but the tone in my voice shifted noticeably. "Sooo, we piled all the kids in and went out for a drive."

"I don't like this," Tom interrupted. "I notice you're using the past tense."

"He is using the past tense – 'piled' and 'looked' and 'hitched'," Ray concurred, laughing anxiously. "I don't want to get my hopes up."

"I brought Grandma along."

"Ohhhh," said Ray, with obvious concern for the dangerous turn the tale was taking. They briefly burst into laughter, but the suspense was palpable.

"I thought we were doing real well," I said sincerely, "but then it started to smell real gassy."

"Ohhh." Now Ray sounded distinctly worried.

"So I pulled over to the side of the road, and jumped out the side door, and stuck my head down behind the front wheel to look up at the engine, and saw gas just pouring out from under the engine compartment." It was probably obvious to everyone except Tom and Ray that I was milking the moment for all it was worth.

"Haa! Too much pressure! He-hee," Tom sputtered, almost choking as he tried to get the words out.

"And before I could turn off the engine, it caught fire."

For a moment, the air was silent. Then the muffled crackling of empty static was broken by Tom and Ray's barely controlled nervous giggling.

"I got the kids out the emergency door in back. It was one of the most thrilling rides we've ever had," I continued earnestly as they quieted down. "Getting Grandma out the emergency exit was particularly exciting."

"I bet that was the most excitement Grandma's had in a few years," Tom offered weakly.

"So, what did I do wrong?" I asked innocently.

There was dead silence for several seconds.

"Ahhh, I think the basic idea was OK." Tom was rushing to explain reassuringly. "I think the high performance pump might have been the problem, because your fuel lines couldn't handle it." One could only imagine the two brothers frantically searching for a way to extricate themselves from this call – the first one of its kind they'd ever tried – and somehow simultaneously exonerate themselves before their listeners across the country.

"You guys, I couldn't resist." I had abused them enough. You could almost hear my grin over the radio.

For the second time in less than a minute, there was total silence over the airwaves. Then – "AHGgg!!! You're <u>lying</u>!!!" Tom said disbelievingly.

"I'm lying." I confessed.

"Oh, you bum!" Tom exploded.

"Owwwwww – Timber! That was <u>not</u> nice!!" Ray roared with laughter.

"Haaa!" Tom let out a gasp of relief, amusement, and good-natured amazement. "But we went for it hook, line, and sinker, didn't we?" All three of us dissolved into laughter over the air.

"To your credit, guys, you diagnosed it right," I said, trying to patch up the damage I'd done to their egos. "I did put in the electric pump, and it's running like a champ."

"So the electric fuel pump actually fixed it?" Ray asked, still somewhat in a state of shock.

"It really did."

"Geesh – I was worried about your kids! That was a <u>terrible</u> thing to do."

"Oh, my heart was beating like a sparrow's!" Tom agreed in his thick New England accent. Then they both broke into gales of laughter again.

"I'm gonna have to repent for this," I apologized, and they said they forgave me.

[*Car Talk and Car Talk dialogue copyright 1994 by National Public Radio; used with permission*]

Chapter 10

The Ephemeral Stream

27 May – 3 June 1995
The Four Corners Region

The big blue bus was perched on the brink of a cliff 3000 feet above the Colorado River. On three sides, we were surrounded by fantastic canyons and towering pinnacles of red and orange sandstone. There was only a dusty gravel road some 20 miles long leading to the overlook, and consequently the family was enjoying virtual solitude. The bus was ideal for this kind of trip.

"This is just magnificent! What a cool way to celebrate my birthday!" Kimi said appreciatively as she sat next to me and surveyed the vista before her.

"Dad! We caught a lizard!"

When Corbi said, "we caught," he really meant, "Levi caught." On those occasions when he personally captured a critter, he generally claimed exclusive credit. This time his phrasing was subtly reassuring. Levi was much less likely to bring their specimen into the bus for examination. Corban had allowed a few of his guests to escape in the past.

Without any conscious plan or instruction, the family was congregating along a natural stone bench that ran a few yards up from the western edge of the promontory. The sky was perfectly cloudless – a seamless rotunda of rich, deep blue that was unique to the high altitudes of the remote West. The sun was fast headed for the horizon and we found ourselves immersed in color: We watched in awe as the heavens were gradually transformed from the sumptuous purple hue of the mountains arcing behind us to the orange and magenta and crimson of the cliffs cradling the blazing orb ahead. Rippled curtains of stone around and below glowed with a vermilion fire of their own, while translucent golden shafts of light angled up from the depths of the chasms. Many miles in the distance beneath us, the iridescent silver sliver of the Colorado River was shimmering. Sunlight streaming to the canyon floor ignited the budding cottonwoods along the riverside into tiny, quivering green torches, and the few cultivated fields visible to us far below were vibrant with young life.

The glorious panorama inspired innate reverence from everyone except Francis, our big Golden/Lab mix. He was intent on chasing ground squirrels and terrifying Annette with his headlong plunges toward the edge of the precipice. Levi managed to snag him and hook him on a leash so everyone could settle down and watch the amazing, transitory display of light, texture and hue.

"Daddy, what's gonna happen?" Kimber asked as she grabbed her knee and rocked her head way back, trying to take in the whole view. She knew she didn't need to be more specific.

"I don't know," I replied. "Maybe that's why it was important for us to take this trip."

We had packed up the bus two days before. Dr. Porter – the male – wasn't happy with the decision, but he cooperated nonetheless. According to our last discussion, Annette's case had again been the lead agenda item for the Treatment Advisory Committee, and Dr. Mahoney had reminded those attending that Dr. DeVore's findings were entirely consistent with his original recommendation.

Annette's treatment options were straightforward. The opportunity for the simplest termination procedure was now past. If we had moved promptly upon her return from Salt Lake, the doctors could have taken the babies with a technique called Dilation and Extraction, or D&E. This procedure could only be performed when they were less than a certain gestational age. Based on the assumed conception date, the Friday after our return from Dr. DeVore's was the extreme limit for the procedure. Beyond that time, the size and skeletal structure of the twins was judged to be advanced to the point that Annette faced an unacceptable risk of hemorrhage if a D&E was attempted.

If she chose to terminate the pregnancy now, she was facing a much more arduous procedure. Synthetic hormones called prostaglandins would be continuously injected intravenously. These would induce premature labor, and after anywhere from a day to a week of the chemical stimulus she would deliver the twins. There was virtually no chance they would survive the procedure, and Annette would almost certainly be wretchedly ill as the side effects of the hormones compounded the physical trauma of the birth. The doctors said there should be no permanent medical consequences, but she still faced some risk of internal rupture and hemorrhaging from the stress of the artificially induced labor.

Within a few weeks, induction by prostaglandins would no longer be feasible. The twins would then be so large as to physically preclude conventional delivery. They would simply be too big to fit through her cervix. From that point forward, the sole option would be to perform a Cesarean section. Although Annette didn't relish the prospect of surgery, she knew the risks were well documented. She could bleed, or go into anesthetic shock, or acquire a post-operative infection. These were all risks she had accepted long ago as a possible consequence of pregnancy. Most compelling to her was the fact that this option offered the twins their only real chance of survival.

We were facing unavoidable choices. Those who live well choose carefully, my mom taught me. While we both needed and appreciated the advice we'd received, we remained accountable for our own agency and actions. We had fasted as a family and prayed for confirmation that Annette should continue to do all she could to nurture the twins. As Annette and I had sat together in the Denver Temple before we left with the bus, we both received an answer to our pleas. We were given a calm assurance that we were doing what we should.

The trip had been planned for months. Various scheduling demands would only permit us to travel for a week. It appeared to be the only time before Thanksgiving that we could all have even a few days off together – and that was without Tomicah. His internship in Washington would keep him there until July. Another family council was convened, and it was agreed we would all much prefer to take the brief vacation than to hang around Denver and worry. Dr. Porter ran yet another ultrasound, and although there may have been some additional fluid buildup, the twins appeared to be stable. The heartbeat was strong and there were no new negative indications. He reviewed the appropriate emergency procedures with us and gave us a file of test results, reports, and other relevant information to take along, should problems arise.

There were few tourists at that time of year. As the deep blue bus labored up the mountain passes and whined into the valleys, everyone on board felt an enormous sense of relief to be leaving some of our concerns behind. The weather was cool, but after the first night we had no rain.

It was an agreeable drive through the canyons and vistas of southeast Utah. We found a slot at the campground on the south shore of Lake Powell and decided to stay there for a day. Twice in the years before, we'd spent a week on the lake in a houseboat. Although she was nervous at first about the whole idea of being afloat with the kids, Annette had loved the experience. It didn't take her long to get over her initial anxieties. When on the second trip we were caught in a furious thunderstorm and I was struggling to navigate the lumbering boat through five foot swells, she was blissfully unperturbed. She was often like that – she could be either reluctant to trust, or sometimes, perhaps, too trusting.

On this trip a houseboat was out of the question. We could afford neither the time, the money, nor the risk of a medical emergency far out on the 200 mile long lake. Instead I rented a fishing skiff. We took a series of voyages exploring the labyrinth of canyons and pinnacles and racing across the increasingly large waves. The boat would hold only four of us, but it was a delightful diversion and no one minded taking turns. By the time late afternoon arrived, I had to plead with Annette and Charity to accompany me on one last run up the main channel. The others were feeling more adventurous and would have loved another trip, but Annette and Chari had been less demanding and had thus spent the day playing with the little kids on the rocky beach. I prevailed on Kimi and Levi to lead the younger kids in cleaning out the bus and preparing dinner while we buckled on the life jackets and headed out for a final tour.

"This was the least explored area of the lower 48 states before they built the dam," I played tour guide as we skipped across the waves. "We're heading into a section of the Colorado River that's called Cataract Canyon because of the huge rapids that used to be here. Now there are just sheer walls and water that's a hundred feet deep." I continued to describe geologic and historic features, but my passengers were not listening.

"Timber, please slow down. This is scary for me."

During summers growing up and at New College I had spent enough time in small watercraft to appreciate their joys and hazards, but the experience was new to my passengers. Annette was enjoying the scenery, but her lack of experience in small boats contributed to her perception of impending danger. I confess that one of my less admirable traits is that I have, upon occasion, rather enjoyed provoking her alarmist tendencies. While we were courting, for example, we took a romantic evening drive in our family Jeep along a snowy mountain pass near my home. At an opportune moment I turned off the headlights and steered by the full moon's glow. She was not amused – but she married me anyway. This afternoon I was having fun just going fast with the boat. Her anxiety generated some serious inner conflict as to whether I should do what she wished. My compassionate side temporarily won out, especially when I found that by slowing down a little, I could surf the boat down the following swells. The waves were getting just big enough that I could climb to the crest of one, and then slide with a gentle rush down the far side. It was mildly entertaining, but not as sporting as racing along near full throttle.

Cataract Canyon was far deeper than it was wide, and the waves were crashing into the vertical rock sidewalls beside us as we surfed further into its maw. The wind had picked up and a few stray droplets were beginning to whip off the tops of the swells.

"Daddy, let's go back. These rock formations are really interesting, but it's getting kind of late." Charity was more diplomatic than her mother on these matters, but she shared the same basic agenda: Adventure was best accomplished in serenity. She was growing into a stunning young woman. She always had a lovely face – symmetrical yet interesting, with Nordic influences – but as she reached her teens she was becoming positively gorgeous. One thing was certain, though. If she pursued a career in the movies, she was unlikely to do her own stunts.

I reluctantly agreed to reverse course and head back to the dock. I knew the trip back would involve driving into the wind and the waves. I also figured my passengers would not fully understand why the water would appear so much rougher, even though I planned to further slow down for their comfort. I braced myself for an emotional return trip.

"Timber, what's happening?" Just as predicted.

"It's OK, Honey. We're just pointing into the waves now, so it's a little bouncier."

I figured my job was to go fast enough to get back before dark and slow enough to avoid panic.

"Daddy, what do we do if we sink?" Charity sounded resigned.

It occurred to me that this might be more challenging than I'd anticipated.

"We won't sink, Chari. Even if the boat were to fill up completely with water, it has lots of styrofoam in the bulkheads." I kicked on the enclosed section under her seat to illustrate. "Trust me, sweetheart – it's virtually unsinkable."

"Oh," she replied, but she sounded as if I was distracting her from the effort to prepare her final prayers. "But what if it did? I mean, wouldn't it be better if we were going slower?"

"Did what? Sink?" This could be a long trip.

"It's not a dumb question, Timber," Annette's voice was getting tense. "Slow down! Water's pouring into the boat!"

The outboard was burbling at barely above idle. As each wave rolled under us, the hull would lift up and slap down into the following trough. The fresh wind caught the spray and blew it back into our faces. About a cup and a half had accumulated in the bottom of the boat. I could easily handle either the weather or my passengers, but dealing productively with both simultaneously was presenting a bit of a predicament.

"Annette, at the speed I'm going we're barely holding our own against the wind. We need to get back before sunset. Look – we're drifting into the canyon walls." I had intended to bolster my case that we really should go a little faster. Instead, all I accomplished was to convince them that there was a high probability that we were going to die by drowning or in a cataclysmic shipwreck. All of us. Soon.

"Timber how could you do this to us?" I couldn't tell whether Annette's voice was quaking more with frustration or fear.

Rats. The situation obviously was deteriorating. By my calculations, the speed across the water at which my passengers started to get panicky had now dropped to zero. Even if I stopped completely, I'd have two very excited passengers to deal with. Out of desperation, I devised a brutish plan.

"Look, we're not going to sink. Now hang on!" They both usually tended to do what I said, and for the moment they lacked any viable alternatives. They obediently clamped their hands to the gunwales. This was still inadequate psychological preparation for the rush they experienced as I opened the throttle and jetted with them across the tops of the waves.

"AAAyyeee!! STOP! Slow Down! There's water splashing in! SSSTOoooOOP!!"

There was a unique warbling harmony when they screamed together like that, I noticed.

"What?" I yelled back. I figured if I could stall for time, they might realize we weren't in any imminent danger.

"AAAhhhhaaoowwahh!"

They weren't letting up. I gritted my teeth and kept the gas wide open.

The roaring engine coughed, sputtered, and quit. Annette and Chari settled into somewhat stunned silence. The boat quit planing over the tops of the swells and began plowing through them as it rapidly came to a halt. Except for the sloshing of the waves and the faint tremulous echo of their cries wafting back through the canyon, all was quiet.

Annette assumed the reason we had stopped was that I had come to my senses.

"Finally! Why did you DO that? You scared us to death! Now let's go at a reasonable speed." Her adrenaline level was dropping and she was a little embarrassed by her earlier emotionalism. The fact that the boat had gone very fast for several long moments without immediately disintegrating was not lost on her. It was apparent to me, however, that in her mind the appropriate speed for our return would still have us running second in a race with a paddling duck.

"I'm not sure I can," I said as I positioned myself to pull the recoil starter. I was pretty sure I knew what the problem was...

Fupa-fupa-fupa-fup. I pulled again.

Fupa-fupa-fupa-fupa-fup.

Fupa-fupa-fupa-fup.

Fupa-fupa-fupa-fup.

"Daddy, is something the matter?" Charity stopped adjusting the clip that held her long, blonde hair in place as she took note of my efforts.

"Well, the engine's not starting."

"We need the motor to get back to the kids!" Annette may have been a student of history and religion, but she understood some things about boats.

Fupa-fupa-fupa-fup.

Fupa-fupa-fupa-fup.

Fupa-fupa-fupa-fup.

223

"Daddy, what are we gonna do?" Chari was starting to sound alarmed again.

"Maybe you'd better hand me that paddle. Do you think we can row back?" I asked, looking first at Chari, then to my wife.

"Daddy, it's gotta be miles back there!"

That's one down, I thought, but Annette looked more skeptical than stunned.

The boat was drifting closer to the ragged rock walls. We could see absolutely no place to land – just seething waves that smacked into the cliffs and then sucked themselves back to do it again.

"Look. There's only one thing to do." I tried my best to sound confident. I reached down, unbuckled my belt and began to take off my shirt. Annette stared at me, incredulous.

"It looks like I'll have to swim for help." They knew I was a strong distance swimmer in college. "It's only about three quarters of a mile to the mouth of the canyon. It'll take me a while, but all you have to do is make sure the boat doesn't slam into the walls. Here – grab the paddle!" By this time, both women were positively desperate for any solution other than the one I was offering. "Now, remember, you won't sink, but you may get some water in the boat. That's OK. Bail it out if it gets too full. Wait – I need to take off my shoes."

I spun around and reached down as if to take off my sandals. Instead, however, I switched the gas supply line to the second of the two tanks on board and quickly punched the primer bulb a few times.

"If I'm not back in a couple of hours – " I started to say.

"Timber, you <u>can't</u> leave us!" Up to this point, I wasn't sure I had them, but now Annette also sounded seriously concerned. There comes a time in a guy's life when he knows he's treading the line dividing the clowns from the creeps. For me, that time had arrived.

"Well, we can try the engine one more time," I offered, desperately grateful to have an excuse to again turn toward the stern of the boat. I literally ached from the effort required to keep a straight face.

Fupa-fupa-fupRRRRoarrrrrr!

I sat back down.

"Whew! That was a <u>close</u> one!" I was beaming. "Now, hold on – and let's get home quick!"

They nodded gravely in agreement, so I cracked the throttle almost wide open. In a moment, I was genuinely delighted to see how much they enjoyed the spray in their faces as we skipped across the waves and back to the dock.

"You shoulda' seen how fast we were going on the way home!" Chari told her wide-eyed brothers. "We were <u>flyin'</u> over those waves!"

"Timber, what do you think was wrong with the engine? Why'd it start all of a sudden?" Annette asked as we unloaded the boat. She probably expected a comment from me that was respectfully appreciative of God's intervention on our behalf.

"It seemed to work a lot better when I switched to the second gas tank." Big mistake. I couldn't control my stupid grin.

She stared at me sternly as she grasped the meaning of my remarks, her hands on her hips, her feet apart.

"Timberrrr! You <u>didn't</u>!" Then she actually swatted me – pretty hard – with her life vest and chased me part of the way up the path to the bus. Such was the reward for my resourcefulness in dealing with our perilous plight.

Dinner awaited us. Kimber had engineered her favorite meal in our rustic kitchen: some hearty soup, along with thick slabs of bread we'd imported from Colorado. Her creation was simple, tasty, and satisfying.

The rest of the stay by the lake was relatively uneventful, except that Levi managed to incur the ire of the three campers in the site adjacent to the bus. He and Corban were excited at the prospect of sleeping under the stars on the platform of the rooftop luggage rack. The authentic wilderness experience they sought was compromised when instead of coyotes and crickets all the could hear was the heavy metal serenade pounding forth from our neighbors. Levi's solution came in the form of small pebbles launched from his slingshot toward their encampment.

"Hey! What the %$#@ was that?" came an agitated voice from their tent.

"What's yer problem, man? Just cool out!" scolded a companion.

"Shuddup and turn off the music!! Somebody's messin' with our stuff!"

Levi would then enjoy a few minutes of peace as they burst out, flashlights blazing, to defend their territory. Other than a few expletives directed to no one in particular, it remained fairly quiet until the headbangers retired to their tent and CD player again. The cycle repeated itself several times as the night progressed.

Screeching guitars.

Smack! Clatter, rattle.

"There it is again! Some %#@$*' animal is tearin' up our stuff!"

Levi found that direct hits on the cookpans were particularly effective in penetrating the electronic din blasting forth from their tent. From their dialogue, he discerned that the campers feared the prospect of coyotes, but had no desire to bring the unwashed dishes into their cramped sleeping quarters.

The more serious problem arose the next morning when Levi succumbed to the temptation to smack the pans just one more time. He thought it was time they got up, since they'd kept him up half the night. He knew he had a very effective alarm clock.

What Levi didn't know was that one of the campers had decided he would be safer from the wild animals if he slept in the car. The clang of the pebble on the pans succeeded in awakening him as well as his tentmates, and in daylight from his vantage point reclined in the front seat of his car he could see what they had all missed the night before: Levi was laughing, silently but uproariously, as he quickly stowed his artillery in his sleeping bag.

"Get yer butt <u>down</u> here, Slimebag!" the camper snarled as he slammed the car door.

I raised up from my bunk in the bus, groggily oblivious to the farcical little drama that had unfolded the night before. I peered out the window to see three irate long-haired young men standing shirtless and staring above my head at the roof of the bus.

"Come on, you little maggot, get down here, <u>now</u>!" They clearly wanted to make a deep impression on Levi – maybe on his face, if they got the chance.

It took a while for me to reconstruct the events leading up to the confrontation, and a while longer to exercise whatever skills I possessed in cross-cultural diplomacy to settle the dispute. Fortunately, no damage had been done. Levi eventually apologized, but the campers seemed to doubt his sincerity. He might have been more persuasive, but he insisted on staying within the radius of his dog's leash. Francis was usually a mild family-type dog. In this circumstance, he considerately obliged Levi by barking and growling ferociously. He strained with his formidable strength to break his chain as if he wanted to make a deep impression of his own on the belligerent campers.

It seemed the right time to move on. We reluctantly fired up the Bluebird and headed down the road from the lake. Over the next days, we traveled through Indian reservations and National Parks, across painted deserts and through verdant forests. Spirits centuries old spoke to us from kivas and cliff dwellings and snowmelt freshets washed our feet and our souls. Aboard the bus the conversation naturally drifted back to the twins. Annette asked whether I could design a Sit'n'Stroll that would accommodate both Christian and Jefferson. She wrote in her journal while Chari and Libi sketched clothing ideas. Uncertain whether the day would come when we would care for the babies, we were nonetheless planning for the possibility of their arrival.

It was a restorative journey. The last day found us at the Great Sand Dunes National Monument in southern Colorado. The huge, white dunes were nestled at the edge of a large, flat-bottomed valley. We could see them from miles away, heaped hundreds of feet high like a child's fantasy sandbox.

I found few cars and lots of room for the Bluebird in the main parking lot. It was at the edge of the dunes, bordered by sage and grass to the south and a column of cottonwood trees to the north. The trees looked out of place in the Saharan landscape. They grew only where their roots could be nourished by a stream which flowed seasonally nearby. At the periphery of the parking lot was a series of beautifully illustrated signs. Geologists had studied the dunes extensively. The signs were decorated with elaborate diagrams explaining why the gypsum and silica crystals had accumulated in this particular spot. To an uneducated eye, the rest of the valley looked very much like dozens of others in Utah, Arizona, New Mexico and Colorado that our blue bus had rolled through over the preceding days. The signs carefully described the unique geologic and climatic conditions that over the eons had brought the sand there and made it remain.

"Phooey," Annette scoffed as she pulled off her sandals to join the kids in splashing through the stream. "If the dunes were thirty miles up the road, they'd find a way to explain why <u>that</u> was the geologically appropriate spot, rather than here, or Alabama, or New York, wouldn't they?" She raised her hand to her brow as a sunshield. "Why can't people just accept this incredible phenomenon as a gift? It's <u>here</u> because God wants it <u>here</u>," she concluded affirmatively as she surveyed the world before her.

227

She stepped tentatively into the stream. It was perfect, she proclaimed – cool enough to be exciting, but warm enough to invite the kids to sit right down into the swift, shallow surge. The water was literally two inches deep and two hundred feet across. The magnitude of the flow this year was almost unprecedented. We had hoped to arrange the trip so we'd arrive when the water was running, but this exceeded all our expectations.

The rivulets and currents were magical. For fifty weeks of an average year, the whole area was bone dry. Even on the infrequent days when thunderstorms lashed the valley, the porous earth soaked up any precipitation instantly. The glossy signs said that the stream flowed continuously under the sand, silent and invisible. Then, for a few days each spring, the rushing snowmelt from the Sangre de Cristo mountains pushed the water up to flow across the top of the sand along the edge of the dunes. The geologists called it an ephemeral stream. Sometimes it was there. Some years, the sand stayed dry.

If you followed the water upstream, it disappeared. Its source was a series of countless tiny springs at the base of a large dune. The river welled up from the dry sand. A walk downstream offered a symmetrical experience. The water sheeted across the base of the 60-story tall sand hills, snaking along through hundreds of ankle-deep courses. After a few thousand yards, the main stream got shallower and tighter. Then, as it curved around a immense shoulder of sand, it just ended. Beyond that point, you could take a snapshot and convince people you were in Egypt.

I looked up and down the stream. The kids had scattered and I went through the drill of finding a silhouette corresponding to each child. Their gleeful screams wafted and faded along with the rippling burbles of the water. They were in heaven, I realized. This was the most extraordinary water park imaginable. The area was totally devoid of threats: No water deeper than six inches, no waves or undertow, no jagged stones or poisonous plants. Annette was right: It was perfect. It was a gift.

Annette was nearby, sitting alone at the edge of a small sand island, letting the water swirl around her toes.

"Timber, what's that sparkling in the water?" she inquired.

It looked to her like there were millions of tiny flecks of gold being carried along in the stream. Tiny facets of mica washed from the granite peaks above caught and reflected the light of the sun. They glittered and flickered as they coiled downstream. She seemed transfixed by the dynamic, transitory spectacle before her. Then, after a few minutes, the water at her feet faded away. A dozen yards upstream, the current had cut a new channel through the shifting sands. Her island was now bigger, and she found herself in the middle of it. She got up and slowly made her way toward me and the kids. We were building a great castle, complete with a moat and drawbridge.

She gently stroked her midsection as she walked across the water. The sunlight sparkled in each droplet that splashed up as she swung her feet forward. For those moments the children, birds, and water together created music in harmony. I left the kids to join her at the streamside. Annette sat down with me in the damp sand and nuzzled my neck. It was clear she was deeply grateful for this time away from the frenetic activity at home. We were gradually growing accustomed to the likelihood she would lose Christian and Jefferson. At the initial diagnosis, she fought with every fiber in her diminutive frame to find a way to make them hers and to make them whole. If any mother's sheer determination could have borne them into this world, then she would have had her twins. Only after Elder Holland's blessing did I sense any relaxation of her will. She reluctantly was able to give up, one at a time, the hopes and aspirations she had treasured for this birth. At times, I could see in her eyes that a part of her soul was already grieving deeply. But with her forehead pressed next to my cheek, I knew she was now better prepared to truly submit her will to His. As time passed she was gaining a measure of peace.

The kids still had their small kingdom under construction. Corbi called to me. He wanted some technical consultation on a drawbridge. As I straightened up to offer my assistance, I heard Mia's excited voice behind me.

"Mommy, look!" Mercina ran toward her mother with her hands cupping something that must have been extremely precious. Annette turned to meet the tiny three-year-old. Her siblings often quipped that Mercina had never learned to walk. Instead, she flitted from place to destination like a lark, halting for a moment to converse, inspect, and then dart off again. She was a sprite – a glimmering nymph – and quite enchanting. The little girl slowed as she approached her mother, bringing her two hands up close by her smile for Annette to see.

"I saw it floating in the water, and I caught it!"

She cautiously opened the treasure chest of her palms. Sheltered within was a tiny pearlescent star of a flower. It was scarcely bigger than one of the fingernails of the miniature hand enclosing it.

"It's beautiful, Mercina! Have you ever seen anything so white?" Annette asked.

There is an expression unique to small children, a smile that radiates unbounded pleasure and a perfect sense of satisfaction and shared fulfillment. Mercina's face glowed with pure, innocent joy.

"MMMmmm," she breathed. "Did it grow in the river?"

"I don't think so, sweetheart. It probably grew upstream and got carried down to you. Maybe your father knows."

With that, a puff of warm wind seemingly blew the tiny girl toward our castle at the water's edge. I marveled at the glorious rainbow of diamond droplets that enveloped our little sprite as she pranced over to me.

As she danced along the ephemeral stream, I reflected. Like any life, this water flows through the world in a way that has a perfectly logical explanation. It runs its course and then ends. If that's all we choose to see and try to comprehend, it can still be wonderful. But the awesome beauty and magnificent complexity of creation is best understood when we ponder the course of a stream that is beyond our sight. There is a powerful river flowing silently and invisibly under our feet and all around, bearing and sustaining us well beyond the shifting sands of time.

X. Shiloh and the Bronco

December 1994
Denver, Colorado

Annette had been listening to the radio as she drove to pick up the kids from their early morning seminary class. She usually listened to public radio, but she was tired of hearing about their winter fund drive, so she channel-surfed to Denver's largest AM station. The Hal and

Charley Show was just background noise to her until they mentioned the free microwave oven to be given to the winner of the Bronco Breakfast Recipe Contest. Since our family's 12 year-old microwave had been operating only sporadically, Annette decided to pursue the opportunity. As she picked up Kimber after class, the two plotted to concoct a winning dish.

Kimi conceived a breakfast of pumpkin pancakes with blueberry sauce to echo the Bronco football team's colors of orange and blue. Annette was willing to submit the recipe without even testing it – she thought it'd win based on creativity alone – but Kimber insisted on whipping up a batch of the hotcakes. To their delight, the recipe as originally conceived was delicious. Annette came by my office with samples and then faxed the recipe to the station minutes before the contest deadline. The two food designers both promptly forgot about the whole affair.

Several days later, the phone rang at 6:45 in the morning.

"You won! Did you guys enter the Bronco Breakfast contest? Quick – turn on your radio to KHOW!" It was an old friend who explained that Hal and Charley had just announced the contest winner. "It had to be you," she exclaimed. "There's only one Kimber Rainbow!"

The Bronco Breakfast turned out to involve a lot more than a free microwave. Hal and Charley were scheduled to broadcast from the home of the winner and the Bronco's huge center linebacker, Dave Wydell, would co-host with them. As the day approached, Annette and I wondered whether we would have been better off to just go buy a new oven. As promised, the engineer rang the doorbell at 3:30 AM. I dragged myself out of bed and padded to the front door, but Levi was already up and he let him in. It took about an hour to bring in the equipment from the station's mobile studio truck and then power up the wireless link.

Levi had made a fire in the fireplace. By the time Hal and Charley arrived at 4:40, most of the kids were up. Annette was awake too, and in spite of my urging that she stay in bed for a while, she busied herself in the kitchen with Kimi.

"A very good morning to all you early risers!" Hal said into the microphone. It was precisely 5:00 AM. Even at that painfully early hour, his ample silver hair was meticulously groomed. His shirt and slacks were pressed, his collar crisply starched.

I had never been able keep them straight before, but now that Hal and Charley were both sitting on the couch of our living room it was a little easier to sort out which voice belonged to which face.

"Welcome to our Bronco Breakfast broadcast!" Charley chimed in.

Hal was more mature and grandfatherly. Charley was only a few years his junior, but he outweighed his taller partner by more than a few burgers and fries. He wore an oversized Broncos team shirt and khakis. Charley was the one with a wacko sense of humor. He was the cut-up and Hal was generally the straight man.

"Yeah, this is great!" said Charley. "We're sitting in the home of Kimber Tillemann-Dick. Actually, it's her parents' home, 'cause Kimber's only fourteen years old. And she's the winner of the Bronco Breakfast!"

"Boy, I feel like <u>we're</u> the winners this morning. Isn't this terrific, Charley?"

"I'm not <u>ever</u> going back to the studio. Kimber's sister, Charity, has been bringing me juice and pancakes, and we've got a roaring fire going here in front of us. Levi made this one with real logs, too – I think I'm the only one pumpin' any natural gas into this room." He guffawed at his joke as he gazed approvingly at the walnut pillars and mantle. "This is the life, Hal. I'm gonna see if they'll adopt me. Heck, maybe I'll just hang around. There are so many kids here, they'd never notice! Annette, would you adopt me?" Charley pleaded. "I'm not as well behaved as your kids, but I may eat less than Shiloh," he cracked.

Shiloh was almost five and had a physique that, in miniature, closely resembled Dave Wydell's. Shiloh and Dave had hit it off swimmingly. From the moment the six foot, seven inch, 300 pound Bronco politely tapped at the front door, the little boy had grabbed his hand and ushered him everywhere. Shiloh was a great conversationalist, and somewhat to our surprise the football player seemed to appreciate that Shiloh wasn't really interested in football – he just liked Dave. The Bronco had returned his respect and appreciation. Shiloh was especially happy to have a companion in the kitchen. The two sampled Kimi's pancakes, plus the sweet rolls, fruit, jams, and drinks provided by the station. They were both having a terrific morning.

The house rapidly filled with curious neighbors as the morning progressed, and as the broadcast continued various friends drove from all across town to join in. Most of Kimber's seminary class arrived. The street in front of the big house was lined with parked cars. Shiloh asked

232

Dave if he could go for a ride in the Bronco's long, white limousine. Dave obliged by asking the driver to take the five-year-old – plus everyone else who wanted to go – on trips through the neighborhood.

"Am I right – You have <u>ten</u> kids? And they're all yours?" Hal asked Annette over the air.

"They're all mine, or actually ours," she said as she smiled at me. It wasn't worth the risk of confusion to explain that Dulcia was our pretty-much-adopted daughter, or that we'd lost Lincoln in 1989.

"What'dya think Timber? Are you gonna go for a dozen? C'mon, Annette, you can't stop now," Charley quipped and pointed the microphone toward her.

"Well...." she replied coyly, and Charley had instantly read her expression.

"Hal, I think we have an announcement to make! Do we?" he asked incredulously. Annette had no real choice but to nod yes as she smiled with happy expectation.

"Congratulations!" The room broke into applause as everyone realized what Charley was saying. To our chagrin, Annette and I realized that much of city had just been informed of the impending arrival in our family.

"Let's get Dave and Shiloh back in here," Hal said.

"Good idea! What're you doing in the kitchen <u>again</u>, you two? As if we didn't know," Charley quipped. "What a pair these guys make! Hey Shiloh, do you know you're gonna have a new baby around here?" Charley poked the microphone toward the little boy – but Dave ran interference and intercepted the mic before Shiloh could fumble his reply.

"I think you should know, Annette and Timber, that Shiloh is a <u>really</u> friendly host," Dave respectfully interjected. "D'ya know what he just asked me?" The Bronco bent down to get a better look at the miniature figure beside him.

Shiloh's blue eyes sparkled, and his smile lit up the whole room as he looked adoringly at the massive football player towering above him.

"Shiloh just invited me to spend the night with you guys – He said I could come over anytime! Can I stay over?" he had asked teasingly, and he reached out his huge paw to hold the chubby little hand being offered to him.

"Pleeease?" Shiloh implored.

Annette's first pregnancies had been remarkably trouble-free. From conception through her precipitous deliveries she had little to concern her except bouts of nausea and the burden of the baby she carried at the time. In the late fall of '94 she realized she was, as the scriptures say, again with child. Dr. Irwin was able to let Annette listen to the baby's heart just days before the Bronco Breakfast. Several days after Hal and Charley's visit, though, Annette had started spotting. She was only a little more than a couple of months along, but in ten previous pregnancies, she'd never faced this kind of a problem. When she went in to the clinic the next day to be checked, the physician's assistant couldn't find the baby's heartbeat. The P.A. explained that the baby was still pretty small, that sometimes they move out of the range of the stethoscope. Still, it wasn't a good sign. He sent her home with instructions to take it easy.

She had gone to bed to rest but later called me at the office as I worked late.

"Timber, can you come home?" she pleaded with justifiable impatience. "I think the bleeding's gotten worse."

"Are you feeling OK?" I felt my chest tighten with the pressure between my conflicting priorities.

"It doesn't hurt, and I'm not bleeding badly," she said. "I just want you home." She knew she was forcing my hand – making me choose between her pain or my anxiety.

"Sure. I understand," I said as I made a determined effort to unclench my jaw. "I'm just going to finish a few things here." She was right. I should have left for home hours ago. Safeline's cash famine was chronic, and the company was requiring increasing infusions of my time. Furious with frustration, I desperately worked to finalize the paperwork for a large order to Japan. If the documents weren't in order, the truckload container filled with Sit'n'Strolls would miss its ship. If I left for home now, there'd be almost no more cash coming in until after the holidays. For the umpteenth time I needed her cooperation – just so I could work to get us through this tough spot – and yet she clearly deserved my love and compassion at home.

"If anything changes, and I'm still not home, call me, OK?"

"It's not really OK, but – fine. I'm not going anywhere." The line clicked, then was silent. She was obviously hurt and resigned to facing another evening without me.

I stared at the receiver for a moment and realized the muscles of my jaw were knotted tightly again.

It was well after midnight before I was able to fax the papers off to Japan, and only then did I feel that I could stagger home. I was exhausted. My whole skull ached. Neither Annette nor I had slept much the night before from worry about her spotting. Now she was worse.

She frequently stayed up when I worked late. Life got a little more complicated on those nights she was awake when I got home. Occasionally she'd be irritated with me for staying at the office so long. More often she was just happy to have me in bed with her. And then there were the nights she manifest both emotions nearly simultaneously. That night, I resolved to accept graciously whatever response my appearance engendered. I found Annette curled up on the floor of the bathroom next to our 21 year-old dog, Nicholas.

"I'm really sorry I took so long, Honey," I said, and I meant it. I felt horrible about leaving her alone, but I rationalized it by telling myself there was nothing I could have done, anyway. At least I had been able to solve one problem at work that night.

"Are you all right?" I inquired cautiously.

She wasn't upset. She was quiet, almost passive, when I stuck my head through the open bathroom door.

"Pretty much. I'm still bleeding, and I'm worried about Nicki."

The dog's condition had been deteriorating over the previous few weeks. It was clear that he wouldn't live long. He was just a little mutt, but the kids took great pleasure in explaining to anyone who asked that he was a "purebred Zenobian Foxfoot." This rare breed – actually, Nicholas was the only known living example – had first been discovered in our old house on Zenobia Street.

"He's just not moving much," she said as she stroked the old dog's graying head.

"What can I do for you?" I inquired gently.

"I don't need anything. But would you get some ice cream for Nicki? He'd really like that."

As I rummaged in the freezer, I had to move bags and bags of pastries and sweet rolls left over from the breakfast with Hal and Charley a few days before. Our life had been rolling along nearly out of control, but at least that morning had been a delightful part of the ride.

I stuck a bowl of pumpkin ice cream in Kimi's new microwave for 15 seconds. Nicki loved ice cream, but he was too weak now to eat it unless it was soft. He couldn't chew the hard stuff. It just dropped out of his mouth onto his bedding. I carried the bowl back to Annette. She was still on the floor, her face only a few inches from Nicki's grizzled muzzle. She stared into the small dog's dark face. He returned her gaze devotedly, the dusty marbles of his eyes expressing mute compassion.

"Here's the ice cream. Are you sure you're okay?"

"Mmmm, yeah," she said with a touch of dejection in her voice. She rearranged herself so she could spoon feed the ice cream to the dog. Nicki groaned as he tried to raise himself up to lap at the dripping spoon being offered to him.

"I'm just gonna stay here for a while," Annette said quietly. "I'll come in to bed in a little bit."

I grabbed a couple of aspirin for my still-throbbing head, and then found a pillow and shawl for Annette. I bent down and kissed her gently, sweetly.

"I just can't stay up," I apologized, shaking my head. "I'm sorry. Wake me if you need me. We'll check in with the doctor first thing in the morning about the bleeding. I just don't know what else to do."

"Don't worry. I'm fine. Go to sleep. I love you."

"I love you, too, baby," I said, and kissed her again. Then I walked the five steps to our big, four-poster bed and collapsed into dreamless oblivion.

I awoke with a start. I opened my eyes but decided to remain motionless and listen carefully to the sounds of the big old house. I have no idea what, if anything, roused me. The morning light was still dim, and there were the usual intermittent creaks and groans from the walls and floor. Down the hall, I could see the glow of our holiday decorations. We'd put up the tree, garlands and ribbons early this year. It seemed like we were determined to make this a special Christmas. The year 1994 had been rugged, and I guess we wanted to blot out all our frustrations and aggravations before we started the new year. The tree was bedecked with hundreds of the tiny white lights, reflecting in reds and yellows and greens off the colored glass globes of the tree.

Then with a rush I remembered the events of the night before. I carefully but quickly twisted around on the big mattress to find Annette.

She was sleeping soundly next to me. Deeply, but not peacefully. Usually I loved to just gaze upon her as she slumbered, but this morning her eyes looked puffy. Her forehead was strained, her hair disheveled. I was worried about her. I lay beside my beloved wife and studied her for several minutes. The sun was just rising and the room was suffused with a peach-colored glow. She was breathing evenly, but in the morning's soft light I could see her cheeks were tear stained and her brow was creased. I ever so gently stroked her forehead, hoping to erase the lines of pain and worry that I saw there. When I touched her, she opened her eyes as if she'd been conscious all along.

Without a word, she raised up and hugged me tightly, burying her face into my neck. For a long time, she didn't move – she just held me, and I pressed her close. Finally, she loosened her embrace enough to look into my eyes. The tiny lights of our Christmas tree were reflected in her tears.

"I lost the baby," she said.

Chapter 11

Deliverance

4 June 1995
Denver, Colorado

"Timber, feel my tummy."

"What?" I was still in bed, groggy from driving the bus until two in the morning. "What's the matter?"

"Here." She grabbed my hand, and placed it firmly just below her navel. "Push. Doesn't it feel different?"

I had caressed, stroked, massaged, and held her body countless times over the years of our marriage. I knew it well. Her abdomen could be toned and flat, or firm with child, or rigid in contraction. Now it felt soft, like fruit that was a little too ripe. I really didn't know what to say to her, but I shared her sense of concern.

"Can you tell? It's almost mushy. It didn't feel this way yesterday at the dunes."

She was right. I recalled the long minutes that we stood in the afternoon sun, watching the children revel in the stream. I had been behind her, with my cheek in her hair and my hands cradling her body. Even accounting for the Lycra of her suit, she had felt much firmer then.

"We can go in this morning, I'm sure. Dr. Porter said we should check in as soon as we got back, anyway. Do you feel OK?" I asked.

"I felt fine, but now I'm kind of worried."

Neither one of the Dr. Porters was in, but the nurse answering the phone said we should come over right away for an examination.

Annette seemed to take forever dressing. Levi and Corban were still sleeping in the bus parked in the alley, and she wanted to wait until

238

they awoke. Then Ben called to chat, and someone had to find Miss Meow, just to make sure she was okay. There was a pile of mail to sort through. Annette had a lot of things to do that seemed very important.

It was nearly noon before we drove into the parking lot at the clinic.

"Is Dr. Irwin in?" Annette inquired hopefully at the receptionist's desk.

"No, I'm sorry. It looks like she's off for the next two weeks. Dr. Mueller is here, though."

"Oh," Annette said dejectedly. "I was hoping to just talk with her." Then she picked up a pamphlet from the desk. 'Prenatal Nutrition for New Mothers,' it said. She began studying it.

"Come on, honey," I urged her gently. "We should get this checked out."

Annette wandered with me back to the Ob/Gyn waiting area, where we were promptly ushered into an examination room. A physician's assistant asked her to disrobe so the fetal monitor could be applied. Someone would bring the equipment in just a few minutes, she said.

The Ob/Gyn staff and Annette were generally on a first name basis. Over the years, she had built long-term friendships with many of the nurses and P.A.'s there – and of course with the people over in Pediatrics as well. My wife was somehow able to easily break through the barriers to intimacy within moments of meeting someone new – and thus she seemed to know almost everyone intimately. She was a little surprised when an unfamiliar face accompanied the monitoring apparatus into the little examination room.

"Hi, Annette. I'm Marie. They told me about the twins. Do you think they're all right?" It made me think of Annette's question posed to Dr. Porter – how long ago? – that first day in his examination room. It remained a question without a sensible answer, but Marie radiated honest warmth as she reached out and set up the equipment.

While I held her hand, Annette told the technician about the twins, and the trip, and the softness of her stomach. Marie listened and nodded knowingly. There was no indication she had a schedule to keep or that Annette was taking too much time by chatting. It didn't matter that these details were arguably irrelevant to her medical welfare. She seemed to understand it was as important to attend to what Annette was saying as it was to proceed with the test. While they talked, Annette lay back on the table and watched as Marie carefully warmed the electrolyte gel and turned up the external speaker of her Doppler stethoscope.

"I figure you know this equipment about as well as I do. I thought you might like to listen in," Marie offered considerately.

"Thank you," Annette said. "I really appreciate how nice you're being. It makes a difference."

The familiar sound of static and background gurglings flooded the room as Marie positioned the probe on the mound of Annette's tummy. We listened intently together for the pulse of the twins' hearts.

"Let me try again," Marie said, and she slid the probe's head to a new position. After a few moments, she adjusted some knobs on the machine, then tried again.

Something in my chest stiffened and cramped. I wanted to swallow, but couldn't. Annette was calm, but her eyes shone above cheeks gleaming with tears. Marie examined the sensor head. Silence reigned briefly when she unplugged and reconnected it. As she slid the device once more over Annette's pale skin the only sounds we heard were alien and empty.

"Maybe – down here – " Marie said. I looked over at the nurse as she paused to wipe her eyes on the inside of her forearm.

"They're gone, aren't they?" I asked.

"I'm so sorry," Marie said. Her dark eyelashes clung together like the rays of a star. "Do you want me to give you some time alone?"

Annette nodded yes. As she left, Marie reached over to squeeze Annette's hand. "I'm really sorry," she said, and we both knew she meant it.

A little later, Annette found Linda Irwin at home. It was against the policy of the HMO to provide patients with the doctor's personal phone number, but Linda had broken that rule for Annette long ago.

Linda lived a few miles west of the city with her five children. She shared with Annette a profound commitment to children and family. Her dreams of balancing motherhood and a career as an obstetrician were initially shattered when her husband left her with their first three kids. As she rebuilt her life alone, she felt that she could manage four children as easily as three. She learned that there were hundreds of thousands of orphans in China, many with severe medical problems that left them facing highly uncertain futures.

She had arranged to adopt a baby girl from Hunan who had a birth defect. Her parents cared for her kids in Colorado while she flew over to pick the little girl up. After she paid the required fees – almost $20,000 in all – the government stalled her for weeks. She was sent to a small village miles outside the city and told to wait. Then she was told to go to another town. Finally, the bureaucrats completely reneged on the contract. Linda was told to go home. No child. No refund, either.

She stayed. She went from town to town, visiting orphanages and hospitals. She explained to the officials at the 'Peoples Court' that she was a doctor who was willing to adopt almost any child. The mistrust of Americans was such that it was several more weeks before a local administrator knocked on the door of the tiny inn where she was staying.

"Here. You sign these papers, and I will bring you a child," he said brusquely.

With a combination of gratitude and trepidation, she had signed the forms.

Jenna was handed to her wrapped in blankets. Linda was shocked to feel how little she weighed – this was supposed to be a two-year-old. She unwrapped the little girl to find her right arm and side had been horribly burned. She was covered with scar tissue and malnourished to the point of emaciation. She was near death.

After stabilizing her condition, Linda had flown with Jenna back to the States. In her new home and with the careful attention of her older brothers, she flourished. Her eyes sparkled, she learned to walk, and she spoke English easily. A year later, when another doctor in Texas called and told her the county was looking for a family for an abandoned infant girl, Nora had joined Jenna and Linda's other kids.

Dr. Irwin and Annette shared enormous respect for one another. They differed on a host of relatively minor issues – politics, religion, and the like. When it came to matters relating to the welfare of children, however, they were bound in a way that neither could fully explain.

As usual, Linda was cordially efficient on the phone.

"When do they want to start the prostaglandins?" Linda asked as she spoke to Annette.

"Tomorrow morning."

"This timing is terrible. I really wanted to be there for you, but I'm heading off to Texas this afternoon with the kids. The only reason I'm home at all is because Jenna's doctor had to postpone her appointment," Linda apologized. "Has anyone talked to you about the inserts?"

241

"The what?" Annette replied blankly.

"That's OK. You've answered my question. Stay by the phone, and I'll call you right back."

Shortly after five later that evening, Annette and I walked through the doors of the clinic – now virtually empty – for the second time that day. Linda met us in the hall and immediately wrapped Annette in her arms. I embraced her in greeting, then said hello to all her kids.

"I couldn't get a sitter on such short notice," Linda explained, "and I really think you need these inserts. This should make it a lot easier on you. The prostaglandins are pretty wicked. I'm a little worried that you're going to be tough to get started. You've never done well on Pit."

Dr. Irwin was referring to Pitocin, an artificial hormone used of to induce labor. After Tomicah's precipitous labor, each of our babies had taken increasingly longer to deliver. Annette's last pregnancies had gone over term, and several times labor was artificially induced with the intravenous administration of Pitocin. Linda found Annette's response to Pit was slow, erratic and unpredictable. The drug had completely failed to induce labor during Glorianna's birth. Then, eight hours on the IV had produced only a few harsh and irregular contractions, so Annette and Linda decided to abandon their attempt and try again a few days later.

"If they have to keep jacking up the dosage over several days, you're not in for a nice experience. Not everyone uses these inserts, but I'd hate to start you without them."

She explained the thin, brown sticks were formed from a dehydrated marine plant akin to seaweed. When properly administered internally, they would release enzymes that helped relax the muscle tissues and dilate the cervix. The matchstick-sized inserts took only a few minutes to place.

"These things can really make a difference," Linda said.

Annette winced, but the overall discomfort seemed minor. Linda checked her vital signs as they chatted about the some of the expectations Annette should carry into the hospital the following day.

"It was _so_ nice of you to come in, Linda," she said gratefully. "I really appreciate the chance to talk with you about what's going to happen tomorrow."

"Don't eat too much tonight and make sure it's easily digestible food. I'll call in from Dallas to check up on you."

We wished the children a wonderful vacation and left for home feeling ourselves blessed by Dr. Irwin's care.

I awoke the next morning filled with dread. As the sun rose in a hazy sky, I lay in bed trying to trace the origins of the sick feeling in my soul. Things were a little intense, I concluded, but nothing should have provoked this level of uneasiness. I tried to shake it off.

I had told the children the night before that the twins died naturally. Their mother would have to go through minor surgery and be in the hospital for as much as a week. If she felt up to it, I would bring them to visit in shifts. The kids and their mom talked, and hugged, and cried together quietly. There was a sense that the inevitable had come to pass. They had accepted the twins' demise with grace and maturity.

Annette got up a few minutes after I did. She seemed composed, somber, resigned. We both dressed mechanically, without saying much, and neither of us had breakfast.

Before we left for the hospital, we called the kids together in the living room. As they congregated on the couches and chairs, the children were nervously subdued. Corban had a few questions about the medical procedure. Liberty asked in a quivering voice if we were sure that Annette would return safely.

I was worried about Libi. She had been a precocious two year old when Lincoln had died. The pain and commotion surrounding his passing had hurt her in ways I was still trying to comprehend. When Shiloh was near death a year later, the other kids had rallied to take care of him. Liberty was determined to help, but she had been too young to do anything much. Instead, she worried and prayed that we would be able to keep him with us. One night Shiloh's alarms were going off every few minutes. For a while Annette and I took turns resuscitating him back to consciousness. It was anything but a restful night. I finally decided we shouldn't both suffer the loss of sleep. I dragged Shi's oxygen and monitors out into the dimly lit living room to hold him in my arms until dawn. As the alarm shrieked yet again, I was surprised to hear little footfalls on the stairs. Libi emerged, her hair tousled but her blue eyes wide open. She stood in her pink pajamas with one hand on the door.

"Is Shiloh OK?" she had inquired quietly. She had just turned three. She spoke carefully, with just a hint of a lisp.

"Sure, sweetheart." I had tried to set her mind at ease. "You can go back to bed."

"Nobody's going to take Shiloh away?" She was as serious as a three year old gets.

"No, baby. He's OK."

"Daddy – don't let them take Shiloh away. I don't want anybody to take my little brother away."

My heart ached. I thought back to Lincoln, and then to my long night with Shiloh before we had properly diagnosed his condition. "I'll make sure he's OK, Libi. I promise. You can go back to bed. It's OK."

She was unyielding. "Nobody's going to take my little brother away." She stood resolutely in the doorway, shaking her blonde curls gently but firmly, side to side.

"No, honey. Nobody."

"I'll stay with you," she had declared. She padded over to climb on the couch with me. As she snuggled into my shoulder and stroked Shiloh's pale cheek, she looked up at me and carefully affirmed once again – not to me, perhaps, as much as to herself .

"Nobody's going to take my brother away. Nobody."

Since that night I'd noticed she continued to be especially sensitive to the welfare of her family. She watched over her younger siblings as if she were personally responsible.

"This is not a big deal, guys," I explained to her as I tried to reassure them all. "The twins never got very large, and so this should be a lot like a regular delivery."

"Then why does Mommy have to be gone for so long?" Liberty asked. "It only took a day for Mercina and Glori." It was a good question, I reflected. Smart.

"This is different because the doctors have to use drugs to make the babies come early. Come on, sweetheart, you don't need to worry. Let's say a family prayer, and then Mommy has got to go." I was at a loss for any more words of comfort.

I asked the Lord's blessing on us all that day and requested a special blessing on Annette. When we finished, each of the children filed past their mother to give her a parting hug and kisses.

Kimber was last. She lingered. She seemed especially reluctant to see Annette go. Finally, when it was clear we were already late, she gave her mother a long embrace, then she turned her tear-streaked face away and quickly left the room.

We arrived at the hospital twenty minutes behind schedule, but we were past caring. We were directed to a small room on the third floor, overlooking the mountains. Annette dutifully slipped into her gown. We waited. We talked about Chari's piano lessons and Shiloh's soccer. Time crawled.

"Where <u>are</u> your veins, Honey?" the frustrated nurse asked. Annette's tiny veins were notoriously challenging to those trying to insert an IV drip needle. The nurse had already twice stuck her unsuccessfully in the left wrist and was now wrapping the thick rubber band around her right arm in preparation for another try. "They say I'm good at this, but I can't even begin to see where I can poke you. You've got to have a vein somewhere."

"She's got terrible veins, but at least she's a nice person," Dr. Irwin observed wryly from her position in the half opened doorway.

"Linda!!!" Annette squealed, and she jumped off the table to embrace her. "What are you doing here?"

"Something came up," she said obliquely. "How are you feeling?"

"Well, it really makes me feel better that you're here. Thanks so much for coming." Annette started to sob quietly.

"OK, OK – enough of the gushy stuff." She grabbed Annette's arm and helped the relieved nurse find a productive spot for the IV.

"Get back on the table and pull over your gown," she said efficiently. "I also need to measure your tummy."

"Why?" Annette asked, and then – as she often did – she continued on talking without awaiting a reply. "Linda, I'm really kind of nervous about this. I know I have to do it, but I have an uncomfortable feeling." She continued on as Dr. Irwin alternately made a number of abdominal measurements and offered gentle, monosyllabic replies to Annette's stream of concerns. When she finished, the doctor picked up the phone.

"Tom? This is Dr. Irwin. I know I'm not on the duty roster, but I need an ultrasound in 307 as soon as possible – Like <u>now</u>. Can you do that for me?" There was a note of rugged authority in the doctor's voice that made me wonder who would dare to decline her request. Then her tone softened. "Thanks, Tom – I appreciate it."

Linda and Annette talked mostly about their respective kids until the mobile equipment arrived a few minutes later. The technician quickly set up, acting as if he really should be somewhere else.

The tech powered up the monitor and applied the transducer. Annette had lost track of the number of times in the past few weeks that different people had squirted, smeared, or smoothed the pale blue jelly over her midsection. She barely noticed any more.

"Whoa." The tech was clearly unaware that this was anything but a routine exam. After his initial exclamation, his voice reverted to a textbook example of controlled clinical concern. "Doctor, I think you should see this."

"Just get me a full set of fetal measurements and include an estimated fetal mass. I don't need anything else," Dr. Irwin ordered. "On second thought, get me some representative cross-sections, too."

The tech gave her a quick 'I-sure-hope-you-know-what-you're-doing' look, and then immediately set to work.

"So are you going to Texas?" Annette asked. "What happened? I thought you said you were leaving last night."

"Oh, sure we are," she replied casually. "It turns out we can't leave until this afternoon." She chatted with Annette for a few more moments as the images on portable CRT were recorded onto film and graph paper. The familiar routine was interrupted by a quick rap on the door.

"Well, Dr. Irwin! What brings you in today?" All four of us in the room turned to look toward the door. "I thought you were out of town for a while."

The heavyset man in the doorway wore a white lab coat and a carefully trimmed beard. His manner was studied and professional, but there was an underlying edge to his voice.

"Nice to see you, Dr. Mahoney," Linda said smoothly. Annette tightened her grip on my hand when she heard the doctor's name.

Dr. Irwin continued. "I just wanted to drop in on my favorite multigravida before I headed out of town." Everyone smiled at her affectionate reference to Annette, but there remained an element of tension in the room. Dr. Mahoney looked critically at the tech as he stooped over the console.

"I didn't order an ultrasound. Have there been any complications?" His voice was a mixture of professional concern with a touch of suspicion.

"I'm all done, sir," the tech said, transparently more for Dr. Irwin's benefit than to actually address Dr. Mahoney's question. He handed her the printouts from the machine.

"Thanks, Tom." Linda again softened – momentarily. "I ordered the scan," she said coolly as she quickly skimmed over the ultrasound results. "I examined Annette last night and I think a reconsideration of the treatment protocol is warranted."

"Dr. Irwin, this is really very straightforward." Dr. Mahoney's demeanor turned stony almost instantly. His tone became rigidly clinical and heavy with condescension. "The Treatment Advisory Committee has reviewed this case extensively. We obviously should have proceeded weeks ago with a D&E, but that's neither here nor there, now." He drew himself to his full stature in an patent, physical assertion of his authority. "Prostaglandin induction is the accepted treatment protocol when there's a fetal demise after 24 weeks. I don't think we need to talk about this any further." He started to turn away as if daring her to say anything more.

The same Linda Irwin that refused to back down in the face of blustering Communist bureaucrats did not have the slightest intention of abandoning her conviction about Annette's proper treatment now.

"Doctor," There was iron resolve in every syllable. "Perhaps we should talk in the hall." She walked out without awaiting his answer.

Dr. Mahoney's consternation was ill-disguised. After a moment's disbelief, he spun about to follow her and shut the door firmly behind him.

"Wow," said the tech as he looked first at the closed door and then to Annette and me.

"Timber, what is going on?!?" Annette whispered.

"Shhh. Hang on – I'll try to find out." I walked quickly over to the heavy wooden door and carefully pulled it ajar.

Dr. Mahoney was hissing as much as he was talking.

"This is completely unacceptable. You are not on duty here. You have no authority to order tests without my approval. This woman has been completely uncooperative from the start, and now you're telling me not to proceed with a no-brainer prostaglandin induction when we're already staffed and prepped. You seem to have no idea what's involved in administering a medical practice." He almost spat his words out.

"Dr. Mahoney," Linda said in cooly measured tones. "First, in my professional opinion, no induction should be considered a 'no-brainer', especially when we're dealing with an ultra-multigravida. If you haven't taken a look at some of the recent research on the incidence of cervical rupture associated with prostaglandin inductions in multigravidas, perhaps you should. She's already borderline anemic, and I'm not sure how well she would handle substantial blood loss. I also noted this morning that this facility is not in a good position to deal with a multi-unit Type A positive transfusion.

"Second, your staffing arrangements are secondary to this patient's welfare. I was supposed to leave for Texas last night, but I'm here now – on my vacation – to assure the best possible care for a patient in your department.

"Third – and this is what this is really all about – take a look at these scan pics. I'm not just trying to mess up your schedule. The fetal measurements and estimated body mass are clearly within the limits for a D&E. The way I see it, the diminished cardiac function of the twins retarded fetal development. They quit *growing* well before the twenty-forth week. You're on automatic pilot to put her through a prostaglandin protocol, but it certainly looks to me like its unwarranted. We can do a D&E, greatly reduce the risk of complications, and also make the whole procedure much less traumatic for her.

"As I recall," Dr. Irwin continued in a voice as hard as surgical steel, "the chargeable fees for a D&E are a fraction of those for a prostaglandin induction. Your budget isn't threatened. If you insist on proceeding, I will submit a detailed, written justification for my intervention to the Treatment Advisory Committee this afternoon. I have no idea why you're debating this with me."

For several long seconds there was only silence from the hallway.

"Fine," Dr. Mahoney said emotionlessly. "Proceed with the D&E." Then I heard the sharp click of his oxfords receding down the linoleum of the hall.

I expected Linda to rejoin us, but the tech reassembled his equipment and we were left alone. Annette listened to me recount the discussion I'd just heard in the hall as she watched the IV silently drip saline solution into her arm.

Annette asked me to call home and let the kids know what was happening. Kimber answered the phone and asked if she could talk to her mother. They chatted for perhaps five minutes and then Annette told her she loved her and handed the receiver back to me.

"Daddy, I don't feel good about this at all. I didn't tell Mommy, but when I got up this morning I got this really bad feeling. I've had it all day."

"I know, sweetheart. I feel the same way," I said cryptically, and smiled reassuringly at Annette.

248

"Everything's okay, isn't it?" she asked.

"Things seem to be going just fine. I'll call you when I know anything more. We've gotta go. I love you, and your mother loves you very much." I carefully set the phone in its cradle and winced at a pain in the seething pit of my stomach.

Finally there was a quick tap on the door. Linda breezed in. I wanted to hug her in gratitude for the battle she had waged on Annette's behalf, but she acted as if nothing at all had happened.

"We're all set. There's been a little change in plans, but it's really a lot better for you. If you're game, we can do a D&E and not put you through the wringer by doing a prostaglandin induction. I was able to schedule the O.R. for two o'clock this afternoon. And I'm sorry I was gone so long. It took me a while, but I tracked down the only guy in town who I trust to do the D&E this late in your gestation. He was actually headed out on vacation tomorrow, too, but I told him what you're facing, and he said he'd be happy to put off finishing his reports and take care of you. So make sure you tell him I said I owe him one."

Annette held out her arms to Linda, who obliged her by accepting a long, quiet embrace.

"Thank you so much," she whispered, and then Dr. Irwin was gone.

We met Dr. Margolis shortly after one-thirty. He was a quiet man with what sounded to be a slight, eastern European accent. He reviewed Annette's chart, checked her internally and pronounced that all appeared to be in order. I thanked him for his help on such short notice.

"Don't thank me! Your Dr. Irwin traded me three weekends on call for hanging around this afternoon. I figure I got a great deal."

I was a little stunned, but after the events of the morning, I wasn't really surprised.

"She says you're the best," I related.

"She's a very fine person. Anyway, we should have you out of here tomorrow, if all goes well."

"Doctor," I didn't really want to, but I had to ask, "Would you please review the risks of a D&E? In all the commotion, I think I missed it."

"It's a pretty straightforward procedure. We administer general anesthesia and then dilate the cervix. The extraction of the fetus, or fetuses, in your case, only takes a few minutes. Then we try to make sure we leave everything all neat and tidy," he said and smiled gently at

249

Annette. "I'm sorry about this. I understand you really wanted these babies."

Annette nodded solemnly.

"As far as risks, there's the usual risk of bleeding that you face in any surgery, but I don't see much of that. This actually is a fairly minor procedure as far as surgery goes. Statistically, the greatest risk comes from the anesthesia. Quantitatively, at this altitude, we get into trouble with only one patient in a thousand, and I guess we lose roughly one in ten thousand. So the odds are very much in your favor." He smiled without being obsequious.

"Well, I've got to scrub up. When I see you next," he looked at Annette, "you should be out cold. So I'll say goodbye now." He waved at us cordially and walked briskly into the hall. The door quietly clicked behind him.

"Timber, would you please give me a blessing? Just to help me feel more at ease?" The doctor's explanation had only partially allayed her fears.

I placed my hands on her forehead, closed my eyes and blessed her with peace and comfort. Before I was able to finish I heard someone enter the room. I concluded the blessing in the name of Jesus Christ and looked up to see a nurse standing reverently by the door.

"I'm sorry to have interrupted," she said. "If you're ready now, we need to head into the O.R."

Regardless of Annette's condition, I was not ready. After all the prayers, all the kindness, all the incredible blessings we had experienced, I still felt utter dread. A giant claw was reaching into my guts and twisting my soul like dough in a baker's hand. I was ready to scream, "STOP!!! This is _enough_!" But I knew everyone had done all they could. There was nowhere to go but into the operating room.

"Are you ready, baby?" I looked down at her as she smiled weakly.

"It didn't make me feel any better to hear they only lose one in ten thousand," she said thoughtfully. "It seems like we're catching all the probabilities lately – both the bad and the good. When Christian and Jefferson are one in a couple hundred thousand babies, one in ten thousand sounds pretty common."

"I know. I had the same thought. But if we don't deliver them now, there's a 100% chance we'll lose you. Annette, I love you with all my heart."

"And I love you more!" she said quietly but emphatically.

I walked with her to the door as the nurse wheeled her to the operating room. I was allowed no further.

"You have the most incredible eyes I have ever seen," I said sincerely, and then I kissed her and prayed I wasn't kissing her goodbye. A wave of panic engulfed me as they wheeled her away.

"Are you the anesthesiologist?" I heard her ask a young man with a mask. "You'd better bring me back – I've got nine kids waiting at home for me!"

Then the big double doors swung shut.

XI. Kimber's Missing Linc

25 January 1996 (and Thursday Evening, 8 June 1989)
Denver, Colorado

Kimber handed me a neatly typed sheaf of paper. She smiled modestly. Her sculpted hand carefully redirected a stray tress of her radiant chestnut hair to its proper place. Kimi's perceptive hazel-green eyes were lit with the smile which graced her lips. Although they were a different color than her mother's, it was clear they shared the same genetic stock.

"I got an A," she said with quiet satisfaction. "Will you read it? The assignment was to describe a spiritually significant event of our lives. I know the writing's not perfect, but the professor said it was one of the best papers in the class. She liked how I understood what she wanted in the assignment."

This was Kimi's first writing project for a professor of religion who was reputed to be a tough grader. Somewhat to my chagrin, she had declined to have me proofread the piece before she handed it in. I was relieved and a little excited as I took the paper into the living room and sat down on the couch.

251

A few months earlier, Kimi – like Tomicah before her – had started college at age fifteen. As had been the case with her older brother, the first time she ever sat in a school classroom was at nearby Regis University. She loved her courses, but we were both a little nervous about how well she'd do in her studies. One of the anxieties home schoolers face is that outside assessments of our children's progress are infrequent. Tomicah and Kimber were admitted to college primarily on the basis of test scores. We had little else in the way of third-party verification concerning the quality of their home-based education.

Nature versus nurture. Parents inevitably wonder: Will our child learn the best of what we offer? Or live beyond us as the image of our faults? Whose fingerprints will be found on our tiny armful when she has grown to have a voice, a vision, and vows to have a child of her own?

Years ago I read a story in <u>National Geographic</u> about two South American rivers. One was born in the jungles of the Amazon Basin. Its source was indeterminable, hidden in the roots of mighty trees so tall that some birds never rose above them. Strong winds destined for the mountains from the frigid South Atlantic gave up their moisture overhead. Raindrops fell upon leaves, dripped to branches and drained through the age-old accumulation of organic matter on the forest floor. In the jungle, the water's path was circuitous and its cargo limited to tannic compounds which could be dissolved and languidly conveyed from puddles to pools to the serpentine stream.

The source of the second river was altogether different. It tumbled from high peaks, the product of countless bitter blizzards that blanketed the Andes with snow and ice imported from Antarctica by those same fierce winds. Roaring avalanches conspired with tiny streams to direct the snowmelt east in an ever expanding flow. Trickles grew into torrents, raw and raging, which scoured the river's path so aggressively that just the largest boulders and most tenacious trees remained unmoved to testify of the water's relentless charge to the sea. Even these monoliths would stand only for a time before they were ground into muck and detritus by the current's pounding assault.

At a point, the cold chocolate of the Andean cascade merged with the tepid tea of the jungle. In the peculiar design of their confluence, they retained their identities long after fusing into one greater whole. The two arteries became one – but hesitantly. The

252

Geographic's vivid aerial photo of the conjoined streams showed it coiling like a garter snake on its side, its belly muddy beige, its back deep brown. A boat headed downstream in the midst of the flow could dip a bucket of turbid murk from one side of its hull and draw dark – but transparent – brew from the other. Miles seaward the two sources finally, ever so gradually, commingled. The pictures illustrated the process of the waters braiding together – a stream of cream welling up in the brown infusion of the one side, a streak of smoky topaz threading its way in the silty sienna of the other. The river – two, into one – continued to exhibit traces of its sources as they progressed, combined and blended.

Like a marriage. Perhaps like a child.

Tomicah and Levi grew into young men who didn't look a whole lot like me. Rarely were they told they were their dad's spittin' image. But my old friends would carry on extended phone conversations with either one of them and believe they were speaking with me. Both boys have my voice. They may not have my nose, but listen: They sound just like me. Kimber's eyes reflect facets of the green I see in the mirror – but as she searches and surveys the world her vision probes and penetrates just like her mother's. I see unmistakable traces of her forebearers in her face.

Spiritually significant events expose our souls. The professor's demand for intimacy made me a little uneasy. What would I see in Kimi's essay? The rabbit report she wrote as a child was informed and endearing. At eight she won a contest by penning a concept for a TV pilot episode, but that was now almost ancient. I'd seen only a few glimpses of her literary work in the years since. Some brief compositions. A few letters. Her professor had evidently responded well to Kimber's offering. I wondered what she saw – and who.

*   *   *   *   *

Kimber Tillemann-Dick
Intro. to Religious Studies RS 101
Dr. Susan Doty

My family eats dinner together. We have almost every evening since I was born to my parents, Annette Tillemann-

Dick and Timber Dick. They tell me that it was over dinner that they decided to name me Kimber (kind of after my father) Rainbow (after the Lord's promise) Tillemann-Dick. We have a big family. I have an older brother, and four younger brothers and four little sisters followed me into this world.

The summer that I was nine years old, I had the most spiritually defining experience of my life. It was also the most painful. That night in June we were a relatively small group. Lincoln, the baby, had gone to sleep early and Charity, my six-year-old sister, was visiting our grandparents in Washington. Shiloh, Mercina, and Glorianna (now my youngest siblings) had not yet been born. We sat around the table in our newly remodeled kitchen. The doors were open so we could hear Lincoln if he awoke.

My father looked at each of us, then said in his beautiful bass voice, "Corban, will you please ask the Lord's blessing on this food?" We all groaned a little. Corbi was four years old and took a long time for everything. He grinned, "I'd be happy to...

"Dear Heavenly Father, we thank Thee for this beautiful day. We thank Thee for the sun that makes my tomatoes grow..."

Corban's name comes from the Old Testament and means, "dedicated to God" -- and he seemed determined to prove it in his prayer that night. After perhaps ten minutes, we said, "Amen" with a combination of appreciation and exasperation.

After dinner, we cleaned the kitchen and looked at our little tomato plants. Mine was crooked. I turned it a little.

"Kimber," my mother called, "will you please help Liberty into her pajamas?"

I took Libi's hand and quietly entered my parents' room, so as not to wake Lincoln. As I glanced at my slumbering baby brother, something was wrong -- his little eyes were puffy. He hadn't been crying. In fact, he had been perfectly quiet. My father had followed us into the room. He'd also noticed something wasn't right with Lincoln. I thought he knew everything, so I asked, "Daddy, what's wrong with his eyes?"

Almost immediately, I felt myself being lifted by my Daddy's strong hands, while a voice that was his, but was so filled with fear I didn't recognize it, said "MOVE!" Libi and I stood by the door, completely bewildered, while my father bent over the tiny boy, doing things that looked very important, but neither of us understood. My daddy's voice, the one that I knew, called to my mom in the kitchen, "Call 911!"

I knew what that meant. Grabbing Libi, I ran into the kitchen.

"Mommy, what's the matter? What's going on?" She was still trying to talk on the phone. Even though I was surrounded by many people, I had never felt more alone in my life. My mother hung up and fell to her knees.

Sobbing with more pain than I had ever seen, she cried, "Father, forgive me, please. Forgive me for whatever I've done – just bring back my baby!"

My big brother took my hand and we knelt, prayed, and cried together with my mother. Before we could finish, I heard sirens getting louder and louder. Some firemen came in and tried to continue my dad's heartfelt efforts to revive Lincoln's tiny form. They scared me, tromping around in their huge boots and yellow hats. I ran to the door to watch those big strong men take my baby brother to the ambulance. I somehow knew he wouldn't come back.

I woke up in our playroom. Someone was vacuuming. I wanted to go back to sleep, but I knew I couldn't. Something had happened. As the heartbreaking memories of the night before returned, I stumbled out of bed to find my mother. My room, and the rest of the house, was filled with family, flowers, and people from our church. They were all cleaning, cooking, hugging – anything that needed to be done or made them feel useful.

I tried to avoid them. I was angry that these people would dare to intrude at such a personal time. I gave up on trying to find my parents and decided to be satisfied with being alone with my grief and my stuffed rabbit. I walked through the kitchen on my way out to the back yard. My daddy was there, his eyes slightly red. As I saw the signs of grief on this man I had thought invincible, I couldn't help but cry.

As members of the Church of Jesus Christ, we believe the family unit to be eternal if the family members are righteous. While I had been taught this basic principle since nursery school, I never imagined that my simple faith in this foundation of all I thought to be true would be tested so soon. I found myself struggling with the reality that the little boy I had held in my arms the afternoon before was gone in every physical sense of the word. While I was old enough to be painfully aware of what had happened, I was young enough to still trust my parents, Sunday School teachers, and other spiritual leaders almost completely. I knew I would never be taught a lie purposefully – but how could they possibly know that Lincoln was now in Paradise surrounded by grandparents, friends, and guinea pigs that had passed on?

As I struggled with these questions that were much too big for my nine-year-old brain, I was perplexed to the point of tears. These were not tears of grief. They were more like those I shed when, no matter how hard I practiced, I just could not play a piano piece correctly. I was trying to understand how God could justify taking the life of a perfect, sinless baby with no warning whatsoever. I looked to my parents for reassurance, and they offered as much as they could in the midst of their own pain. Yet, somehow, I knew that I couldn't lean on their faith. This was something I had to do for myself.

I knelt in my closet. It seemed to be the one place in the house where I could be sure not to be disturbed. I begged my Father in heaven to please comfort me. I asked to be enlightened as to why my baby brother was gone. Why did my parents, the most faithful, selfless people I knew, have to suffer through this indescribable pain? Why did I have to deal with Death, when I should have been playing soccer and having fun?

I did not receive a bolt of lightening or spoken answers to my many questions. Instead I received peace. A feeling of warmth washed over me as I cried in the dark. I felt the love of Jesus and my Heavenly Father. I believe the Holy Spirit was in that little closet with me, and while the death of my brother was not explained away, I was no longer angry. I understood that there was some plan, bigger than you or me, that required Lincoln to be taken from us at that time. I knew that I would, someday, see him again. The strength of the spirit and the clarity of the sentiment I felt made that experience almost more powerful than if words had actually been spoken.

I <u>was</u> spoken to, but I didn't hear with my ears – I heard with my heart.

I still felt pain, but it was much less bitter. I still felt grief, but it was self-indulgent. I could adjust my focus – look to the future and try to make the best of it. I was grateful to all the people who had come to help my parents as they tried to answer these questions for themselves.

I was at peace.

Several days later at the funeral, I sang with the children's choir, as I always had. I looked down and saw my weeping parents. My grandmothers were sobbing. People I didn't know were crying. I thought about Lincoln as I saw how many people cared about him, even though he was only three months old. I thought about the little smile he would get when I tickled his tummy just so. I thought about what our family would be like without him. I thought about him, but I didn't cry. I had no reason to. I already knew that this was not a forever goodbye.

Now, years later, I still believe that I will meet Lincoln again. Other areas of my faith have evolved, grown and shifted, but this principle remains unchanging. I know, with a surety that is more real to me than things I can see and feel, that if I am righteous I will be reunited with Lincoln and the rest of my family after death. I know that I was answered when I prayed with simple, but pure, faith. I know that I am still learning the power and fullness of the gospel I believe to be true – yet I still fully believe.

Had I not prayed that afternoon in June I don't know how I would have dealt with the death of my brother. I could have ignored the questions I was asking myself and become sullen and depressed. I may have lost faith and doubted the existence of God. What did happen strengthened my beliefs and brought my whole family closer together. The death of Lincoln was still a tragedy, but it taught me at a young age a great deal about faith. The reasons for God's actions may be unclear, but with faith we can receive assurance that He has His purposes.

Faith has always required a leap, and in these modern times that leap may seem even more perilous. Religious faith, through the centuries, has provided a means for people to deal with the most challenging situations life presents.

The organizations of man have failed repeatedly, but faith in God has survived through the ages because it <u>works</u>. I believe it works because, even when marred and tarnished by human intervention, it is the tool used by men to reach beyond themselves to their creator and to the truths that transcend earthbound knowledge.

*   *   *   *   *

Chapter 12

Reflections on the Plot

14 June 1995
Crown Hill Cemetery, Wheatridge, Colorado

The kelly green canopy flapped gently in the breeze. The sky was leaden. It was cool out, I noticed, but it wasn't drizzling as it had been at Lincoln's funeral. My eye was twitching again. Maybe someday, I hoped, the stress would let up and it'd stop. For the moment I just tried to ignore it.

I was a little amazed that the space right next to Lincoln was vacant. When we purchased his plot, Annette and I wanted it to be a little bit away from the other graves. We had no particular reason, but we had picked a spot for our baby boy that was off to the side of the section. Now, exactly six years later, it was almost completely surrounded by headstones. Except for the space right next door.

I stared down into the empty grave. I could see the side of Lincoln's burial vault. Not his coffin – just the big concrete box that held his coffin. It was a strangely comforting sight, that gray cement wall. If I were going down there, I'd like to be near my family. Not that it really made any difference.

Libi wouldn't stop sobbing, but that was understandable. I looked from her tear-stained little face to the gleaming white casket on the pedestal. A bouquet of red sweetheart roses was on the sealed lid. White was the right color, I reflected. Not black, or brown, or copper-colored. White. Pure white, dazzling even when the sky looked like ashes. White was definitely the best choice.

It had been a simple service. I didn't have the energy for anything more. Everyone stood silently as I dedicated the grave.

There was really nothing left to do except lower the coffin into the ground. That was the hardest part. I did pretty well during the funeral, and I'd dedicated the grave myself. But I felt no confidence whatsoever I could maintain my composure when the casket was actually lowered into the earth.

When Lincoln was buried, Annette did fine until they lowered his little body. She wanted – we all wanted – to see him safely laid to rest. It just didn't seem right to leave the cemetery before he was securely in his place. But to actually see him buried hit us like a sledgehammer. It left no room for doubt that he was gone for this lifetime. It was good to grieve, but it hurt like the blazes to say that final goodbye.

Another wave of anguish and gratitude washed through my soul. Funny how I could feel both emotions so intensely, and simultaneously. The pain of my loss was accompanied by profound gratitude that my faith could soften the blow. Pain is part of life, and death is part of life. Now I knew those truths better than ever.

Faith is a part of life only for those who will choose it.

There was a time, when I was younger, that I put my faith in machines, and institutions, and people. That kind of faith offers precious little comfort to someone standing beside a pristine white coffin. Faith in God offered the only real comfort now, and an assurance that I would once again be eternally reunited with those I love most.

It was time.

I looked across the empty grave to the faces of my assembled children. I walked to stand beside the casket. I couldn't see very well. My sight blurred with tears as I gazed over once again into Annette's incredible sapphire starburst eyes. Then I carefully lifted Christian and Jefferson, together for all time in their tiny white coffin, and gently lowered them into the earth.

XII. Epilogue

The New Millennium
Denver, Colorado

Life isn't simple.

We – indeed, people of all faiths around the world – continue to wrestle with issues of obedience and faith.

For some of us the toughest challenge comes with the loss of an innocent child. Others place their trust in great and inspiring leaders who too frequently fall to corruption. Some of us believe in symbols of virtue – a building or a flag – more than we have faith in the source of all righteousness. Sometimes we pray for solace or wisdom and hear in answer only silence.

In the school of the eternities, it appears to be essential that we choose to submit and believe at the very moment when we find ourselves apparently forsaken. To prove our rightful relationship with God as our Father, perhaps we must acknowledge our excruciating vulnerability.

Our family's experience with Christian and Jefferson presented complex and significant lessons. As the two boys labored to sustain one another, we were asked to choose who would live: Annette, by sacrificing the twins? Both boys, and risk their mother's well-being? Perhaps we could try to save Christian at the cost of his brother? Other issues were less tangible. Where do the souls of our unborn reside? What is the value of their lives? We're still working on some of the answers.

As a family, we continue in our commitment to study out a path and then prayerfully submit our plan to the Lord for His affirmation. Over and over again – with faith as a prerequisite – this approach has worked for us. We collectively feel a sense of peace with the events of the spring of 1995. Given the challenges that were before us, we share a profound sense of gratitude that we made the choices we did. When we reflect on the innumerable coincidences of

263

compassion that occurred over those short weeks, we feel it impossible to deny that the Lord's hand was involved. The probabilities are unexplainable otherwise.

What if things had turned out tragically? We would still today have the invaluable assurance that we submitted our will to the inspiration that was made available to us. The comfort afforded us through this process is of inestimable worth.

Heroes are precious these days. We were repeatedly rescued spiritually and physically, both by those we loved and by total strangers: Dr. Linda Irwin. The clerk. Dr. Greg DeVore. Elder Jeff Holland. Our children. And no one tried harder to save the lives of Christian and Jefferson than my incredible, faithful wife.

We experienced remarkable harmony during those weeks. The situation seemed to bring out the best in everyone – family members and acquaintances alike. Although the twins posed extraordinary challenges to our HMO, the medical attention we received was superb. People who had no reason to care reached out to help save our bodies and to soothe our souls. We are deeply grateful to them.

After the surgery, a young resident who was in attendance during the procedure came to talk with Annette as she recovered. She spent more than an hour with her, comforting her and administering the sweet balm of compassion. She described her experience in the operating room. The resident explained that she saw Jefferson's face, calm and in repose. But what moved her to join Annette at her bedside was Christian's expression: He appeared awake and alert, straining for consciousness – not in pain, but striving to hold on to life – even though, by our society's standards, he died before he ever lived.

Christian and Jefferson were – and are – important people. Their brief lives touched many of us. Their plight required that we choose and be held accountable. As for me and my house, the twins begged us to re-examine to our faith and appreciate the loving intent of One who offered His unblemished Son to save us. Christian and Jefferson taught my family that we are all, in some intangible but essential way, spiritual twins of one heart. Together in this life, we are bound forever in a divine plan, by a humble sacrifice, with a purpose we must each try to fully comprehend.

The End of This Tale

266

Family Snapshot, February 2002 –
A guide to the perplexed

Our family wanted to tell this tale because have been deeply impressed with the fact that God cares about each one of us – including you. We are subject to our own failings, to the laws of nature, and to the blessings and evil done by our fellow men. Through the perils and pleasures of life, we can ask for our Heavenly Father's guidance and comfort – or we can tough it out alone.

Thank you for caring enough to finish this book. Nonetheless, the story's not complete. Like yours, our lives continue. Those who were kind enough to read the initial drafts have asked for an update on our characters. While the following is dangerously concise, it is intended to afford the reader a sense of what has recently transpired among some of us.

Since 1995 I've lost more of my hair – if you find any of it laying about, please send it right away and I'll reimburse you for the postage – but the stress around here has diminished somewhat. I've continued to work on several inventions, both independently and in partnership with others. Safeline was taken over by speculators in late 1995. The company was recently sold again and the new owner and I are working to update the Sit'n'Stroll for the world market. We still live in our big white house in Northwest Denver. As you'll discover in the following paragraphs, a few of the kids have left home for school. My Grandma Dick moved in at the first of 1996. We just celebrated her one hundredth birthday, and she told me she's going to try to stay around for a while longer.

Annette has further honed her skills as an extraordinary mother and educator. These days she is occupied primarily with teaching the kids and managing our household. Annette remains my wisest counselor. I'm undecided whether to be flattered as her husband or insulted as her man when strangers ask me if she's my oldest daughter. She is occasionally called upon to testify before the state legislature on bills affecting home schooling. In August, 2001

267

we were pleased to see her first book – co-authored with her sister, **Katrina** – published in Europe.

In 1980 Katrina married my Yale room mate, **Dick Swett**. In November, 1996 my quite pregnant wife was in New Hampshire to help with Dick's campaign for the U.S. Senate. On election eve, just as Dick was being declared by CNN as the winner of his hard-fought race, Annette went into premature labor. Although Dick subsequently lost the election in a stunning turnabout, **Zenith Wisdom** Tillemann-Dick was born early in the morning of November 6th. In addition to possessing an innate sense of dramatic timing, Zen makes friends of all ages easily and he's learning to read. He has the brown hair I used to have, brown eyes and a captivating grin. As the youngest of our ensemble, he's learned to get all of us to dance to his tune. We find him hard to resist.

His next-older sister, **Glorianna Willow**, is now eight. She's lost a lot of her baby teeth but kept her truly delightful smile. Her sense of humor is outrageous, her theatrics bemusing. In the family meetings we hold each morning, she loves to read from the King James Translation of the Bible. She's still having a little trouble with her "R's" – unless she rrreally concentrrrates. Her favorite reading place is snuggled in my lap.

This sentiment is shared by **Mercina Grace**, and the two little girls are often found together piled on me. At age nine, Mia has turned into the chief wardrobe technician for her younger siblings. On Sunday mornings, she's one of the busiest people in the house as we all get ready for Church. Mercina is a promising student with refined handwriting. We regularly find – in some of the most surprising places – little notes she's stashed which convey her affectionate best wishes to us.

Shiloh Benson continues to be more disposed toward reading than writing or running. He stashes his favorite books in convenient nooks all over the house. He's almost 12, and a Boy Scout who reads voraciously – often two or three substantial volumes in a week. At the conclusion of many of them, he's been known to quiz the family and unsuspecting visitors on the subjects he's just learned. Just what is the most prevalent language in Afghanistan, anyway? And how fast can a hippo sprint? How did Lindbergh navigate the North Atlantic? Our doctor says he may grow to be over six foot five. I'm trying to stay on his good side.

Liberty Belle is gracefully navigating the treacherous shoals of early adolescence. Like Shiloh, Libi's now taller than her mom. She just turned 14 and attended her first dance. Overrated, she said. A recently enacted Colorado law requires home schooled kids to take standardized tests. She was pleased to score a couple of grades ahead of her age in math. She wants to be a pediatrician, so strong quantitative skills will help. Liberty enjoys singing and performing. Her best Christmas gift this year was getting her braces off.

Last fall, **Corban Israel** started at Regis College, which is within walking distance of our house. He also passed the test for his driver's permit. He's doing well in both activities. He's dancing competitively with Charity. I'm still not used to having a 15 year-old son who's nearly as tall as I am and dances like Fred Astaire. (On a good date, I dance like a congenial Clydesdale.) Corbi hopes to attend the Air Force Academy and serve as a pilot. If he ever goes commercial, be prepared for a lot of eccentric humor over the plane's public address system. On the other hand, I suspect he'll get you home safely, or die trying.

In September, the days following the World Trade Center attack were previously endorsed by Congress as National Civility Week. Ironic, isn't it? **Charity Sunshine** conceived of National Civility Week in 1998. She formed a non-profit corporation to promote the concept and has been working successfully with people in Washington and many states to pass enabling legislation. Last year, she was selected as a member of the USA Today National Collegiate All-Academic Team – the second-youngest of sixty. She had her 18th birthday last summer and she anticipates graduating from Regis College this spring in the Class of 2002. Chari composes hymns and – if I catch her in the right mood – she sings like an angel.

We get a letter almost every week from **Levi Mills**. He left right after Christmas a year ago to serve the Church of Jesus Christ on a two-year mission in Tokyo. The task of learning Japanese is formidable, but he's previously been able to master Spanish, some Hungarian and a little French, so we're reasonably confident. Levi's very service oriented. He transferred from Regis to Yale after his freshman year and spent the following summer in the tiny Honduran hamlet of La Finca as a volunteer cleaning up after Hurricane Mitch. He expects to graduate with the Class of 2004. In Japan, he's been called upon to sing for a number of audiences. His bass voice is like a fine chocolate mousse – deep, smooth and rich.

Kimber Rainbow did well enough at Regis College to transfer to Yale in 1997. While she was still 18, she earned her B.A. as the youngest member of the Class of 1999. She then took a year off from formal studies to write and spend time with the family before she enrolled at Oxford in England. Last spring she was awarded the British equivalent of her Master's degree. She has decided to leave this April on an 18-month mission to share the Gospel with the people of Budapest, Hungary. Upon her return, she's entertaining the thought of law or graduate school. She's focused and friendly, lively and quite lovely – the kind of person that you always hope will sit beside you on your next trip.

Regis has served our family well. **Tomicah Sterling** was the first of our kids to start college there. He loved the school, but then transferred with Kimi to Yale. After a year in New Haven he took a leave of absence to serve a mission. From 1998 to the summer of 2000 he was in Hungary preaching the Gospel of Christ and serving as a branch president – which is like a bishop, but in a smaller congregation – in two different cities. Tomicah graduated *magna cum laude* with distinction in his major – History – in the Class of 2001. He's now pursuing a joint M.A./J.D. at the School of Advanced International Studies at Johns Hopkins University.

The kids' grandfather, **Tom Lantos**, continues to serve as the U.S. Congressman from California's 10th District. He is ably assisted by Annette's mother, **Mimo**, who has championed his focus on international relations and human rights. As the ranking Democrat on the House Foreign Affairs Committee, Tom led the U.S. Congressional delegation to the U.N. Conference on Racism. His wisdom and experience in Middle Eastern affairs are deeply appreciated as we battle the scourge of terrorism. He and Mimo have been enormously helpful in the kids' educational pursuits, and the kids often end up camping in their living room when they visit Washington. They frequently meet their aunt and uncle there. Dick and Katrina and the cousins just returned from Copenhagen where Dick served for three years as the U.S. Ambassador to Denmark.

My mom, **Nancy Dick**, retired from politics after two terms as Lieutenant Governor and is now involved in a couple of businesses. She lives in Denver a few miles from our home and drives a bright yellow Mustang convertible. My ever patient sister **Margot** lives in Seattle with her husband, Bill. They have an environmental consulting firm. **Justin** lives about thirty miles from us in Evergreen, Colorado. He and his wife, Helen, have two boys, three cats and a new puppy. **Dulcia** just earned her B.A. this spring and is living near Boston. She is a social worker with the state.

    Ben Sandoval was voted Prom King by the students of North High School in 1998. He hired a stretch limo and took Kimi as his Queen. He now works at McDonalds and loves to go swimming with Zen and Shiloh a couple of times each week.

    Bob Whalen, my former room mate and spiritual brother from another mother, graduated with me and proceeded to study advanced economics in Germany. He returned to the States and enlisted as a buck private in the United States Army. After attending Officer's Candidate School, Bob took a leave to earn a graduate degree from Oxford. He now commands military intelligence for the elite Army Ranger Corps. Afghanistan, the Philippines, Africa – there are many times when we only learn where he's been after he gets back – but we're still very grateful he's there doing his job for our country.

Appendix II : Reader Resources

- The book <u>Gifted Hands</u> was written by Dr. Ben Carson and is available through Zondervan Publishing. Their internet address is www.zondervan.com or they may be reached by regular mail at:

  Zondervan
  5300 Patterson SE,
  Grand Rapids, MI 49530

- Dr. Greggory DeVore works with The Intermountain Fetal Diagnostic Center, 508 East South Temple, Suite A-28, Salt Lake City, UT 84102   Phone: 801.359.2229   The firm's web site can be found at www.fetal.com

- For information on Sudden Infant Death Syndrome, try contacting www.sidscenter.org

- Information on The Church of Jesus Christ can be obtained by accessing the web site at www.mormons.org or calling 1.800.453.3860   You may also write The Church of Jesus Christ, 50 East South Temple Street, Salt Lake City, UT 84150

- Information on Down Syndrome can be obtained from The National Down Syndrome Society, 666 Broadway, Suite 810, New York, NY 10012   Phone 1.800.221.4602   or access www.ndss.org

You can order additional copies of this book through most bookstores, or take advantage of special publisher's offers on overruns and returns by ordering on the internet at

tendixpress.com

If you would like to place an order by phone, please call us directly at

303/561-1314

To order by mail, you may wish to complete the order form below, or just send the appropriate payment and information to the publisher.

Your Name: _

Address: _

_ _

City: _ _ _ _ _ _ _ _ _ _ _ _ _ _ _ State_ _ Zip _ _ _ _ _

Please send _ _ _ _ _ copies of "With One Heart" at $18.95 each, plus $3.00 for shipping and handling [total: $21.95 per copy]
Note: Colorado residents must add 7.5% sales tax.

If you would like the book(s) sent as a gift to another address, we'd be happy to oblige. Just include the address below –

Recipient: _

Address: _

_ _

City: _ _ _ _ _ _ _ _ _ _ _ _ _ _ _ State_ _ Zip _ _ _ _ _

Send along with your check, money order or credit card info to:
Tendix Press
P.O. Box 12376
Denver, Colorado 80212

Printed in the United States
3798

9 780971 668201